Hold Back the Night

Rosemary Kingsland is a novelist, ghostwriter and journalist and has written for the *Sunday Times* and the *Evening Standard*. Her late husband was the journalist and castaway Gerald Kingsland, with whom she has three sons. She lived in Nashville, Tennessee for ten years before moving to London, where she lives today.

You can visit her website at www.rosemarykingsland.com

Hold Back the Night

Memoirs of a lost childhood, a warring family
and a secret affair with Richard Burton

Rosemary Kingsland

arrow books

Published by Arrow Books in 2004

1 3 5 7 9 10 8 6 4 2

First published in the United Kingdom in 2003 by Century

Arrow Books
The Random House Group Limited
20 Vauxhall Bridge Road, London, SW1V 2SA

Random House Australia (Pty) Limited
20 Alfred Street, Milsons Point, Sydney,
New South Wales 2061, Australia

Random House New Zealand Limited
18 Poland Road, Glenfield
Auckland 10, New Zealand

Random House (Pty) Limited
Endulini, 5a Jubilee Road, Parktown 2193, South Africa

The Random House Group Limited Reg. No. 954009

www.randomhouse.co.uk

A CIP catalogue record for this book
is available from the British Library

Papers used by Random House are natural, recyclable products made from
wood grown in sustainable forests. The manufacturing processes conform to
the environmental regulations of the country of origin

ISBN 0 09 9 45798 9

Typeset by SX Composing DTP, Rayleigh, Essex
Printed and bound in Great Britain by
Bookmarque Ltd, Croydon, Surrey

*For my mother and father and
Richard Burton, with love*

Acknowledgements

This is a deeply personal memoir. It is the kind of book one probably would shut away in one's memory, since it is so private and at times has been painful to write. However, sometimes, circumstances or planets collide and strange things happen which act as a key to unlock the past.

I was staying with Cathie Pelletier, an American novelist originally from Maine, who has lived in Tennessee for many years. I had first met Cathie when I had also lived in Tennessee for eight years during the 1980s and we became close friends. One evening during my visit, a tornado blew through the state.

Cathie's husband, Tom Viorikic, was away. We were alone in her beautiful home just outside Nashville with just her numerous rescued dogs and cats for company. Having lived for so long in the South, we were used to tornadoes and knew the havoc they could wreak. We hurried to put the dogs in the basement but the cats refused to budge, so we stayed in the den with them drinking wine. The wind grew stronger, the sky turned black. In the middle of the afternoon, it was as dark as night. Then the lights went out. We lit candles and opened another bottle. In the south these impromptu celebrations in the teeth of danger are known as tornado parties. It was cosy indoors and exciting, listening to the roar of the wind, the crashing of trees.

'What's that tea kettle sound?' Cathie suddenly asked as a banshee shriek headed our way. Moments later, the wall of the storm hit. The windows blew out, the cats streaked around the room as if they were on one of those fairground walls of death. The shriek of the wind blew louder, more insistent. We all dived behind the sofa for protection and huddled together in the dark. During the next half hour as the storm raged, we told each other our secrets, as people often do when faced with extreme danger.

The memories that had surfaced during the tornado were too strong to ignore. Cathie suggested that this was a story that should be told. I started to write. When the book was finished, I sent the first draft of the manuscript to Cathie, who is a brilliant and highly respected literary novelist. A second draft emerged, which Cathie sent to Betty Prashker, a legendary editor at Random House, and the book was on its way.

My sincere thanks go to Cathie Pelletier; and to Random House editors, Betty Prashker and Rachel Kahan in New York and to Hannah Black in London who had faith in the manuscript and saw it through to publication.

I have changed many names to lend those closest to me some privacy. People's perceptions of events that happened so long ago can be different. If my brothers and sister in particular remember things a little differently, my defence is that these are my recollections, the memories of my childhood and youth and I have made an honest attempt to portray events as I remember them.

Rosemary Kingsland
London 2003

HOLD BACK THE NIGHT

One

❦

My brothers and I were born in India, during those last tumultuous days of the Raj. Jimmy was two years older than me, Freddy was two years younger. I, the girl, was in the middle, born in 1941 in Jutogh, high in the Himalayas, a far and distant world from England. Our life in India had been one of ease, with servants standing by to answer our every whim. We had made one trip back to England, in 1946, when Mother had taken my brothers and me and sailed home for a sabbatical with my grandparents, in South Wales. Our second journey to England was fraught with tension and, this time, a great sadness, for we knew we were leaving for good. It was in 1948, and after three long centuries of rule, Britain was giving India back. By this time, my maternal grandmother had left my grandfather and had removed herself to their second home on the South Downs, where we stayed.

I can still remember arriving at the docks in Liverpool, my hands hurting so much from cold I cried while we waited for our luggage to disgorge. I was miserable and frightened by this bleak, grey country. It was like a war zone, pockmarked with bomb blast, rusty iron girders, and deep holes, with remnants of destroyed buildings standing out against the skyline of a squat, dingy little city. Above it all, a bitter wind whistled in from the estuary, tossing newspapers about, flapping and rattling corrugated iron. I wanted the blue skies and hot bright sun of India, the noise and rich smells of the bazaar in Delhi, the scented pine forests of Simla. I wanted the clean, soaring snow peaks and glaciers of Kanchenjunga, which glistened with a brittle light far above Darjeeling.

Seeing me about to freeze to death, a watchman of some kind – he was huddled over a glowing coke basket in his hut by the quay gates – held my hands against his hot mug of tea to warm them. Just then, our great heap of luggage came hurtling down the chute from the side of the ship. I watched as Mother tried her best to gather it all together on the docks. That was when I started sobbing and couldn't stop.

My father arrived early in 1949, and that's when it was apparent to me how much my grandparents disliked him, mostly because he had gained quite a reputation in India amongst the ex-pats as a womaniser. He was a handsome man and could be enormously charming, but, as I had often heard Mother's family say, that didn't take them in for a moment. I later learned that they had sent my uncles to bring my mother home, but too late, she was married. He worked at the Commonwealth Relations Office in London at this time, and so was not always at home. The peace was kept for a time until the tension grew and he and my Uncle John – a real war hero known as 'Bunty' – ended up in a fight. I can still remember the two of them tumbling down the stairs at Brighton, breaking a grandfather clock on a landing at the bend. The next day, Father took a train from work, stopped at the first suburb he liked the look of, which happened to be Wimbledon, and bought the first house he was shown. We were in it by the end of the week. A few months later Jimmy and I found a dead baby wrapped in a brown paper parcel in one of the big ponds on Wimbledon Common and my mother panicked and wanted to leave the dangers of the city. So Father sold the house to a married ex-girlfriend at a loss.

We moved to Downside, a little village in Surrey that I liked, since I was soon given the task of pumping the church organ. I fell in love with a children's graveyard there, next to the tragic memorials to the village sons who had fallen in battle, but Father soon began an affair with a local woman and Mother must have found out as it wasn't long before we moved again.

Just before my little sister, Gracie, was born, we settled in Guildford. We had no car and so never ventured far from the town itself. Mother was very ill that summer with some mysterious disease called 'white leg', something to do with her being pregnant with Gracie. When I think of my mother before her pregnancy, I remember a tall and angular woman who walked fast, so locked into her own misery as to seem almost a stranger to me. She was quite beautiful, with bobbed wavy chestnut brown hair, fine bones and a beautiful mouth, but the spark had gone from her. The past was closer to her than the present. There were a few moments, when she gardened or played the piano, when she seemed almost happy, and at those times she told me some fascinating stories about her early life. Mostly, she was depressed. At times, hysterical outbursts against us and my father, floods of tears and shivering fits made her seem quite mad. When she became pregnant, medical problems caused her to gain a great deal of weight and with it came self-loathing. Then she retreated to bed and rarely moved, attended once a day in the mornings by the district nurse, who happened to live next door. I was still only ten, but during the long summer break I did the everyday work of looking after the family. My father made breakfast before he went to work, but I shopped at the general store at the end of the road and made all our other meals, which usually consisted of macaroni cheese, corned beef salad and bread and butter and jam at teatime. A proper little housewife, I swept and dusted and sometimes made the beds. When the laundry piled up, I'd cart it all into the bathroom, fill the tub with soapy water and throw the lot in. Smaller items weren't too bad, but I struggled with the heavy sheets and towels. To help me, I'd get into the tub with Jimmy and Freddy and like the laundry wallah I remembered from India, we'd stamp up and down on the washing until the room was awash with suds and dirty water. My mother, in the next room with her head buried beneath the covers, somehow perpetually managed to sleep through the screams of laughter and splashing noises.

Trouble brewed when my father started an affair with my best friend's mother. We had to move once more, and again the house was sold at a loss in a hurry. By now, and with another financial calamity at our heels, we were so broke that a move to Cornwall was the cheapest option – and Mother foolishly believed that in the Cornish hinterlands Father would be miles away from his favourite city women. A house was found, cheap and bursting with furniture so old that no one wanted it. Father made arrangements immediately and off we went again

By 1953, we were neatly tucked away in the remote county of Cornwall. The weather across England was atrocious for most of that year. In January, torrential rains, an unusually high tide, and onshore gales had caused the North Sea to breach the dikes along the east coast and flood far inland, drowning hundreds of people. By June, when the young queen Elizabeth was crowned, the rain still fell in a steady downpour, washing out most of the street parties. Only the news that Mount Everest had been conquered by a New Zealander and a Sherpa, both of whom were conveniently considered by the British to be British, raised the nation's dampened spirits a little. As bells rang out, people talked of a new Elizabethan age, of a new prosperity, a new birth.

I was a solitary tomboy given to roaming the wild country around our Cornish home, dreaming of adventure and exploration, not of romance and sex. I wasn't coltish and leggy like my best friend, Pamela, a solicitor's daughter, who had tumbling fair curls and come-hither dark-blue eyes that had the boys chasing her in droves. Small and sturdy, I was built like a moorland pony, with shaggy brown hair and the apple cheeks of a country girl. Circumstances had not yet placed me in the right place at the right time. I was waiting in the wings, the stage still empty, the curtain not yet risen on a terrible and painful love affair. Mostly, I felt unsettled, a sense of groping for the unknown, of my body developing an inner life of its own, beyond my control. I couldn't ask anyone what was going on, certainly not my mother, who was not the cuddly, confiding type.

It was a time when sex was a taboo word between the generations. Somehow, my friends and I muddled along, the entire subject concealed in whispers, a carefully guarded adult mystery so impossible to penetrate that we were constantly searching for clues. Even the most obscure references to body parts and suggestive activities in the dictionary, the Bible, or Shakespeare assumed pornographic proportions, which, if read out loud in class, invoked furtive whispers and giggles as notes were passed beneath desks. Anything could set us off.

In an attempt to use rules as a method of chaperonage, grammar-school girls and college boys were banned from walking on the same side of the street. It didn't make sense when most of the girls had brothers at the college, as I did. Jimmy often filled our house with rowdy classmates. Consequently, mornings and evenings when we flooded to and from our respective schools, the pavement on one side was filled with giggling girls, the other side with loud boys, horsing about, throwing conkers or paper darts to catch our attention. Rumours flew around the school like wildfire when someone said she had seen our head girl out walking down Lovers' Lane at dusk with the opposition's head boy. Was she stupid enough to let him do it? we asked. Another rumour flew: she was pregnant, her life was ruined, she'd have to leave, her parents were sending her away. Being ruined was the big thing we had to avoid at all costs. Even French kissing could ruin a girl – and if a boy whispered the words 'French letter' into your ear, slap his face and run. None of us was sure what French kissing was, let alone a French letter, but the knowledge that just a kiss could have such disastrous consequences was terrifying. How could you tell if you were being French kissed? And who to avoid? Suppose your uncle kissed you, or, heaven forbid, your father? For a time, until we forgot about it, hysteria set in. It seemed our world was full of pitfalls to be avoided, even though we didn't know what most of those pitfalls were.

'Doing it' was high on the list. We were always on the

lookout for people who might be doing it. The boys' headmaster came to see our headmistress – whom we called Auntie Moo – in her study, a regular weekly event to compare notes on our linked schools. Suddenly we were convinced his walk was more unsteady than usual when he left, and her nose was red at the tip. A bottle of sherry was seen in the bin. When I volunteered to listen at the study door, a girl at the top of the stairs standing 'cave', I heard the sound of laughter, and, what to me sounded like many suggestive silences. No doubt about it, as far as I was concerned, they definitely did it behind the closed door.

Someone else said they saw Mr Nash, the art master, kissing Mam'selle, with her dimples, scarlet lips, and saucy dark eyes. From then on we convinced ourselves they were doing it all right, doing it in the games cupboard, in the library, up in the attics, in the summer house by the tennis courts. God, how they did it, everywhere and all the time: under the dark piney overhang of the cedar on the front lawn, behind bushes in the walled garden, in his great beast of a car parked down by the potting sheds, which were out of bounds to us.

Thinking it hilarious, in art class we asked when we were to be allowed to paint nudes. We dropped subtle hints in French lessons: 'Excusez-moi, Mam'selle, what does 'baisez-moi' mean?' Then, we would scream with laughter. They must have thought we were mad. Pam and I asked Juliet, the third member of our triumvirate, to quiz Mr Nash subtly about Mam'selle on Juliet's way to and from school with him each day from Bude, the fishing village on the north coast where they both lived. Juliet's father was an artist like Mr Nash, so the families were close. Juliet looked like a Spanish gypsy with long jet-black plaits, her hair parted in the centre and pulled very tight, flat to her scalp, almost as if her hair had been painted on, as it is with a wooden doll. Her skin was warm honey, and, most striking of all, across her nose and cheekbones, she was so deeply freckled she looked as if she wore a highwayman's mask.

Half in love with Mr Nash ourselves, we envied Juliet her intimacy with him, a man – a Mr Darcy with his unruly black curls and aquiline features – who wore corduroys and a thick white fisherman's sweater with a red kerchief tied at a slant. When we asked her what it was like, being so close beside him in his car mornings and evenings, in her deep slow voice she said, 'He drives very fast over Bodmin Moor, scattering the sheep and ponies, and he sings.' What does he sing, we giggled, French love songs? No, she said, Scottish ones, very loudly, like 'Yeho My Nut Brown Maiden', and 'Sail Bonny Boat Like a Bird on the Wing', and 'Roamin' in the Gloamin'. Does he roam in the gloamin' with Mam'selle, do they walk along the shore arm in arm, do they do it behind a sand dune? we asked, and laughed at our wit. Nobody knew where Mam'selle lived nor went to on her own in the evenings. She had a little French Citroën – a Deux-Chevaux, grey and dappled with rust, it looked like a lopsided tin box – in which she rattled off at the end of the day, turning out of the drive in the opposite direction from Mr Nash, an obvious ruse to throw us off the scent, we said knowingly.

However, if, during all this hysterical fun, anyone had said to me, 'Do you know what it is they do when they do it?' I would have been unable or unwilling to reply, my otherwise fertile imagination always stopping short of reality. The shock, then, was all the greater in the last week of spring term when my form was told that instead of gym we were to have a 'hygiene lesson'. We were not to bother with changing into shorts and plimsolls, but were to remain in our classroom.

We called Miss Cadwallader 'Jolly Hockeysticks', although she was never jolly. Tall and rangy, with lean muscles still preserved from the days when she played for England at hockey before the war, with just a glance she subdued the excited buzz when she strode in, wearing a tattered black academic gown like a wizard's robe over her habitual baggy shorts. This was serious. She took her place by the blackboard, the kind on stilts like an artist's easel. Her eyes ranged over the class, her face devoid of expression.

'Today, I am going to read to you,' she started, holding up a booklet. 'I will not countenance giggling or lewd comments. Do you understand?'

'Yes, Miss Cadwallader,' we chorused.

Our immediate reaction had been that one of us had done something so dreadful, expulsion was on the cards, but this was something else. For some reason I carried a guilt complex so strong that I was always convinced the finger was pointing at me. That thought in mind, I immediately developed hiccups. There was a delay while Miss Cadwallader brought me to the front of the class. She told me to lie flat on my back on the floor, which I did. To this day I remember the smell of the dusty floorboards, the strange angle of the blackboard, her sinewy legs, and the shredded edge of the black gown as she stood over me.

'Hold your breath and count to fifty,' she commanded.

The entire class chanted with me as I hiccuped my way through the count. I stopped at forty, gasping for air like a landed fish. The hiccups continued.

'Again!' she urged. 'Take a deeper breath.' The count started again. After a while, I realised I was cured and got up.

Her face glowed, her horse teeth smiled. 'It works every time,' she crowed. 'Now, Rose, back to your seat. We have wasted enough time.'

She held up the booklet again, opened it at the first page, and in a flat, expressionless voice, started to read. A mask had dropped over her face; the frivolity was over.

At last, we learned what 'doing it' entailed. The activities, whether real or imagined, of the boys across the road, the head girl, Mr Nash and Mam'selle, Auntie Moo (heaven forbid!) were exposed. What Miss Cadwallader read was beyond our smuttiest dreams. It was so astonishing, so unlikely, so embarrassing – so unappealing – that very little registered. Sometimes, she stopped to draw on the blackboard. When she had finished each diagram, dispassionately, she indicated key points with a ruler. Then, she paused barely long enough for us to gawp, trying to make sense of it, to connect it with our own anatomy or that of any male we knew, before she erased it with a few quick swipes. Any stray embarrassed giggle that started was quelled with a single fierce glare.

At the end of the lecture, Miss Cadwallader said, 'Now girls, any questions?' Numbly, we shook our heads. 'Very well. If any of you have a problem, you may ask me privately. For the sake of modesty, you will not discuss this with your fathers or your brothers, nor any male of the species, although some of you might care to ask your mothers for more details in due course. If you managed to comprehend a word of what I said, you'll know when that time comes. Very well, class dismissed.'

We filed out in an orderly way before bursting out of the main doors on to the terrace where, free at last, amid shrieks of laughter, we mimicked Jolly Hockeysticks. As for her offer of going to her for a private conversation, it was too terrifying even to consider.

When I was walking home to lunch on my own a few days later, a car drew up to the side of the road and a man leaned over to ask the way to Egloskerry. I put my head in the window to tell him I didn't know, and quick as a flash he threw open his coat. He hadn't a stitch on underneath.

'Here, little maid, have a feel of this,' he invited, tongue stuck out of the side of his crazily grinning mouth.

I stepped back and, having been taught always to be polite to strangers, said, 'No, thank you.' Remembering what I'd also been taught about never running away from mad dogs and angry bulls but to keep my head, I put my nose in the air and walked on, ignoring him. He loitered a bit, shouting rude things out of the car window, then drove off. We never talked about sex, or anything remotely close, in our house, so I kept it to myself until later in the afternoon when, bursting to tell someone, I mentioned it to Pam.

'He was naked?' she said, eyes wide.

'Well, he had a mackintosh on.'

'But nothing under that?' I shook my head. 'What did it look like?' she urged. 'You know . . .'

'It was so quick . . .'

'You must have seen! Go on, tell me,' she demanded.

'I thought it was a rat.'

'A rat!' We burst out laughing.

'Come on,' she said. 'You have to report it. The man's obviously a maniac.'

There was no arguing with Pam, there never was. She marched me to the school secretary, who immediately telephoned the police. When they asked me what I actually saw, I could only gaze at the ground, my face on fire.

'It's all right, my dear, no need to be alarmed, we'll catch him,' said the sergeant, patting my arm in a fatherly way.

'Men like him should be put down,' my mother said. 'Girls aren't safe any more.'

With indisputable logic and very little detective work, the police drove straight to Egloskerry, where the flasher was caught red-handed – he'd found the way after all – running up and down the village street and flinging open his mackintosh at every female he passed.

Morgana, our unpaid cook, was comforting in her matter-of-fact way, but then, very little disturbed her. As she often said, she had seen it all in her seventy years on this earth. 'He be un of um loonies, eh, my dear? They be lots of um round theyze parts, allus showin' off, it be they inbreeding, you zee. Now zet you do-an, haave a hot zup of tea and a zlice of my lardy cake and be puttin' it out of your mind, ther'z a good maid.'

But there wasn't much putting it out of my mind because a similar thing happened shortly afterwards. A week earlier I had been at a favourite spot deep in the wood, watching a great green woodpecker drill a hole in a rotten trunk. The trees were still bare, so the bird had been easy to spot with its magnificent green, red, and yellow plumage. Country people call it the yaffle because of its loud, ringing cry, like laughter echoing through the woods. I returned to the same spot, hoping to see it again, perhaps to find its nesting site, and was astonished with the glory of bluebells that seemed to have appeared from nowhere. The blue carpet hazed in every direction, alive with the sound of bees, the colour and perfume so strong that I was overwhelmed with the kind of piercing joy felt only by the young. Lost in one of those unanswerable existential teenager's debates with myself about why such beauty was created for so fleeting a time, often never to be seen, I didn't notice the man standing partly concealed behind a tree. Suddenly he jumped out, waving his thing at me, shouting, 'Lookee 'ere, I can do ze waggle-dance like 'um bees getting honey.' I froze. His mad red face, the lock of dark hair hanging into his eyes, the torn tweed jacket, and the wide-gaping trousers were embedded on my mind like a photograph. Then I turned and ran, leaping through the undergrowth, not stopping until I reached the lane and the safety of some farm labourers cutting the hedge. I knew if I mentioned this second event, I would be banned from exploring on my own, so I said nothing when I reached home.

Sex, it seemed, came in all sorts of weird packages.

Our small market town lay on the westerly flanks of Dartmoor, where the River Tamar formed a wide valley that divided Cornwall from Devon. Grey was the predominant colour, an overwhelming grey of granite and slate, livened with the occasional bright splash of double-decker green buses and scarlet post-boxes. Old-fashioned stores, whose window displays hadn't been changed since 1900, clustered around an ancient cobbled square with a pagan granite cross surrounded by looped iron chains, once the site of the butter market. To one side there was a pump and a trough gouged out of a massive block of granite where horses still drank. The railway station had been built below the town, into the side of a cliff next to the cattle market. Right at the end of the yards was the dreaded slaughterhouse where, out of a mixture of bravado and curiosity, I went once with my brother Jimmy. As we peered in through the open doors, we saw a cow's stomach being cut open, with gallons of still steaming bright green grass gushing over the concrete. The sight haunted my dreams for years.

The climate in that part of Cornwall seemed far different from that of the rest of England, almost as if Cornwall were a different country, which in many ways it was. Sometimes, the sun didn't shine for months on end. Mist seeped down from the moors and even in early summer harsh flurries of snow blew from the distant black hills and sharp crags. Up there, said Morgana, putting the fear of God into me, dangerous criminals were locked up for life: you could hear them rattling their chains and howling like dogs when the wind was in the right direction.

Morgana had turned up at the door one day shortly after we moved to Cornwall, asking for a job. She said she'd worked in our house all her life since the age of eleven, working her way up from scullery maid to cook. Constantly aware of our dire finances, my mother said she didn't need anyone, but Morgana said she didn't want to be paid. All she wanted were her meals and the fat off the ham to take home.

'Well . . .' my mother had said slowly. That was enough for Morgana.

'Well thun, my dear, I'll be 'ere in the mornin', do-an you be worryin' 'bout a thang,' Morgana said. She quickly patted my mother's arm. Mother could only nod wordlessly, but I could tell that she felt relief that here would be a friend, someone who would tackle the monster kitchen range that gobbled up coal and burned food. And then Morgana fixed her dark, sunken eyes on me as she pointed a crooked finger vaguely down the street.

'Ask anyone, little maid, th'ull show you my hou-az,' she said, speaking with a soft country burr that had long vowels inserted. I took this as an invitation to visit her, and nodded that I would. Then I watched as Morgana, bent in half like a witch, hobbled away. I knew in my bones that life would now be a bit easier for us all.

An old woman, Morgana had never been further than Bodmin. As a maid of fourteen, she had walked the twenty miles there to the goose fair with her sweetheart, who won her a china cup with two handles. He did this, Morgana proudly told me, on the coconut shy. If a lucky soul could knock the coconut out of its stand, a prize was won.

'It be a loving cup,' she said. 'Well, my dear, he guv it tay me, to drink zider at our wedding, he said, but it wunt tay be. Poor laamb, he died in Africa fightin' ze Boass.'

Her tiny cottage was shingled all over with slate – roof and sides alike – as though it were a sleeping armadillo. It lay down a narrow cobbled alley known as Blind Hole. On my very first visit, Morgana showed me the cup. It was filled with paper spills in a muddle of bric-a-brac on the sooty mantelpiece. She picked it up, spat on it, then rubbed it clean with a corner of her apron. Painted pink ribbons emerged, twined around a date: 1895. Ambushed by love on the long way back from the goose fair, Morgana became pregnant but her lover was soon gone to join the army, never to return.

'I be too old, my dear, to be shy. I be caught by love many times, and nary an 'uzband to my name. Now they be zixteen grandchilun and more great-uns thun can be counted.' She glanced at me with an impish smile. 'Do-an you never be go-an tay Bodmin my dear, not wuth no young zoldier-boy.' She was proud of her memorable day out and what was to be her first and last look at the distant sea from the heights of a tor.

Her stories made me want to go to the goose fair, to see geese with orange legs and tarred feet. The tar was supposed to act like little protective shoes as they were driven along stony roads, sometimes all the way to London. 'September, the fair be,' Morgana said. 'Come Michaelmas, my dear, uz'll find a nice zoldier and uz'll go.'

'She's pulling your leg, Rose,' my father said. 'Those old traditions have died out.' But, cut off from the rest of England by the River Tamar, the Cornish were a people with an orphan language and dark secrets. They were convinced that they lived on an island that held their traditions safe. Merlin had never left Camelot, Guinevere and Lancelot still dallied in sunlit meadows, and Arthur was the once and future king, ready to return when called to the fray. They still burned the wicker man and worshipped the green one. Every week a pannier market was held in the square where country people would bring in the baskets they wove from willow wands. Old folk like Morgana put out a dish of cream at night for boy fairies they called piskies, and there was still a goose fair at Bodmin, even though the geese were taken there on the back of carts and in old vans and no longer driven in great flocks, a hundred strong.

In spring, as part of ancient fertility rites, with almost the entire population of the town, we danced the floral dance, the girls dressed in long frocks with flowers in our hair, following pipers throughout the town. We started and ended at the White Hart Hotel – its doorway was almost a thousand years old and stolen from the old priory in the vale – where barrels of cider were rolled out to be drunk. In a remembrance of sun worship, the May queen, with her maids-in-waiting, danced around the maypole on the castle green, plaiting bright ribbons in intricate patterns, each pattern shaping an age-old story. The round hill on which the castle keep stood was artificial, the earth dug by a Norman earl from what became a deep hollow filled with sweet chestnut trees. In the autumn, the fallen nuts in their spiky green shells were so thickly scattered on a deep litter of leaves that people came to scoop them up by the sackload to sell at the market by Southgate.

The hill where we lived caught the wind and, whatever the season, we froze in our draughty old house outside the castle walls. I have no idea at all who once owned the big house. When we found it, it was empty of people but full of furniture, floating on the hilltop in the mist as if it were the *Marie Celeste*, a ship abandoned. Nobody wanted heavy, old-fashioned furniture back then, but my father had bought the lot because we still had very little of our own. Everything we possessed had been burned in riots at the docks in Bombay while awaiting shipment home, back in 1948.

It seemed as though nothing had been altered since the house was built. The wallpaper was dark with soot where candles and oil lamps had smoked for generations. In the bedrooms the paper was sprigged with pastel flowers. Downstairs, some of it was hand-painted on ragged silk, with huge bunches of poppies and dusky peonies, flamingos, parrots, and bamboo grasses. The heavy velvet curtains with bobbled fringes were tempting to my baby sister, Gracie. Her small fingers were forever pulling the fringes off, leaving gaps behind, like missing teeth. The tables had soft chenille covers down to the floor. When we crawled in underneath, they became small caves where we could pretend that we were somewhere else. Acres of mahogany gleamed in the firelight. There were massive mirrors, velvet chairs, cracked leather chesterfields, and black, leather-cloth dining chairs, their deep buttons full of dust. There were feathered birds, waxed fruits, a squirrel, and a rainbow trout, all suspended in time beneath glass domes. The walls were hung with faded watercolours of luminous-eyed women and cracked varnished oils of long-nosed men seated on one-dimensional cut-out horses. Throughout the house, huge mottled mirrors reflected us as if we were misty, silvered ghosts from a bygone age. I remember, too, a great sideboard with a wine rack inside which – for a giddy period of indulgence our first Christmas there, and as an echo of his previous life – contained claret for my father, until it was all drunk. On the top was lined up sherry and port for visitors, as well as Stone's green ginger wine for my mother. For my brothers and me there were jewel-coloured bottles of Corona: dandelion and burdock, cherryade and limeade.

Two eagles sat on pillars and guarded the gate at the front of the house. A short path led up to the grandiose front door. Around the side, dangerously worn steps led down to the basement door. This was the tradesmen's entrance, where milk, bread, and fish were delivered and coal was tipped into a chute, leaving gritty black clouds hanging in the air. The gloomy basement kitchen, full of terrifying dark shadows, soon became known to us as 'the dungeons'. It contained long slate sinks along one wall, a massive dresser sixteen feet long and ten feet tall, and a vast range that lurked in an inglenook like some medieval instrument of torture. This terrible place became Morgana's fiefdom, and she would never leave it, however much my mother tried to lure her above stairs to do a little dusting. The plain food she cooked was put on to a dumbwaiter and hoisted up on a pulley to the dining room above. But we would never see Morgana herself above the level of the kitchen.

Our financial circumstances became clear to me the first day the fishmonger came to the tradesmen's entrance, his straw basket heaped with the latest catches of the day. Morgana called my mother to come down and do the purchasing.

'Now, here be a real nice lobster, caught fresh this morning at Polperro,' the fishmonger said, and held the clawing creature aloft. My mother looked at it longingly, no doubt remembering the mild lobster curry with mango chutney she used to enjoy in another world, but at 7s 6d it was far too expensive.

'How much are the herrings?' she asked. As it turned out, herrings were cheap, a penny a pair when brought to the door in the straw basket. The fishmonger seemed to understand instantly that his lobsters would never get as far as 'the dungeons', much less to the gleaming mahogany table on an upper floor. This is when he suggested stargazie pie, a Cornish speciality made with herrings.

'Whatever is it?' Mother asked. It sounded wonderfully poetic.

'You'll find it right tasty, my dear,' the fishmonger said with a wink. He quickly handed over sixpenn'orth of herrings to my mother, who in turn took them to Morgana.

'For stargazie pie,' my mother explained.

That evening, a dozen herrings in their entirety, heads, fins, and innards, were placed upright on their tails like mermaids in an oval dish and covered with pastry. Openings were made for the heads to stick through. When it came to table, twelve scorched heads gazed blindly at us in their crisp golden crust. At first, we thought it was a joke. Gracie and the boys refused to eat it, but, ever the adventurer, I tried it, only to discover that it was full of bones. I was forced to spit it out into my napkin.

'That old woman's impossible,' my father exploded. 'She does it on purpose.' Mother dared not tell him the stargazie pie was her idea.

Morgana got to take the pie home, so it wasn't wasted. In our house, nothing was ever wasted. A Sunday roast was eaten cold with salad and pickles on Monday, curried on Tuesday, rissoled on Wednesday, the bone boiled for soup on Thursday, and any leftover scraps were turned into Cornish pasties.

Next to the kitchen was the disused servants' hall, a dusty sepulchre where we played ping-pong on the long table that once had seated a dozen maids and footmen. At the back, on a sloping hillside that led directly to open meadows running down to the river, were the terrace and the lawns, surrounded by a flint wall that was practically hidden from sight by black-berried ivy. There were dead shrubs in tubs, and yew and holly bushes where blackbirds fed on berries and sang a song so sweet it filled me with yearning. The lawn sloped dangerously steep, too wet to walk on, the grass so vividly green it looked like a bog, surrounded by beds that were full of dried-up flowers that rustled in the perpetual wind. One boundary of our garden was, in fact, the ancient wall of the castle, fifteen feet thick and built in the time of Edward III. Within its thickness was a small prison cell we could walk across in a couple of strides. It was guarded by a clanging iron gate that was never locked. My brothers and I used this as a den, and even though people walked to and fro under the adjoining castle arch, it still felt private, a place where we could play our games and, in the dank cobwebby gloom, scare each other with ghost stories. It meant little to us that George Fox, founder of the Quaker faith, had been imprisoned in that very cell. We didn't stop to consider that his severe black-garbed behind had sat on that same chestnut plank we sprawled on so carelessly in our light modern clothes. Nor did we think that perhaps the ancestors of the black spiders that were lurking in the stones above us had once woven their dense webs above George Fox's head.

When we first moved in there had been on the property a decaying glass house filled with a grapevine that must have been hundreds of years old. The grapes hung down in heavy purple bunches, but the entire vine was thickly covered with a white mildew. Ignoring my mother's comment that it should be sprayed with copper sulphate solution, my father, who couldn't tell a daisy from a buttercup, said it was diseased and cut it all down. He didn't stop there; he went on and wrecked the glass house, setting fire to it all in a massive bonfire, sparks from which went shooting over the ancient roofs of the town. He had an obsession with fires, my father did, and I often think he destroyed things as an excuse for a blaze, which he would stoke for hours, the glow of the flames reflected in his horn-rimmed spectacles.

Myra Boscowan's mouth was pink and soft and damp like a dribbling baby's. She seemed to blow soft bubbles when she spoke. Her cheekbones were wide and flat, her mousy hair was tied in bunches with ribbons, and her pale eyes had a faraway look, as if washed with rain. She followed me around at school like a puppy, her feet too big for her body in the wide flat sandals she wore. Myra had a great curiosity about me, and about how my family lived. She let it slip to me that she often walked past our house and peered in through the black iron railings. I suspect that she was romantically misled by the haughty eagles with outspread wings on the gateposts, and by the overexalted front door, which was all she could see beyond the untamed shrubbery. No doubt imagining grandeur inside, she longed to be invited in for tea.

'We're not rich,' I told her, ruffled, for I wished we were. 'It's like an empty box wrapped in silver paper.' But Myra refused to believe me and kept pressing until one day, foolishly, I relented. 'I'll ask my mother if you can come next Tuesday,' I said, knowing very well that I wouldn't ask.

Myra's face glowed. 'What time shall I come?' she asked.

'You could walk home with me,' I said. 'We have tea at four-thirty.' When I realised what I'd just offered, I quickly added, 'But let me check with Morgana first.' I honestly believed that Myra would forget by Tuesday.

'Who's Morgana?' she asked.

'Our cook,' I said, which only reinforced the delusions of our grandeur in Myra's mind. I could see this on her face, and perhaps that's why I, too, bought in to the notion. 'I'll get her to make some petits fours,' I invented, so suddenly that I could almost taste them. I had often envisaged my grandmother's petits fours, which were made from hoarded marzipan and little squares of sweet cake dipped in chocolate. In a dreamlike fantasy I suddenly wanted to share them with Myra Boscowan. Pam, Juliet, and I often played such games, talking of the unimaginable treats we would stuff ourselves with once food, especially chocolates and sweets, came off ration.

Nothing more was said, and, relieved, I put it out of my mind. The following Tuesday evening there was a knock at the front door and there stood Myra, in a straw bonnet and a frilly white garment bound with a wide pink sash. With her was a fresh-faced muscular man who seemed to burst out of a shiny suit that perhaps had fitted him once, but was now much too small. The top button of his shirt didn't meet the buttonhole, and the space was covered by his tie. Filled with panic, and madly wondering if they would leave if I shut the door quickly, I stared too long. They both shuffled awkwardly under my gaze. Finally, the man nudged her, prompting Myra to thrust a warm, squashed box of chocolates into my hands. I looked down at it. It must have taken a month's ration of their sweet coupons.

'I've come to tea,' Myra said. 'My father left work early to bring me. He's a stonemason.'

'Howdy do,' the man said, removing his hat. He stared at a mirror on the wall behind me as he smoothed his hair and wiped his shoulders, as if expecting a fine layer of stone chips to cascade down on to the doorstep.

From the garden, my mother called out, 'Rose, who is that?'

I took Myra and her big clumsy father through the open garden doors of the library, out on to the terrace where Mother was watching Gracie. Terrified, I introduced my visitors.

'They've come to tea,' I explained.

Mother put away her darning. 'Tea?' she said doubtfully. 'You'd better ask Morgana.'

'It do-an zeem like you be expected,' Mr Boscowan said to Myra. His eyes slid to the small box of chocolates I was holding, as if he would like to snatch them back. Quickly, I passed them to Mother.

'Oh yes, of course you were expected, Myra. Will you

stay to tea, Mr Boscowan?' I asked, crossing my fingers behind my back.

'Not tay eat when I baint 'un asked,' he said, but not resentfully. 'But I baint zaying no tay a zup o' tay. Bain' a stonemason, they alluz be dust.'

'Oh, what kind of stone do you cut, Mr Boscowan?' Mother asked him. In no time at all, effortlessly, she winkled out of him the fact that he was a monumental stonemason working in the undertaker's yard by Southgate, carving headstones, angels, and crosses. 'You come from a long line of fine craftsmen, Mr Boscowan,' Mother said. 'Men such as you built that castle above us, and the priory down in the vale.'

'Zat' be so!' he exclaimed. 'Zem carvings on the church, hard granite theym be. I restored 'um.' He held out his callused hands for us to look at. Leaning forward he confided, 'Michelangelo, he be the one.'

'Perhaps you should live in Italy,' Mother suggested.

He sounded surprised. 'Italy? I wuz there in the war. I baint go-an back.'

'Oh, I should love to go! Oranges and olive groves. Art and music! Away from this dreadful climate and poverty of spirit,' my mother said, her voice more animated than I had heard it in years. I was surprised. I had never seen this side of her, this passion for life. She was usually so depressed that she gave no hint of the scope of her knowledge and interests. But there had been a few clues that I had missed, particuarly when I struggled with homework. Her grasp of every subject was quick and her help, skilful. Now, listening to her talk so vivaciously to Myra's father, for the first time I saw a woman who had suppressed her dreams. It left me unsettled, as if I didn't know who she really was.

I took Myra down into the dungeons, where just twenty

minutes earlier my brothers and I had descended like locusts and had consumed almost a loaf of bread with strawberry jam, leaving nothing but crumbs upon the table.

Hopefully, I asked Morgana if there was anything left for my friend. 'Ull find zomething for the maid,' Morgana said, 'if I be emptying the mouzetrap tay feed her, thun, I be do-an it.' Myra's unhappy gaze shifted around the gloomy kitchen, as if expecting to see the place overrun with vermin. 'Now sit you down at the table, my dear,' Morgana said. 'I expect you be hungry.' While I made fresh tea in the best silver pot and carefully carried up a nicely laid tray for Mr Boscowan and Mother, Morgana prepared for Myra the food intended for my father's supper: eggs poached in vinegar water and a few slices cut off the remnants of the ham bone. When I returned to the kitchen, Myra and Morgana were gabbling away in the Cornish tongue and for the first time, Myra appeared at ease. They switched to English when I came in. I sat at the table opposite Myra and watched her eat. Unaccountably, my mouth started to water and I stared avidly at her plate as the rich golden yellow of the egg yolks broke and flowed over the pale pink slabs of ham.

When she finished she pushed the plate away and said, 'We have ham and eggs for breakfast every day at home.'

'The little maid be thinking thud be afternoon tea on they terrace with zugar cakes and 'em zandwiches,' Morgana said slyly. 'Baint thaat be zo, my dear?'

After tea, I got the cards out and we played snap. Somehow an embarrassing and tedious hour passed and eventually Myra and her father left. The next day in school, she abandoned me to rejoin the coterie of Cornish-speaking girls she used to hang out with before she got a crush on me. I was very relieved. Having an admirer had been quite a strain.

—

When my father told me that he was taking me on a trip to London, I couldn't believe my luck. He was fond of me and often treated me as far more of a friend and confidante than he did my mother. He talked to me about poetry, music and plays, but if my mother ventured an opinion he would impatiently brush her aside, or mock her cruelly. Usually, she retreated into her shell, but occasionally she would flare up and my brothers and I would disappear while the row blazed. We went in February or March 1954, and it must have been half term or I would not have been allowed to go. With me in my school uniform – I had precious little else to wear as best – we left from the railway station, next to the cattle market. The train pulled out in a cloud of smoke to the chorus of the bleating of sheep and the lowing of cattle. I remember peering out of the carriage window to see the long line of animals patiently waiting to enter the slaughterhouse. Then the town fell away behind us, suddenly lost in a downswirl of thick smoke from the engine. I was excited to be going back to London, a bit older and wiser than I had been during the short time we had lived there, after our return from India.

Trains always fascinated and scared me. They spoke to me of danger, yet they also spoke to me of travel, adventure, and escape. The powerful action of the pistons, working furiously yet in smooth harmony, thrilled me. I loved the excitement of journeying somewhere and the swaying movement of the train. It seemed like a giant dragon that smelled of soot and smoke and carried us across vast distances in the comfort of its womb, cushioned against the outside world by thick velour seats, enfolded in luxury, soothed to sleep, and in the morning, a place we had never been.

—

It was in a railway carriage at the age of seven that I first heard of the concept of freedom. I also learned that freedom came at a high price. We were leaving Delhi for the last time on the out train. The platforms and carriages were crammed with arriving and fleeing people during the bloody carnage and confusion of Partition, when the British handed India back after three centuries of rule. For the sake of future peace an incredible experiment, a religious division of the subcontinent, was effected, splitting it into two separate nations. Out of Mother India, the two parts of Pakistan were ripped like conjoined twins who were brutally hacked in two, each half stuck on a dry nipple on the plump breast of a fabulously wealthy maharani who hadn't wanted them born. The bloodshed and rape during this transition, when hundreds of millions of angry people were forcibly removed from their villages and towns and shipped thousands of miles away, led to a cycle of murderous revenge that has not diminished more than half a century on.

I remember that our ayahs, or nursemaids, were travelling with us, but only to the docks where ships were waiting to carry us back to England. After that they would be cast off with no employment. For our bearers, our manservants, the station in Delhi was the end of the road. We would never see them again. My personal bearer, a tall, noble Sikh, stood on the step of our carriage in his immaculate white, a red tartan sash at his waist, a proud red puggaree like a cockatoo's crest in his starched turban. As the train slowly moved out, clearing a path through the mob on the line with a massive cowcatcher, I suddenly felt scared for all these mobbing people who faced an uncertain future. My bearer's brown face, with luxuriant black moustache and berry-red lips, was illuminated with a sad smile; his white teeth flashed as he bade a sorrowful farewell to me, his beloved Missy Baba, whom he had taught to ride horses on the near-vertical slopes around Simla. Suddenly a look of astonishment came across his face and he vanished. I stuck my head out of the window and saw him lying on the platform, a scarlet flood gushing from the two severed halves of his body, forming a huge puddle in the dust. The Muslim who had cut him in half with a single mighty stroke stood among a fleeing crowd, his legs planted wide apart like stone pillars to give him balance as he whirled a great curving scimitar above his head. His face, his arms, and his white coat and baggy trousers were vividly striped with bright blood, like the tartan of my bearer's ruined sash.

The sound of my scream seemed to hang in the air like the billowing smoke from the engine. My ayah dragged me back from the open window and covered up her face with her sari, wailing 'Ayee . . . Ayee . . .' behind the folds of the cloth.

'Rose, stop making such a fuss, you're upsetting Ayah,' my mother said, not realising what had happened. 'None of us wants to leave, but we'll just have to get used to it.'

My father, dressed in his lightweight khaki uniform with brass stars on his shoulders and crowns in his lapels, was seated opposite me and had also seen what had happened. While my mother was lecturing me, he had put his hand on his Sam Browne and pulled out his revolver from its leather holster.

'Pull down the blinds,' he said to my mother. She did as she was told, and sank back into her seat.

'What on earth is going on, George?' she asked. 'Can't you see you're alarming the children? We're quite safe, the train is full of our troops.'

My father said, 'We won't be safe until we're home. This country is finished. I doubt if it will survive Partition – damned fool Socialist idea. We should have strung up Mahatma Gandhi while we had the chance. He's already got the blood of untold millions on his head; he'll have the blood of millions more before this is through, all in the name of freedom.'

'Millions have just sacrificed their lives in Europe and the Pacific for freedom,' was my mother's quiet response. Unlike my father, she had been born and educated in India. She spoke several of the languages and had a sympathy for the history.

'That's different,' my father said shortly. They seemed to have forgotten that I was sitting there in shock, that our three ayahs were now clinging to each other, rocking and moaning as if chanting a spell. The train gathered speed; the platform was left behind.

Although I was so young, I recall the conversation, along with every moment of our train ride leaving Delhi, with perfect clarity. My parents' words were repeated at home by them and their friends a thousand times in a thousand different ways over the coming years. Giving up the Raj and the India they knew was very hard for so many colonials. Most of them thought it was a grave mistake; they saw themselves as benevolent parents, ruling fairly and kindly. I don't recall ever being curious – at least, not then – about what the Indians and Pakistanis themselves thought.

On our visit to London, Father and I were to stay in

Chelsea with a mysterious man I knew only as 'Father's chess friend'. He would occasionally turn up in Cornwall for a chess marathon, arriving on his big black BSA motorbike with silver wire wheels and black leather panniers at the side, like the ones used by motorcycle messengers during the war. He would pull up at our house, covered with dust from the journey, dressed in his old RAF sheepskin jacket, heavy flying boots, and one of those brown leather helmets and push-up goggles. I say mysterious because he and Father would disappear into his study and stay there for what seemed like days, playing chess nonstop, emerging only when they were hungry. He said his name was Mr Smith. In Jimmy's *Eagle* comic, there was a daring character who used to speed across war-torn Europe on a similar bike, carrying secret messages with him. Since Father's own military work had included espionage, I imagined that was what Mr Smith had done and perhaps still did. The world of espionage was always there in our lives. Apart from some obscure code-breaking work my father had done in the Army, he would sometimes play pen-and-paper code games with us on a rainy Sunday afternoon, and we always eagerly switched on the radio to listen to favourite programmes like *Bulldog Drummond* and *Dick Barton, Special Agent*, our fingers tap-dancing to the sound of Morse: da-da-da – dah dah dah – da-da-da!

Sometimes I would wake in the middle of the night and hear Father and Mr Smith arguing. Most often, it was Father yelling because he couldn't bear to lose, and I wondered how soon it would be before Mr Smith left. Then, most often at dawn, I would hear the roar of his big bike and he'd be gone.

Postal chess seemed to lead to less contention between them, even though a single game could last for weeks.

Father would have a board set up in his study with the game in progress and a small brown envelope with a window showing the address on a two-sided card would arrive containing Mr Smith's move. I can still see Father now, in the morning after the post came, half-shaved, still in his dressing gown, as he studied the board with Mr Smith's latest move in place. Eventually, perhaps not until the next day, he would make his move and write it down. The card would be turned around to show Mr Smith's address through the window and another stamp stuck on, until the envelope was no longer brown but like a shapeless cushion made of multicoloured papier-mâché. I think it was part of the fun, to see how many stamps they could stick on without having to use another envelope. But even postal chess had its dramatic moments, with Father hurling the entire chessboard and all the hapless pieces across the room if Mr Smith's paper move was too good.

Chess was not to be the purpose of our visit to London, however. Father was investigating some business opportunity or another, although I never discovered what, and we had also been invited by Lord Macintosh – another one of Father's numerous acquaintances from the old days, who passed sporadically through our lives – to one of two private readings of Dylan Thomas's *Under Milk Wood*. The tickets weren't on sale to the general public, so it was quite special, all the more so, said my father, because Dylan Thomas had died the year before, in New York, during a drunken binge, and so, it was believed that this was his last work. In fact this proved not to be the case when later several of his half-finished notebooks were dredged up and published to wide acclaim. It seemed he was far more in demand when tidily dead than roisterously alive.

The performance was being held on a Sunday, when

theatres were normally closed, at the Old Vic, the London home of what was to become the Royal Shakespeare Company. It was a scruffy little building, almost exclusively attended by students, in a near-derelict area by Waterloo Station that used to be the site of a busy and bawdy street market in Shakespeare's day. The market had long since been reduced to a clump of stalls in The Cut and Lower Marsh, which had once been a swamp and foetid sewer inhabited by leprosy victims, pickpockets, and thieves. It had also been the site of Shakespeare's and Kit Marlowe's theatres. Bomb damage was still plainly visible all around, with huge gaps where historic buildings used to be.

We arrived grandly by taxi in a flourish of freezing sleet. To my disappointment, I saw a flat, plain building, more like a shabby grey concrete box than a palace of magic spells. Above the entrance there were a few decorative frills and a massive coat of arms to remind us that the Old Vic was built during the extravagant era of the Victorian music hall. The interior was equally shabby, the red carpet in the foyer worn and threadbare, the curlicued gold and red auditorium so tired it almost looked grubby. It was also very smelly, like a bazaar in the rain – that rank animal smell of warm, perspiring bodies crammed together, an amalgam of cloying perfume, Coty face powder, and Brylcreem. Above it all, there was a waxy smell, almost like plasticine. I didn't know what it was then, but it was to become as familiar as my skin, something that took on an almost erotic significance: the smell of greasepaint.

The exclusive crowd invited was to fill the auditorium, since the gallery, with its backbreaking benches, was not used. All were dressed smartly in evening clothes. I alone was in my everyday school uniform: green gym slip, blazer and beret, white ankle socks, and Oxford brogues. I felt uncomfortable among such elegance. It bothered me that my mother and father were so self-engrossed that neither one of them had thought to buy me something simple and pretty to wear for my first night out at the theatre.

'God Save the Queen' struck up, played by musicians in the pit, their faces underlit like characters in a horror film. Everyone stood to attention and sang lustily. One or two, though capless, saluted. With the war so recent, we were still a very patriotic tribe. The crowd settled down in their seats with an air of expectation. I felt my inexperience, unsure of what was to come. After more music, the houselights lowered. It was the season for colds and sore throats. People coughed. The sharp smell of eucalyptus struck my nose as pastilles were sucked, chocs were passed, programmes were rustled. I sat forward in my seat so I would miss nothing.

Sybil Thorndike, the grande dame of the English stage, came through the curtains to introduce the event, speaking in glowing terms about Dylan Thomas's wayward genius, adding that since he was a Welshman, there had been a quick whip-round to gather together all those Welsh actors who were resting – this raised a laugh – who had offered their services free to honour their great countryman. As the curtains slowly pulled back on a stygian stage, she concluded by thanking us all for our generosity in supporting the performance, the proceeds of which were to go to Dylan Thomas's widow, Caitlin, and their children.

My father leaned over and too loudly said, 'Well, we didn't pay. Do you think we should leave?' He seemed to find his remark funny because when I ignored it, he repeated it, more loudly: 'I said, we haven't paid!'

In paroxysms of embarrassment, sure everyone had

heard, I hissed back, 'Ssh! It's about to start.' My father seemed to find it impossible to sit quietly through a performance, no matter how grand. Like the rabble from Shakespeare's day at the old Rose or the Globe, he liked to be involved from the front. He was a commentator, a chatterbox. In short, a pest.

The curtains drew fully back and sparkly little lights hovered like stars, a low heaven, barely illuminating the scene. At once, I could see it was to be a plain, no-frills performance. The stage was practically bare, atmospherically lit. The actors walked in almost casually. The First Voice began reading and I was hooked, scarcely able to breathe as the little Welsh seaside village and a 'moonless night . . . starless and bible-black, the cobblestreets silent and the hunched, courters'-and-rabbits' wood limping invisible down to the sloeblack, slow, black, crowblack, fishingboat-bobbing sea' was painted with words as surely as if with brushstrokes on the backdrop before us.

'Young girls lie bedded soft or glide in their dreams, with rings and trousseaux, bridesmaided by glow-worms down the aisles of the organplaying wood. The boys are dreaming wicked or of the bucking ranches of the night and the jollyrogered sea.'

This was a poetry I wasn't prepared for, the power and beauty of the language so different from the easy lyricism and sentimental imagery of Tennyson, whom I loved with romantic zeal and could quote by heart.

Most of all, I was mesmerised by the actor reading First Voice; his voice was mellow and rich and fluid, like warm syrup flowing over the audience, soothing us, entrancing us. He was dressed entirely in black, and his muscular build made him appear stocky. His head, from which dark curling hair sprang rampant, seemed too big. It was an actor's face: strong jaw, high cheekbones, mouth mobile and expressive. The audience was captivated from the first word to the last. Even my father fell silent.

'Only you can hear and see, behind the eyes of the sleepers, the movements and countries and mazes and colours and dismays and rainbows and tunes and wishes and flight and fall and despairs and big seas of their dreams.'

Despite the power of the words and the magnificence of his voice, he had a stillness, a power to draw and hold attention even when he stood silently by while other actors spoke. His name was Richard Burton. It was hardly surprising that I'd never heard of him – cut off as I was in our draughty house at the furthermost extreme of England, I'd heard of no one. And, of course, he did not notice a wide-eyed schoolgirl sitting in the darkness of the third row.

Two

War or no war, rationing was not a concept designed for my mother. She had no idea how to budget on a monthly basis and so blew her slender housekeeping allowance in an exciting splurge. This meant that our meals seesawed from feast in the first week of each month, to famine during the last, but, for a few glorious days the house was filled with anticipation, with good smells and laughter. We dined like kings before winding down to stews and shepherd pies and, finally, for days on end, nothing but porridge for breakfast, macaroni-cheese for lunch, and bread and butter for dinner.

Thankfully, in Cornwall Morgana was there to rescue us, at least when it came to meals. She stoically took it all in her stride and, without question or complaint, she cooked whatever was available and delighted Mother by varying the ubiquitous macaroni-cheese with cheesy potato pie, Cornish pasties made with cheese, Welsh rarebit, and cheese risotto. Cheese, you see, was cheap.

In truth, I suppose the problem with money had more to do with my parents themselves than the circumstances around us. They seemed to have had no thought for the future, which was probably a good thing since they also had no training in how to handle what it might bring. During those halcyon days in India, they had carelessly drifted on a river of milk and honey, with servants answering their every whim. Our move to Cornwall had followed another of Father's spectacular business schemes – the details of which we children were never told – which had rendered us practically moneyless. And money hadn't been the only problem between my parents. My mother's parents had greatly disapproved of her marriage to my father, so there was no financial aid arriving from that camp. Right to the ends of their lives my grandparents both remained hopeful that my mother would come to her senses one day and leave my father behind. I'm sure they must have wondered, as I often did, why she didn't just pack up and head back to a better life. I suspect she was simply terrified of life without this man she had married, and so she put up with his numerous affairs, his many broken promises, and his spendthrift ways. Perhaps at rare times she remembered what it was she had seen in my father in the first place: that energetic, gregarious, self-made man, amusing and enter-taining to his friends and superiors, good-looking in a darkly saturnine way. This was certainly what his numerous female admirers saw, for when Father was around other women he was nothing less than charm incarnate, making each and every one of them feel as if they were the only woman in the room, fascinating them with his wit and humour. However, I suspect that as Mother grew to hate him, she saw only a selfish man, a man who reserved a high and mighty attitude for servants and minions, but who had a great esteem for his mistresses.

Perhaps there was the same disillusion on my father's side. Did he remember the beautiful girl with translucent skin, thick chestnut hair, and a slender, graceful figure who had been properly brought up to ladylike pursuits by Irish nuns in a Himalayan convent? Mother might have been a hopeless cook, and our house might have been unkempt and dusty, but she could play the piano with flair and brilliance; her watercolour paintings of plants and birds were delicate and accurate. She could sew a fine seam, she could embroider, crochet, and quilt, and she could knit without looking. If Father did remember these qualities now and then in Mother, it didn't last long. Mostly, he saw a woman who simply never understood how to handle money. Why she couldn't cope when other wives did was a mystery to him, and he pondered it even while ordering another expensive tailored suit and a pair of bespoke shoes for himself. One thing was for certain. Father's strong personality, learned from his own childhood of poverty and neglect, had turned my mother into a shy and nervous woman, a shadow of her former self, one I distantly remembered as being happy once.

Considering these circumstances, it took some kind of bravery for me even to approach the subject of a new swimsuit, but before I could, another argument about money erupted at dinner.

'Other women manage,' Father raged, when he'd been served macaroni-cheese for the fifth night running.

'Their husbands earn more money than you do,' Mother said nervously. She raised her hand to rub the familiar red flush of anxiety creeping up the back of her neck. The explosion, as always, was immediate. Jumping to his feet, Father hurled his plate at the wall above my mother's head.

'Their wives aren't fools!' he yelled. Mother screamed, cowering from the shock of the crash behind her. Father was very touchy about his reduced position and circumstances after years spent lording it over servants and subordinates. No one could lord it like my father.

'I don't know how to shop,' Mother wept from behind her hands. 'I was never taught.'

'You're mad, I don't know why I married you!' my father shouted, pounding on the table so that all the glasses, the plates and the silver jumped and skittered on the polished surface. Mother dropped her hands and stared at him. Instinctively, at that frightening moment, I knew that her greatest fear – greater even than having to beg for credit or having plates of food hurled at her – was being abandoned with four children to bring up in a land where she was a stranger.

As if to reinforce his power over all of us, Father took himself off, slamming the front door on his way out of the house. We sat around the table, subdued by this threat to our security, Mother quietly sobbing and Gracie screaming to be free of her straps. Suddenly, the dumbwaiter rattled and a rice pudding emerged from the depths. The spell was broken as my brothers pounced on it. I sat Gracie on my lap and kissed her wet face, tasting the salt in my mouth as I fed her spoonfuls of the milky rice. Bone weary, eyes swollen, Mother took herself off to bed.

I waited now until the next morning before I broke the news to Mother that I would need a new swimsuit.

'This dreadful climate's far too cold to swim in,' Mother said, then shuddered, as if the very idea were enough to give her chills. Brought up in a land of crocodiles and poisonous water snakes, she had never learned to swim, so saw no earthly use in it. However, it had taken me days to get up enough courage to broach the subject, and so I was persistent.

'I've got to have one,' I said. It was true. At my school we had hockey and netball in the winter, swimming and tennis in the summer. This was regardless of weather since, living on the edge of Dartmoor, we were used to late blizzards and thunderstorms, rain and creeping mists for much of the year. All the other girls had the regulation ones from the school outfitters, trim-fitting little garments made out of navy-blue jersey.

Mother looked stricken. 'You should have mentioned it sooner, Rose. I don't have any money until next month.'

I said nothing as I stood there, waiting to see if this was her final word. I had learned young to be sensitive to the alarm and despair that any request, however modest, could trigger in my mother, sending her off to her bed for days. Somehow, in her anguish, she was able to ignore the fact that she had a toddler and three other children to care for. Early on it became my task to muddle through on my own; to change and feed Gracie, to wash the family's clothes by hand and hang them out on the line, so that Gracie would have clean nappies and my brothers and I clean clothes for school. In contrast to this, and no matter how scarce money might be, my father's shirts and detachable collars, which he changed twice a day, were collected by a weekly laundry service and returned, starched and immaculate.

Mother sighed again. She looked around the room, as if for inspiration. Suddenly, her eyes focused on the book-shelves and she brightened.

'I'll knit you one!' she declared.

God, no, please no.

'There's a pattern in my book, regulation swimsuit suitable for girls or boys,' she continued. 'No one will know the difference.'

Lots of fashion problems had been solved over the years,

thanks to Mother's 'bible', which was an old brown knitting book she'd bought from a jumble sale for sixpence. All these years later, I still have it, Reference 6462 stamped in gold on the leather spine. It contains those patterns for lacy shawls and little dresses and rompers she knitted for my sister, as well as those school jerseys, socks, and vests for my brothers and me. Even back in the early 1950s the book was dated, but Mother lived by the philosophy that fashions in woollens never changed. She was forever buying old garments from jumble sales for a few pence, then 'pulling them down' to make clothes for us. But a swimsuit?

She quickly flipped through the pages until she came to a bikini set for a woman, much too mature for me. The only other pattern was for an almost topless sunsuit for a six-year-old boy or girl. 'Never mind, I can adapt the camiknickers,' she said, pointing to the photograph of a trim blonde woman draped at a dressing table, brushing her hair, wearing a kind of combination vest and panties.

'No! I'll look silly!' I stormed.

'Of course you won't. Trust me.'

She produced an old navy-blue jersey from a mothballed drawer and unpicked it, first winding the scratchy prewar wool around her fingers and then rolling it into a massive, crinkly ball. 'I should steam the creases out,' she said, 'but it doesn't matter much, it'll get wet soon enough.' At the time, her words didn't have the ring of doom about them. Her fingers flew and the swimsuit was finished in a couple of days. She finished stitching the last seam, bit off the wool, and handed the results of her labour to me. Suddenly torn between doubt and hope, perhaps realising that she was casting me in the role of Cinderella, she said, 'Will this do?'

Surprisingly, and although it was itchy and very severe, the finished garment fitted perfectly when I tried it on in my bedroom. To my relief it also closely resembled the other girls' costumes. The difference, however, was brought horribly home to me when I jumped into the swimming pool for the first lesson of the summer term. The wool absorbed water like a sponge and stretched – dear Jesus, how it stretched. When I emerged, gushing blue dye like a flood of ink, the crotch was somewhere around my knees, the bodice exposing nipples shrivelled with cold like little raisins. The girls in my form shrieked with laughter while I died a thousand deaths. Then Pam was there, helping me to squeeze out the water, giggling, but in a companionable way.

'Where on earth did you get it?' she asked.

'Mummy knitted it,' I mumbled.

She raised her perfect brows over her forget-me-not eyes. 'Your mother is weird, but I like her, she's different,' she said. 'Wet wool stretches, you know.'

By now I was almost calm. Pam was the leader of the pack; where she went, others followed. The girls crowded around, trying to help, offering their towels. Their kindness reassured me.

'I've got a spare costume you can have. I'll bring it in tomorrow,' Pam said in a way that brooked no argument.

With such humiliations in my life, it was no wonder that I preferred my own company. My love of nature started as a kind of needed companionship, so I'd roam dreamily through the open fields of the valley. I was fearless in climbing trees and, in order to watch a peregrine falcon at close hand, I even scaled the sheer sides of a disused quarry I had found, deep in the woods where no one else ever went. As I crossed the damp meadows by the river, homeward-bound in the dusk, often I'd see a ghostly barn owl flying low over the grass, hunting for voles. Or I'd be followed by a herd of cows, ambling along behind me, getting closer as their curiosity got the better of them. I can still feel their hot, sweet breath huffed into my hair, a pungent smell of urine and fermented grass surrounding me like a cloud. If I stopped and turned, they would back away, still watching me with luminous dark eyes; one or two would belch. As soon as I moved on, they would follow me, a little more urgently, getting closer. I would stop and turn; it became a game.

My interest in bird-watching originated, as did so many of my early passions, with one of my brother's hobbies. Jimmy collected birds' eggs. They were kept in a large Christmas cracker box, lined with a deep bed of cotton wool in which little hollows were carefully shaped. Nestled within the box were nearly fifty eggs ranging in colour and size from a hedge-sparrow's astounding blue, to the large olive of a pheasant, or the minuscule pearl of a wren. We learned to tell the difference between eggs that were very similar in colour, such as the green eggs with brown freckles of both the blackbird and the mistle thrush. After a time, we became quite good at deciphering the wide range of different-coloured eggs laid by a single species, such as a tree pipit.

It had all started three years earlier when Jimmy was given a secondhand copy of *Birds of the British Isles and Their Eggs* for Christmas. The big book was filled with lifelike watercolour paintings and lit a spark in both of us. Jimmy immediately decided to become an egg collector and appointed me his lieutenant. Until that moment it had never occurred to me that wild birds, as well as tame ones like chickens and ducks, laid egg, nor that they were of such variety. My own Christmas gifts that year, a box of six tartan hair ribbons and a new copy of Edward Lear's *Book of Nonsense*, paled into insignificance next to the magnificence of Jimmy's bird book with its waxed blue cloth cover and title embossed in gold.

We filled our spare hours in the cold months from Christmas until the nesting season began in late March or April, poring over the pages. We quickly absorbed a basic knowledge of birds and became familiar with the rules of 'nesting'.

'Take only one egg from a nest,' Jimmy instructed me. 'Birds can't count, you know, but if you take them all, they will desert.'

'Well, they can count then,' I said cheekily.

'No they can't, but they're not stupid. Even a bird's brain can recognise an empty nest. They think a snake or something has been there and won't go back.'

It never occurred to me that the only kinds of snake we had in England were the grass snake and the adder, and they didn't climb trees.

From his friends, Jimmy had learned how to blow eggs. These friends were farmers' sons who messed about outdoors, rabbiting and fishing and otherwise tormenting the wildlife. He'd prick the egg with a pin at the top and bottom and then gently blow. If the egg was new-laid, before the chick had formed, a watery mess of yolk and albumen would shoot out. A more developed chick would explode out in a mess of broken shell, blood, and slime. Sometimes, you could see the small heart and the rudiments of eyes. Disgusted, Jimmy would kick it away. If he had to climb a very tall tree to get to the nest, he held the egg in his mouth on the way down. Once he took an addled egg and it burst while in there. The taste and smell were so vile that he hung from a branch puking over his boots. It was his ambition to have an egg of every bird in the British Isles, neatly labelled in proper collection chests, the kind made of mahogany with brass handles and corners. I threw myself into this quest, until one day a fledgling jay was blown and lay dying on the grass with its useless stubby little wings decorated with two or three half-formed flight feathers, its flat yellow beak and inky blue eyelids still tightly sealed. I no longer had the heart for egg-blowing.

Jimmy's own interest in eggs was ruined when I accidentally destroyed his entire collection. We had been playing hide-and-seek and I chose the top shelf of his wardrobe to crawl into. This was where he'd put the box of eggs to keep them out of Freddy's clutches. Like an awkward cuckoo, unwittingly I settled myself down on that false nest of cotton wool and cardboard, crushing it. Desolate for a while, Jimmy soon switched his interest to hunting game with his Webley airgun, sent to him by Granny who, although she despised my father, loved her grandchildren.

I adored Jimmy. I admired everything he did and would have followed him blindly through thick and thin. I wanted to be Jimmy, I wanted to be a boy, with a boy's freedoms. When the house rocked with our parents' rows, or when Mother was at her maddest, we took comfort from each other, a little unit of two, often escaping an atmosphere of hate to roam through the fields. At first I was happy to go along with anything Jimmy did, no matter how bloody, dressed in a pair of his grey flannels, which I always returned muddy and saturated to the knees. Only racy women wore trousers and none were made for girls. I wanted to be a proper little trouper, following in my brother's wake, one who could scramble through brambles without getting scratched. We would set off in the pearly light of dawn, across fields still wet with dew, to a warren on the edge of a wood, getting down on our bellies among the rough tussocks until an unwary rabbit hopped close enough for Jimmy to score a direct hit in the head. An airgun didn't have the power of a .22 or the killing spread of a shotgun.

What I remember liking most about those days was the raw land pulsing around me. I remember late snowfalls blowing down from the mountains of Wales, which lay far to the north across the Bristol Channel. Heavy flakes would rime the fields with a fine white icing, encasing every branch, every blade of grass, with ice crystals that sparkled in the pale morning sun. I remember us, Jimmy and me, how we wore balaclavas and gloves knitted on our mother's nightly clicking needles, only our frozen noses and cheeks exposed. I remember how Jimmy always carried the gun and I the hunting bag. I try not to remember the soft rabbits who fell dead before us, or those wood pigeons we bagged – such a pretty bird in shades of grey and pinkish violet with a clean white collar. Like all game birds, pigeons were easy targets. The shock of even a small pellet anywhere on their plump pink breasts felled them at once. No, I try to remember the snow, and the sound of our steady feet upon the frozen earth.

Spring came. On an idle afternoon one May, as I sat on the riverbank watching a pair of grey and white long-tailed tits come and go from their nest in a gorse bush that was radiant with small golden blossom like a pea-flower, a boy I knew, one of my brother's friends, came along the path with a fishing rod. When he spotted me, he stopped.

'Hello, Rose. What are you doing?'

'Nothing,' I said. 'What are you doing?'

'Fishing.'

He settled down on the bank not far away and an hour passed. The female bird was sitting on her second clutch of eggs, so there wasn't a lot of activity. I was content to doze, made sleepy by the perfume of the may blossom that floated overhead like a cloud, and the meadowsweet that lay like snow below, and the golden gorse that was heavy with the sound of bees. A little bit of Morgana's folklore idly drifted into my mind: 'When the gorse be out of bloom, kissing's out of season.' I had noted that even on the coldest day, in sheltered places one or two flowers still nestled within the grey-green thorns. After a while, I heard the quick flutter of wings, a soft call of tupp-tupp, as the bird left the nest. Its tail was so long, it didn't seem possible that it could fit inside the well-concealed mossy dome, but from Jimmy's bird book I knew that somehow it bent its tail right over its body and it all fitted snugly inside. I don't know why, perhaps it was because I wanted to be accepted, but I then did a stupid thing.

'Have you ever seen a bottle tit's nest?' I asked, giving the bird its country name.

'No. What's it like?'

'I'll show you, if you promise not to show anyone else and never ever to take the eggs. Promise?'

'Yeah, I promise.'

The nest was in the centre of the bush, difficult to reach. At first sight it looked like a ball of lichen or mouldy cheese. Inside, it was thickly lined with tiny feathers.

'That's not a nest,' he said scornfully.

'Yes, it is. It's covered with cobwebs to camouflage it. There's a little opening near the top, just big enough for a finger. There's six eggs,' I said, gently slipping a finger into the slit. 'You have to be very gentle, for they're tiny and fragile.'

He copied me. 'I can feel them,' he said excitedly. 'They're warm. Can you take them out? Let's have a look.'

'No, they might break, and the nest could fall to bits,' I said, suddenly scared, seeing by his expression that he wouldn't leave well alone. Back then it seemed to me that all boys were rough and destructive. I breathed a sigh of relief when he took his fishing rod and went on his way.

The next day, the nest was wrecked, sad little scraps of cobwebs, grass, and feathers scattered on the ground beneath the gorse bush, the eggs gone. When I saw the boy again I flew at him like a wild cat, pushing him to the ground. I straddled him, shouting and beating him furiously.

'I hate you!' I screamed. 'You promised!' Then, I started to weep. 'Those poor birds, you don't know what you did. I'll never speak to you again.' I got up and walked away, ashamed to let him see me cry.

'You're nuts,' he shouted after me. 'They're just birds.'

When I arrived home that day, still in tears, I discovered that the spectre of knitting had reared its head again. Mother had entered a knitting competition in *Good Housekeeping* magazine, motivated by a first prize of twenty guineas. She had spent half an hour in the local haberdashery, strongly influenced by some wool on sale. The knitting bible was open to a pattern for a skating sweater in blue with a design of white snow crystals, and she was busy at work. While I was still very upset over the ruined nest, it was a relief to see that Mother was showing animation for the first time in months.

'I can teach you, Rose,' she said, when she saw me staring at her busy fingers. And so, it began. Each evening when I came home from school, she would hold up the piece of knitting to show her progress on the sweater. Then, once I'd helped put Gracie to bed, I would find myself with two needles and a ball of yellow wool in my hands, taking lessons. We would sit companionably around the fire in the drawing room like two old crones at the guillotine, listening to *The Archers* on the radio, while my two brothers built complicated machines out of red and green Meccano upstairs in their freezing bedrooms. I loved our growing closeness, seeing it as a sign that things could get better.

A year or two earlier Mother had decided to teach me the piano, but her method was learned from the nuns who had taught her. She would rap my knuckles with a ruler when I hit a wrong note. When I grew sulky, she said I was lucky, the nuns had also cut an inch off her hair each time she did badly, until she was practically bald. 'What happened?' I had asked. 'My father came for a visit and found me with a chapped scalp and chilblained ears,' she said. 'So he removed me from the school at once. He was angry with me, not with them. He said I was a nuisance, always in trouble.' I must have been a nuisance, too, for my piano sessions with Mother became torment for both of us, until, finally, we ended up screaming hysterically at each other and the piano lid was slammed shut for ever on my musical career. For a long time there had been a distance between us, so now I looked upon her offer to teach me knitting as an olive branch, one I reached for gladly.

As Mother's skating sweater grew toward completion, so did my own slightly grubby offering: a pair of canary gloves that would become my father's Christmas present.

The gloves were nothing compared to the skating sweater, however, which occupied centre stage and was treated with much more respect. It seemed a precarious under-taking, but then a windfall of money depended upon it. I will always remember the special smell of the Johnson's baby talc Mother shook over her hands to keep them dry and clean as she worked. The wool was never allowed to roll across the floor, and at the end of the day it was all wrapped in a white pillowcase to protect it. When we heard my father come in, our work was always put away quickly, her sweater, my gloves. It may be the only time I felt true companionship with my mother, that summer of the bird's nest and the canary-yellow gloves.

While Father fiddled with the radio to find a concert on the Third Programme, regardless of what we had been listening to, I would descend to the dungeon to heat up milk in a saucepan for cocoa. This we drank while he walked back and forth, conducting to the music, which he had turned up loud, or raising his voice above it, reliving his winning streak at bridge or quoting from whichever play was under rehearsal in the Oddfellows Hall for the dramatic society. His energy brought the house alive while draining the power from my mother, like a brilliant light from too small a battery. She sat in her chair with her eyes fixed hopelessly on his face and said nothing. Later, I came to realise that she was always convinced he'd spent the evening in bed with a woman, and in many cases he probably had. When the cocoa was drunk, and the cups and saucers put on the dumbwaiter to be washed in the morning, she retreated upstairs and got into her single nun's bed in the room she shared with Gracie. Father sat in his study along the landing to compose bad poetry until dawn, before lying down on the old army camp cot he'd lugged around the world. His latest demon was in the form of Freddy's teacher at the local junior school, a man named Charles Causley, also known as 'the Cornish poet'. Father had become obsessively envious of Mr Causley's growing fame. He couldn't understand how a humble schoolmaster could achieve what he, a man who had seen the world, could not. So, Father battled nightly with the words that just would not come.

Finally the skating sweater was finished, wrapped in white tissue, and sent off to the magazine. A few weeks later Mother was informed by post that she had won third prize: a hamper. With irate tradesmen dunning at our door for payments owed them, she had been counting on those twenty guineas to pay off a few of her debts. Winning third prize out of an entire nation of knitting women was a real achievement, at least to me, a novice knitter, but Mother was distraught.

'Here,' she said, dismissively handing the sweater to me. 'You can have it.'

Autumn came, colder than usual. We woke each morning to frosty grass and thick mists rising from the river in the valley below. I had always liked that time of year, liked the bittersweetness in the air that made me ache with longing for something unknown. Perhaps the ache is encoded in our genes, dating back to an ice age when we could smell the wind blowing off the glaciers and knew it was time to head south with the migrating herds. Spring always seemed different, a green juicing, a rushing joy that gave way to the headiness of summer. Spring was youth and joy. Autumn was looking into the starry sky and sensing age-old patterns.

On All Hallows' Eve our town held the pagan

ceremony of Halig, which culminated in 'witch burning'. Mother stayed at home, hating the cold so much she would often wear her overcoat in the house. Sometimes, she even wore it to bed. The rest of us were there, watching from the side as the floats and band passed by. A chill moon shone through intermittent clouds, and a cold wind brought flurries of snow, which came unusually early that year. I stamped my feet and sniffled into my mittens. I could feel a cold coming on. The noise and confusion were overwhelming and my head ached. A sudden stitch doubled me over in pain. When it subsided, I slipped away from the throng. Behind me the parade blared by. Fireworks shot into the sky, fires crackled in back gardens, little children shouted, witches and vampires slunk through the shadows. The band was at a distance now, drums beating, brass swelling, everyone cheering. Light-headed, I reached the green beneath the high bulk of the castle keep. I ran, leaping across clumps of grass, swerving past bushes. I was crazy, eyes wide, hysterical. I was as big as the world, as big as the sky, frenzied under the hidden moon.

Suddenly, the noise and the confusion were gone. I was alone. In the centre of the green a huge bonfire was ready to blaze into life at the touch of a taper when the parade reached this point, but now it was quiet and dark. A cold wind blew hard and set leaves swirling. My bones felt scrambled, as if melting and flowing through my body – hot and bubbling. I sat on a cold swing and pumped my legs back and forth, back and forth, the lava flowing through me, a molten sea whose tides echoed the rhythms of the distant band. Swinging wildly up into the sky, head hanging down to the ground, feet pointing up, hair brushing the frozen earth, arms stiff and straight, grasping the cold chains, metal burning through gloves, fingers bent and aching. Upside down.

The parade swung into view down Castle Street, the crowd streaming along with it, goblins and dragons and monsters spilling on to the grass, people shouting, a wave bursting out of the confines of the castle gate into the dark, open space. The bonfire suddenly sparked and crackled into fierce life. Children shrieked, the crowd cheered. Fireworks exploded noisily, rockets arched over the trees, and stars fell. They were burning a witch from one of the floats, a reminder of such burnings a long time ago. The black pointed hat and cloak toppled forward as the flames bit; then the straw centre whooshed into flame as the fire's hollow heart folded and writhed into itself.

Filled with unexplained terror, I fled home. The bath-room was as big and cold as an ice cave, with black and white tiles on the floor, walls covered with white oilcloth and stencilled with black swans, a huge tub sitting on lion's paws, and a demon geyser that hissed and roared like a dragon belting out scalding water. Standing in the steam, I thawed, the blood flowing again, pumping into my frozen hands and feet, into my frozen nose and chin. My ears felt pierced with little arrows of pain. I slowly undressed, and as I slipped my white knickers off, I was unprepared for the alarming stain marking the end of my childhood. I leaned against the mirror, seeking comfort, as if wanting to be rejoined with my lost image. My tears mixed with the steam running down the cold glass. I felt a terrible fear of the future. Who could I tell? Not my mother. We didn't talk about such things. Pam seemed so confident, so assured, that I didn't want her to laugh at my fears. It would be impossible to talk to Miss Cadwallader, who had warned us this would happen, that there would be blood one day, and eggs, fragile and delicate and breakable inside us, just because we were women. Outside, I heard a last sharp roar from the crowd and knew the witch had finally burned, nothing left of her but ashes. The mirror misted and I slowly disappeared. I knew then that nothing would be the same again.

—

December came, bringing ice and blizzards that turned our harsh grey town into a frozen vision, like an ice palace cut from a glacier that floated above the valley mists. The windowpanes in our unheated bedrooms became thickly covered in fern patterns, delicate and beautiful. We could see our breath and the lino was bitterly cold beneath our bare feet. At nighttime, we would take all our clothes into bed with us, so they would be warm in the morning when we wriggled into them beneath the blankets. Then we would stumble to the washbasin and grab a flannel to wash only our faces and hands, ignoring those parts we could not see.

At her wit's end to provide a nice Christmas for us, an astonishing thing happened to my mother. She won a modest fortune. She had surreptitiously been doing the football pools, a penny a line, never really expecting to have any luck. She couldn't believe it when she heard the results on the radio and realised that she had picked every draw. At first, she thought she had won the big one, £75,000, and nearly collapsed at just the thought of it. Warmly wrapped against the cold, I walked with her to the phone box on the corner so that she could report her win. Her fingers were shaking more with nerves than with cold as, fumbling, she fed coins into the box. I waited in painful anticipation as she carefully dialled the winners' number. She spoke to someone, listened, then sighed and replied, 'Yes, thank you.' Slowly, she replaced the receiver.

'There have been lots of winners,' she said, as if resigned to her bad luck.

I felt suddenly hollow. 'How much?'

She sighed again. 'I don't know, it depends how many have won. They'll share it out.'

I really think that for a brief moment she had seen Shangri-la – a modern, easy-to-clean cottage with a proper housekeeper, nice food, decent clothes for us, and no unpaid bills. Disappointed as her dreams of vast wealth faded, she seemed flattened, her spirit gone. She said she'd give Father the cheque when it came.

'No, don't!' I begged. 'He'll spend it on himself.'

'He's your father, Rose,' she said, accepting the inevitable, now that she wasn't to be rich enough to escape his philandering.

I looked at her helplessly. 'Oh, Mummy, you always give in to him.'

She must have loved him because she could never resist him, however selfish he was. It always baffled me how my father would worry so bitterly about money and yet could throw it away so easily. Later, I came to realise that spending it made him feel better, gave him a sense of purpose and achievement. I also came to realise that even while my mother despaired, even while she was angry and jealous, some inner part of her wanted him to have his pleasures because for a while it made him happy.

One of Father's pleasures was in seeing films. He always managed to find enough money for all the big Hollywood movies, especially those starring beautiful women, since he adored them. He told me that when he was in his teens he had fallen madly in love with Mary Pickford. When, as a young soldier in Simla, he met a girl at a dance who resembled her, he proposed at once. Devastated when this girl rejected him, he proposed to my mother instead, at the very same dance. I wished he hadn't told me that story, because it would have been nice to feel that at some stage in their lives they had truly been in love. My mother's version of how they met and married was entirely different, so perhaps my father's wasn't true. He often invented things for effect and later forgot what he had said.

It was during that cold December that Father announced he was taking me with him to the pictures, and that we would see *My Cousin Rachel*. In that cultural outpost we always saw things later than the rest of the nation, but it didn't matter one whit. Since the radio was our sole source of entertainment, just going out for the evening was an event. I had no idea who would be in the film, nor did it matter. It was all thrillingly Hollywood.

'You can wear the skating sweater,' Mother announced to me. 'It's upstairs in your tallboy.'

I knew better than to argue the point, and it was freezing outside, but when I pulled the sweater on over my head in my bedroom, the tight ribbing clung to me, revealing what I had been ignoring. I had developed breasts. They seemed to have grown in the night as mysteriously as molehills on a flat lawn. For some reason, while most of Miss Cadwallader's talk had gone in one ear and out the other, the bit about never telling anyone had stuck. A sense of shame about my body had become deep-rooted. Breasts were a sure indicator that I was growing up, that changes were being wrought, unwanted transformations.

Ashamed, I dragged the sweater off and got dressed again in my shapeless school uniform of all-concealing green gym slip and cream Vyella blouse. The girdle about my waist was also plain bottle green. Other girls, neat, quick, and clever girls like Pam, were awarded monitor's girdles of striped silver and green, but I was a scruffy little thing and broke too many rules.

'Why aren't you wearing it?' Mother asked, when I went downstairs.

'It's too tight,' I lied.

'Too tight? Of course it's not. Go and put it on at once.'

Forced to go back upstairs, I buttoned myself into a liberty bodice to try to disguise my new shape, but it made no difference. I now had undeniable curves. I crept into my mother's room and stole her roll-on girdle. Quickly, in case she came up to see what the delay was, I pulled it on over my chest, dragged the sweater back on over my head, and stared into the mirror. The strong elastic gripped and flattened me in its clammy embrace. I might look as plump as a pouter pigeon, but the defined shapes of breasts had gone.

'How do you manage to make everything you wear look so scruffy?' Mother said, when I finally shuffled downstairs for the inspection. 'If you stood up straight and stopped slouching, you'd look better.'

I wasn't listening. Instead, I had bounded through the door to catch Father, who was already strolling toward the one and only cinema in town. There we stopped to read a faded pair of posters on either side of the double swing doors. When I saw that Richard Burton was the star, I nearly swooned. I felt his name should have been up in lights.

Father must have noticed that I was paying a lot of attention to the handsome face. 'He was nominated for an Academy Award over in Hollywood for this film,' he said with an air of familiarity. 'Not bad for a man still in his twenties.'

Father's tone of voice always made it sound as if he knew many important people quite well. Actually, he did know Daphne du Maurier – her husband, Lieutenant General 'Boy' Browning, had been an old Army friend. He and Daphne lived about twenty miles away in a house by the sea. Father always made a point of reading du Maurier's books so that he could butter her up when they met. Father was very good at buttering up women.

That evening at the cinema my resolution to remain a child for ever quickly dissolved. Breathless and starry-eyed, I gave away my heart from the one and sixes. Struck dumb anew by the beauty of the voice I'd heard in the flesh just once before, by the perfection of the face seen for the first time in close-up, I fell headlong in love with Richard Burton. I nearly wept as he adored Olivia de Havilland almost to the point of madness in that emotional story of jealousy and suspicion. Couldn't Richard, as Philip Ashley, see that Rachel was wicked? Surely he must know that she had murdered her husband? I was so absorbed that I was able to ignore my father's usual loudly voiced comments and questions.

'Well, what did you think?' Father asked, as we left the cinema. I was wrung out and couldn't speak, wanting to live through it all, again and again. He repeated the question.

'She was horrible,' I burst out. 'How could he possibly care about her?'

'He was hypnotised, as men are by wicked women, especially if they are also beautiful,' my father said, amused. 'I must write to Daphne. She'll be pleased to hear we enjoyed the film.'

Personally, I thought Daphne du Maurier probably couldn't care less. When wonderful actors like Richard

Burton starred in your film, why would the opinions of anyone else matter? We stopped again to look at the posters in the glass frames on each side of the double doors. I longed to go back inside and ask someone if there were any to spare, but I didn't have the nerve.

'Let's have a nightcap,' Father suddenly suggested. I tucked my hand in his arm and felt very grown up as we walked through the square to the White Hart Hotel.

People waved to Father as we came into the lounge bar. He certainly seemed very popular. Everyone there knew him. 'George! Over here!' Pam's father shouted. 'Come and join us!'

Too young to go to the bar, I sat in a corner by the door and watched my father cosy up to one of the women. There was a tension about them that was almost electric. Now I knew why we had come here. I was to be his alibi, stuck in a corner like a cipher, pretending I had noticed nothing. I could hardly breathe and felt the studs on the girdle sticking into me. I was so stupid, so, so stupid.

When my father brought my drink, I grabbed for the glass to gulp it down but knocked it over instead. I jumped up from my seat, ginger beer soaking into my skirt. Sobbing, I fled through the front doors of the hotel and into the square. He came running after me.

'It's all right, Rose,' he said. 'It was an accident. They can mop it up. Come back inside.' He grabbed me by the arm, trying to calm me.

'I hate it in there!' I screamed. 'It's smoky and they're all drunk.'

'Don't say you're going to be like your mother,' he sighed. 'Come on, I'll take you home.'

We walked in silence to our front door, past the silent

eagles on their pillars, the magical spell of Hollywood now broken.

'Oh, I left my hat behind,' Father said, and was instantly gone, back to the chattering, flirtatious crowd, back to all the lively, happy people.

—

The money my mother won in the football pools eventually amounted to £10,000, an unbelievable sum, considering that an average house in Cornwall cost only about £800 back then. That Christmas was gloriously lavish. My brothers and I had Raleigh bicycles, toys, and games. A radiogram was purchased for the family to share, a brand-new model just in, they said. It cost £60, a huge sum, far more than Mother spent on food in an entire quarter. Not stinting, she bought stacks of 78 records. Bing Crosby and Rosemary Clooney sang 'White Christmas', and there were many wonderful treasures, such as 'Hernando's Hideaway', with Edmundo Ros, and 'Stranger in Paradise'. Patti Page sang 'Tennessee Waltz' and 'On Mockingbird Hill' and we had Lita Roza's 'Doggie In the Window', which Gracie loved and asked for repeatedly. Freddy's favourite was 'I Saw Mommy Kissing Santa Claus', while mine was 'Secret Love', by Doris Day. There were heaps more records in that treasure trove, all old ones, discs in plain brown paper sleeves that had lingered for years covered with dust in the back of the shop. Hearing them on the radiogram brought back memories for my parents of the lost days in India, when they would dance without a care in the world.

More importantly, Mother's windfall of money freed us to move to London, where my father felt he could get a better job and shine again in a wider social circle. The rest of us didn't want to go. Gracie was too young to count, but my brothers and I loved it in Cornwall. We were happy in our schools and loved the countryside that surrounded us. Mother was terrified of the unknown, of the dangers that she was sure existed around every corner of the city; but most of all she hated the idea of my father plunging back into his spendthrift ways with sophisticated women. But, as always, he got his way. Within two weeks, we were packed and ready to go. All the furniture was to be left behind and sold. Father said he never much liked it anyway. We were still on Christmas holiday when I learned we were moving, so I can't remember telling anyone at school. We had no telephone for me to contact them so I'm certain that, in their minds at least, I must have just disappeared from my desk. Father had obviously made the decision earlier. Of all the people I knew, Morgana was the only one who said good-bye to me. She was utterly heartbroken at losing us and the only job she was likely to get at her age. Vehemently, she pleaded her case, using our futures as her weapon against change. 'Stay here, where it be zafe, let the little maid finish her larnin,' she said. Then, when that argument didn't succeed, 'You do-an want to be go-an to that Lunnun, it be a terrible place to brung up young'uns.'

In her heart, my mother agreed with that, but she didn't confide this in Morgana. However, I knew that something other than the fear of going to London was bothering my mother and soon she told me what it was.

'Morgana has worked for us for nothing for two years,' Mother said. 'I must pay her now I can afford it, if she will take the money.'

'Of course she'll take it,' I said. My imagination took flight. 'She could go away on a holiday! She's never been anywhere in her entire life – except once to Bodmin, and that was on foot.'

So Mother told Father that she wanted to give Morgana £200 and would he get the cash out of the bank. He stared at her as if she were mad. 'Are you out of your mind? What on earth would an old woman like Morgana do with £200?'

'She'd do with it anything she wants. It will be hers, a little nest egg. She's old now and has nothing to show for her work,' Mother pleaded.

'Don't be so ridiculous!' my father said. 'If you must give her something, give her a large ham, she'd like that. One with plenty of fat.'

This time, Mother wasn't going to give in easily. 'It's my money and I want to give some of it to Morgana. She has been an enormous help to me,' she said stubbornly.

'She's been sitting on her backside in our warm kitchen for two years and had plenty to eat, which is a damn sight more than she got at home,' my father snapped, ready to explode. 'Do you realise, Anne, that two hundred pounds is two per cent of our capital? Two per cent! It's a fortune, and she's done nothing to deserve it. Now, just forget it. The answer is no.'

Mother stared silently at him before she turned and walked out of the room. She put on her fur boots and thick coat, and nodded at me to do the same. Then, we dressed Gracie in her white bear suit. The three of us went up to the bank, slipping and sliding over icy cobbles all the way.

'What about Daddy?' I asked nervously.

'Your father, Rose, is a fool. He's sitting at home doing the crossword, full of his own bloated self-importance and none the wiser.'

My mouth must have dropped open in shock at these unimaginably rebellious words coming from my mother.

'Your father's got some big shocks coming to him,' she promised. '*Our* capital, indeed.'

We returned home with the money in a stiff, white envelope and descended to the kitchen.

'Here,' my mother said, handing it to Morgana. 'This is for you, in appreciation of all you've done for us.' Morgana stopped peeling potatoes and wiped her hands on her apron before she took the envelope.

'What be it?' she asked, almost fearfully.

'It's heaps of money!' I crowed. 'You'll be able to take a holiday! You'll be able to go to – to . . .' Because we had never been on a holiday, I could think of nowhere suitable. Then, Paris popped into my mind. 'You'll be able to go to Paris!'

'Morgana doesn't want to go to Paris, she doesn't speak French,' Mother said. 'You can go to Torquay, Morgana, and have a lovely time, being waited on hand and foot for once.'

Morgana opened the envelope cautiously and peered inside. She fingered the money, then took out a single large note.

'Five pounds, this be five pounds!' she muttered. 'Well how much there be in here, then?'

'Two hundred pounds,' Mother said. 'A hundred for each year.'

Morgana sat down and laid the envelope on the scrubbed table, clutching the five-pound note in her lap with gnarled brown fingers. She lifted her eyes and stared at the lone bulb dangling from the ceiling.

'Electricity,' she said slowly. 'They baint never been no electricity in my house, baint never been none. All my life it be oil an candles, soot an smoke, dan' nuisance, tis often I've been afeared I'll be burnt to a zinder.'

'You don't have any electricity?' Mother said. 'We didn't have any in India, of course, but this is England.'

'I'll be after putting zum in, getting zum ease in my life,' Morgana said. Her ancient face wrinkled into a contented smile as she picked up the envelope, replaced the fiver, and tucked it into her bosom where it stuck out at an angle. 'A lodger, I'll be having now, an a wash boiler, zo'as I can be taking in laundry. Thankee my dearies, now life ull be sweet.'

If Mother thought this act was going to go unnoticed she was wrong. When my father found out that the bank had been raided, his anger reached white heat and it was only my brothers and me, shouting and dragging him off, that stopped him from grabbing and shaking her.

'You'll ruin us!' he bellowed at Mother, who cowered back, the brave wind taken out of her sails.

Eventually, because it was too late, and the deed was done, the money given away, Father calmed down. Months later, at a chattering cocktail party, at which he was the life and soul, I heard him tell one of his amusing stories about how he had brought electricity to Cornwall, even though privately at home, he still chastised Mother for giving Morgana the money.

—

We boarded the train for London, leaving behind the stockyards and slaughterhouse, and the bleak grey town sprawling up the hill. The train had no sooner pulled out of the station than Father, energised by his plans for a new life in London, tucked in to the bursting picnic hamper that Morgana had unexpectedly prepared for the family. She had filled it with things she warned we would never see again: ham sandwiches made with fresh buttermilk bread, scones with strawberry jam, honeyed saffron cake, and that morning's clotted cream skimmed from a pan set on a cool corner of the monster stove. She had also packed some of her special pasties wrapped in clean linen, one end filled with meat and potatoes, the other end with apples: a complete meal-in-one that farm workers took with them to the fields. Finally, crisp little russet and gold Cox's pippins spilled from the basket, a reminder of the apple orchards we were leaving behind that every spring blew white and lovely down the valleys of that legendary land. Father was the only one with an appetite, it seemed.

When I think back to the days of what was supposed to be my innocence, those days before adulthood wrested me away from my youthful self, I remember many things, as if they are brightly coloured symbols of my childhood: the knitted swimsuit dripping its blue dye; the tit's nest in ruined, tattered dreams; Morgana's stargazie pie; the night of All Hallows' Eve, when my innocence began to drain out of my young body; the canary-yellow gloves that Father liked so much he even wore them when he visited his mistresses; the sky-blue skating sweater emblazoned with white snow crystals; the sound of my mother's relentless needles, as if maybe she could knit a better life for us, if only she found the right pattern. It's after all these memories wash over me and are gone, that I finally think of Richard Burton, staring out at me from a faded poster locked in glass, on the double doors of the only cinema in town, like those feathered birds and waxed fruits we left behind at the dusty house in Cornwall, all suspended in time beneath their glass domes.

Three

Father was excited, but I could tell Mother didn't want to return to the city. When we had lived in London before, in Wimbledon, not long after we arrived from India, the experience of finding the drowned baby was so alarming it precipitated the first of her nervous breakdowns. We had been walking on Wimbledon Common one day, when my brother Jimmy and I ran off, as usual, and were playing by the lakes. That's when we spotted the half-submerged brown paper parcel. Jimmy started to throw stones at it and I quickly followed suit as Mother approached along the path. The parcel bobbed up and down and floated closer to the sedgy bank until Jimmy was able to fish it out with a stick. Excited, he cut the string with his penknife as I curiously looked on. The dead baby lay inside, white and clammy from having been in the water so long. It was like a wax doll, with blue eyelids and long dark lashes lying gently on colourless cheeks.

'Throw it back in, before Mummy sees,' I urged, but it was too late, she was already there. She gazed silently at the bloated infant for several seconds.

'Tomorrow, your father can sell that horrible little

hovel,' she said, quite expressionlessly. 'We're moving to the country, where it's safe to bring up children.'

I think it was from that moment that my mother began to grow mad. During the time it took to sell the house and move, she grew steadily more ill and agoraphobic, until even the smallest thing seemed too much for her. Panic was always very close to the surface. She had never seen so much traffic before and when a child who lived down the road was crushed under a bus, she became obsessive as to our whereabouts. One evening after school, instead of getting some shopping done as I usually did on my way home, I stopped off to play on a building site. Sick with worry, Mother forced herself to leave the house. While she toured the streets, panicked beyond reason, dinner was left to burn on the kitchen stove. When eventually I crept in, covered with mud, the kitchen was filled with smoke and the sink with burned saucepans. 'I've been worried sick!' Mother shouted hysterically. 'I'll kill you if you pull a stunt like this again!' She waved a carving knife in emphasis. I ducked under her arm to escape the fury and somehow my face came into contact with the sharp blade. My nose was almost sliced in half. Blood spurted everywhere.

Mother ran to the corner to call an ambulance and when it arrived, she insisted that we all ride in it, since she refused to leave my two brothers behind. At the hospital, I was thankful that the wound was not nearly as serious as it looked, and that Father was not there to add his chaos to ours – he may have been on his way home from work, but more likely he had gone straight to his bridge or chess club in town, as he usually did – because the hysteria escalated, for Mother seemed incapable of not crying. While my nose was being stitched in one cubicle, she was in another, a doctor injecting tranquillisers into her.

—

Now, we were on our way back to such unpleasant memories. As the suburbs of London approached, their crowded red-brick houses and bare winter gardens almost invisible through the snow whirling against the train windows, I could sense my mother growing more edgy and nervous. There was a grey and hollow look about her expression, a clenching and unclenching of her hands, a deeper huddle into her coat while Father sat with Gracie on his lap and pointed out landmarks he couldn't possibly have seen, but which he made sound exciting to a three-year-old. One of his most endearing qualities was his ability to empathise with children, mostly because at times he was quite childlike himself, with his sudden enthusiasms, his temper tantrums and his love of jokes. Often, he was never happier than when playing card games with us or games with pencil and paper, like Battleships. The drawback was that he hated to lose, even to a five-year-old; a dark sulk would descend and he would storm off for a while. His sulks would originate from the most unlikely direction. He had taught me to play chess at an early age and, as was usual when playing against a novice, would handicap himself, even to the extent of taking away his queen and perhaps one or two other major pieces; yet, if I happened to win, which was rare, instead of praising me for doing well, he would say 'Well I'll be dashed!' and hit the board from beneath so all the pieces flew into the air. Many times we sat at the table, after he had calmed down, companionably gluing the head of the knight back on. I had learned that a joke – which he loved, always laughing until he cried, having to take off his glasses to wipe his eyes

– or some soothing flattery, would bring him round, and almost in a maternal way, I would gently cajole and tease him until he was ready to play again.

As the train drew closer to Paddington Station, I could sense my mother's dread, and she was right to have such a strong premonition. After all, there we were, a few days into 1955, with blizzards sweeping the capital city, and to top it all off, Father had rented us a flat on a temporary basis, sight unseen.

From the start, things weren't promising. The cab driver outside Paddington Station refused to take all our luggage – some ten suitcases and boxes tied with cord. He quickly pointed out the notice inside the cab: no more than five pieces of luggage unless by agreement with the driver. But Father always knew better. While we stood by, tired and mortified, he positioned himself in the cabbie's face and began to rant and rave. Still, the man wouldn't budge. He merely looked this little red-faced Rumpelstiltskin up and down and beckoned to the next person in line. We were left to skulk to the back of the queue and await the arrival of cabs whose drivers hadn't seen the argument.

'George, you ride roughshod over everyone,' Mother said. 'One day, someone will kill you.' Father merely made a pained moue and stared off into space. I think he realised he'd made an exhibition of himself, but if ever confronted and asked why, he would reply, 'I am what I am.'

Travelling in two cabs through the blizzard, we drove eastward for nearly an hour into an area that grew poorer and more poverty-stricken as we proceeded. I was amazed to see great piles of yellow slush speckled with black soot in the gutters, churned up by traffic and coloured by the filthy smoke from a million coal fires in the city. I felt disoriented and lost as the taxi slowly inched forward, the cabbie peering out of the window as he searched for landmarks. He made numerous labyrinthine turns. Sometimes, people hurried by on the pavements, looking like ghosts in a lost landscape. Other times, a red bus would loom up, suddenly, like a wall. Street lights were hazy and muted. Traffic lights had soft haloes that glowed like fuzzy balloons floating in the falling snow. The thing I noticed most was the peculiar smell of London, of old soot and petrol and grease from cafés, a slight odour of drains and of newsprint hanging in the air, combining together and yet separate, stinging in my nose and gritty in my mouth.

Father was still brooding. He'd lost one battle but was determined to pick another fight. After a while he banged on the communicating window.

'Oy, fellow! You'd better not be cheating me,' he warned. 'We're only going to Dalston, not the North Pole.' The cabbie pulled in.

'Do you want to get out and walk?' he asked, aggressively.

'We've been driving around for an hour,' Father persisted.

'And we'll drive for another bleedin' hour in this whiteout,' the cabbie said. 'Do you know where Dalston is? It's in the bleedin' East End, ain' it?'

It wasn't surprising that Father hadn't known where Dalston was, having as he did an almost naïve, blinkered view of life, which possibly was why so many of his golden eggs turned out to be empty and worthless. To him the only parts of London that counted were the influential areas around Westminster, the glamour of the nightlife in Mayfair, and the West End. Dalston – or more widely, Hackney, with its pestilential marshes and notorious prison – could have been on another planet. When we finally drew up outside a tall terraced house with peeling paint in a shabby street, all Mother's fears were instantly confirmed. She sat in the taxi and said, 'Oh no, no, this can't be it.'

The landlady was an old Greek woman, her face more wrinkled than a relief map of the Balkans. She had dyed black hair and a wicked slash of a mouth. She told us curtly that she wasn't expecting us until the following week. It was a ploy to explain away the squalid, unprepared state of the flat Father had rented, one that didn't exist outside the glowing terms of the advertisement. The furniture was piled in one room like a junk shop. In order to have enough room for all of us, we ended up split between two floors, with another flat between. To go from the living area in the basement up to our bedrooms we had to pass through the floor occupied by a lonely young French-woman. Her sailor-husband was away at sea and she was left with a newborn infant. Father didn't seem to mind this, but Mother and I did. To make matters worse, there was no electricity in the basement part of the flat so that we were in darkness down there. On top of all this, the water was frozen.

'George, this is impossible,' Mother said. 'We're going to a hotel.'

'You pay me six months' rent and you can go,' the landlady said insolently. 'If not, I keep your deposit and your luggage, heh?' She held up the key of the room where all our cases had been put and which she had quietly pocketed.

'It should be against the law to rent out accommodation in such a terrible condition,' Mother said. She added that she couldn't understand how someone like my father, who during his career had had the power of life and death over thousands of lives, could keep on getting it so wrong.

Father scarcely listened. He was only concerned about losing his poetry manuscripts, which were in our luggage, and kept shouting Mother down and saying we should stay where we were.

Finally, because it was so late and we were cold and tired, Mother agreed: 'But only until tomorrow.' We all went back into the house, and Marie Christine, the French-woman, slight and pale with huge grey eyes and as graceful as a dancer, let us warm ourselves in front of her coin in the slot gas meter. She also made us tea and toast while the landlady, who lived on the top floor where she kept a baleful eye on things, roused her son to help arrange the beds all in a row in one of the rooms. We slept that night like a family of refugees in a hostel while Mother and Father whispered recriminations at each other in the dark.

By the light of morning, we saw the full extent of the horrors. The bathtub was in the kitchen with a kind of board that pulled down over it to double as a table.

'What happens when we take a bath?' Mother asked.

'Then everyone must leave the room,' the landlady said insolently. 'Is no problem.'

'Is a very big problem,' Mother insisted. 'This place should be condemned.'

The landlady laughed out loud.

'Ho, yes, then all London is condemned. Ten years ago, is bombing. Still government says is no money, is no materials, is no labour to fix.' Her voice hardened. 'So, like I say, is no problem, pay me six months or I sue in court.'

While Father sorted out his contorted affairs and house-hunted, Mother sat all day with Marie Christine, speaking in French. She learned that Marie Christine's husband had decorated their flat at his own expense, in order to get a roof over her head before the baby was born and he had to

72

return to sea. In the meantime, Jimmy, Freddy, and I roamed the streets, gaining a sense of the life and culture of the East End, home to real Cockneys and also of refugees of many nationalities. It was a busy, thriving, and polyglot area, full of life and different smells and sounds. We discovered poppy-seed bread and Oxford marmalade and little Greek cakes called baklava and shumali in immigrant shops along the Kingsland Road. We also discovered the Geffrye, a museum laid out with entire furnished rooms showing what it must have been like to live in the past, but our favourite was the enchanting, little-known Museum of Childhood, in an old mansion filled with treasures, where we spent long hours wandering about in deep content-ment. The mechanical toys and all the gadgets fascinated even Jimmy, who was restless and bored with most things. I couldn't understand what was happening to Jimmy; we had always been very close, but now he was often moody and intractable and barely spoke to Father. I thought perhaps he missed his friends, and it was partly that, but he was also growing up and he resented being treated like a child. There was something more too, which I didn't learn about until later. Jimmy was closer to Mother than I realised, and in Cornwall he had heard from his friends about Father's sordid affairs. In showing how much he despised Father and considered him weak, Jimmy believed he was championing Mother – but it only made things more fraught and edgy.

One day Freddy and I explored the ugly little garden that led from the basement kitchen, with its leafless shrubs and a sooty tree of heaven uprooting the cemented yard. Two crows sat on the roof of an outside lean-to and rose angrily, flapping their wings when we approached. They did not fly away but settled down again and glared at us balefully. They could have been the landlady's familiars. Under the overhang of the lean-to, what had been mysterious humps when covered with snow in the shelter of the wall proved to be soggy mattresses against a green door. Pulling them aside to see what lay behind the door, we saw bundles of bloody rags, heaving with rats.

At once, I was taken back in time to India, and the little single-track trains going from the plains up to the hill stations. The lines were cut out of sheer hillsides, a wonderful feat of engineering by the Victorians. At night, elephants would rush out of the thick forests and charge the trains, pushing them over the side, where they plunged hundreds of feet into deep gorges. Nobody knew why they did this only at night, but it meant that the trains had to stop at sundown at little lay-by stations. Everyone would get out to stretch their legs and eat food prepared over camp stoves; using cold spring water rushing down from the snows. There was a sense of camping out in low bungalows, which were open to the railway at the front and the forest behind. We slept in long lines on charpoys, while the lower classes slept huddled into sheets on the beaten earth. One night, I was lying on my side and looking out toward the track when I heard a muted rushing noise, like leaves softly moving as the wind got up. In the moonlight I saw something that resembled a bolt of grey furry cloth unrolling toward me. I froze as the first rat ran under my mosquito net and over my thin sheet. Then came tens and hundreds it seemed, a moving torrent a few feet wide of hurrying bodies that flowed over me, in through the front opening and out the back. Even today, I cannot easily describe the horror of the sensation, the sense of lying there rigid, unable to move or to cry out. Worse than anything were the scaly tails that dragged across my neck. As quickly as they had come, the army of rats was gone. My ayah, who had been sleeping curled up in her sheet on the cool cement floor, only a few feet away, never even stirred.

When the police came to see what Freddy and I had found in the yard, we learned that an abortionist who was currently doing time had used the basement premises. The bloody rags were nothing worse than discarded bandages and sanitary towels. Abortion was a word with which I wasn't familiar, but Mother certainly was. Her anger came, too, from knowing my fear of rats and knowing of the disease they spread. She started packing at once. She told Marie Christine that if she had any sense she should leave too, but the French girl had no money. Mother gave her a note to give to Father when he returned in the evening, and said she would write to him, so he'd know where to find us. Then she bundled us and our luggage into a taxi and told the driver to take us to a nice, not too expensive, hotel.

The cabbie, to his eternal credit, said to Mother, 'Well Missus, you look like a literary lady, how about Bloomsbury?'

'Virginia Woolf,' said Mother.

The driver grinned. 'There, I knew I was right. Bloomsbury it is.' And that was how, for a brief golden period, Mother suddenly woke up to the fact that she was a woman of means and came into her own.

We arrived in Russell Square at a Gothic red sandstone hotel that was supposed to resemble a miniature version of a building in Saint Petersburg. It was wonderful to wallow in an endless supply of hot water in deep tubs in private bathrooms, to enjoy crisp clean sheets on comfortable beds, to have warmth and comfort surrounding us.

'I should have ignored your father,' Mother said. 'I should have left that hellhole at once when I wanted to.'

For a moment I was tempted to say, 'Don't write to him. Empty the bank, do it now. Let's disappear!' But I bit my tongue because once such words are said they can't be taken back and I knew she really did love him and in a way, so did I.

The hotel was close to some wonderful places such as the British Museum, and the Natural History Museum, in South Kensington, with its vast collection of animals from a giant blue whale to dinosaur fossils. We children were allowed to travel alone, but only on the bus because Mother had a claustrophobic fear of the Underground. I preferred the bus because I liked to see where I was going and could gaze into the windows of all the great stores along Oxford Street and Knightsbridge as we slowly trundled by. Gracie's favourite place was Coram's Fields, close to our hotel. Once the site of an eighteenth-century foundlings' hospital, it was now a park, and adults were allowed through the high iron gates only if accompanied by a child.

In the evenings, I would dress in one of the knitted jumpers made from secondhand wool – we never used the word 'sweater' back then – that I had brought from Cornwall. I had only one skirt, a new kilt that had been bought from a small old-fashioned shop right opposite the gates of the British Museum, and which swung nicely as I walked. I would sit in the hall with a book and watch the guests arriving at the hotel for assignations in the cocktail bar, or laughing and chatting as they congregated for dinner in the dining room. The women were usually in svelte gowns and furs, the men in dinner jackets and crisp white shirts. Observing them, Mother suddenly became aware that we weren't properly dressed. She seemed to see for the first time that our clothes were too tight, too short, too shabby, and she bemoaned how far her standards had slipped through years of poverty. Jimmy, who took after my mother's tall brothers, had put on a great growth spurt and now towered above my father, who had now joined us. He looked almost like a clown with bony wrists and ankles showing. He possessed no suit, only his royal-blue school blazer and flannels. I, on the other hand, looked that strangest of things: an adolescent still dressed as a child. With fresh eyes, Mother cast a critical eye over the depressing contents of our wardrobes and decided everything was tired and outdated.

'We'd better go shopping,' she sighed. 'We look like scarecrows. Thank God for my win. Rose, can you imagine how our lives would be without it?'

Mother wasn't extravagant. She simply believed in good quality, and good quality – or so she had been taught by her own mother – came from the Army and Navy store, whose catalogues had outfitted the Empire. So that was where we went, to their big emporium on Victoria Street, between the House of Commons and Buckingham Palace. I was bought some decent underwear to replace my liberty bodices and everlasting green school knickers. Then, embarrassing us both, though she tempered it by gazing vaguely into space while addressing the saleswoman instead of me, Mother said I required some brassieres and a suspender belt for my first pair of stockings. The petticoats and knickers were made of cellulose, a new material which slipped and slithered so sensuously in my hands it surprised me to learn that it was made from wood pulp.

Mother had only just started. Next, she selected a couple

of princess-line wool dresses with embroidered Peter Pan collars and three-quarter-length cuffed sleeves, one in maroon and one in a pretty dusty blue, and a scarlet two-piece with a pleated skirt and a jacket with blue frogging. I thought the latter resembled the outfit worn by an organ grinder's monkey, but Mother said it was original and suited me. She bought blouses and two pairs of low-heeled court shoes and finally, a mid-calf, full-skirted, dark-green, shot-silk taffeta shirtwaister for evenings, to be worn with a fluffy white bolero jacket. As she inspected the jacket and gave careful thought to the high price, she murmured critically, 'I could knit this in an evening.' I held my breath in case she changed her mind and decided to knit everything. Then, quietly, she said to the saleswoman, 'Yes, we'll have it. And do you have a warm coat to go over the day dresses? Harris tweed would be nice.' I was overwhelmed, unable to believe that finally I could put aside all my old school uniforms from Cornwall, including the ubiquitous gabardine mackintosh, which even then I was standing up in. At times, I had felt like the Ancient Mariner, doomed to live with that bottle-green albatross for ever.

As usual, while considering our needs, Mother had bought very little for herself, just a couple of tweed costumes and one in brown crêpe for evening, with a velvet collar and a tracing of bugle beads. 'You're not old enough for a full-length evening frock,' she said, now, 'but by the way you're filling out, it won't be long before you'll be demanding lipstick and heels. And I can't believe the way Jimmy has shot up. He's taller than me now.' And taller than Father too, I thought.

Was I the only one who had noticed that Father had suddenly grown a couple of inches? I'd also seen that he no longer strutted energetically about, but had started to limp. He took his shoes off a great deal when he came in, sighing with relief. Without shoes, the bottoms of his trousers dragged on the carpet, and suddenly I saw that they were too long because they had been specially cut to disguise new built-up shoes. It was a confusing moment. Far from feeling scorn, I felt a rush of sympathy. He was powerfully built, his shoulders wide and muscular, his arms strong. Only his puny, hairless, white legs let him down, making him the short man nature had obviously not intended him to be. However, the extra height wasn't worth the pain and the shoes were discreetly lost. In a confiding moment, Mother once told me that he was touchy about his legs, rarely exposing them to public ridicule. He'd had rickets as a child, through a deprived diet, and that was why we never saw him in swimming trunks. In fact, he kept his legs so carefully concealed, I can recall seeing them only now and then by accident. Still, he had told me about swimming across the Brahmaputra – which was two miles wide – every day, when he was stationed on its banks, not realising that it was full of crocodiles.

By now, Father was starting to treat me as a confidante and, almost reluctantly, I was enjoying that inclusion, a sense of being grown up. He had a knack of telling stories against himself that were entertaining, even though sometimes the story wasn't really one a father should have been telling his daughter, at least, not the way he told it. In one, Father related how Edwina Mountbatten, wife of the Viceroy of India, notorious for her sexual conquests of both men and women, had taken a fancy to him, inviting him to stay for a weekend when Lord Mountbatten would be away on a tiger shoot. She left Father to his own devices while she had a massage and her hair done in

79

preparation for her own personal tiger shoot, and he fell asleep, floating on an air mattress on the swimming pool. By the time she eventually came looking for her target, he'd been rushed to military hospital with severe sunstroke and was out of action for the entire weekend. Lady Mountbatten was so angry at being thwarted, she tried to get him court-martialled, sunstroke being considered a self-inflicted injury, but Mountbatten was used to her spite and ignored her. Instead, he took Father on an official inspection of Darjeeling, where he tried to seduce him himself.

'I was between the Devil and the deep blue sea,' Father said, chuckling.

'Who was the Devil and who the deep blue sea?' I asked, amazed by all these goings-on among people I had thought almost godlike in their power and position.

'Oh, she was the Devil without a doubt: Kali, Devi, and Lady Macbeth combined. She was probably the deep blue sea as well. She had the bluest eyes I ever saw. His were a light blue, but hers were deep. Many a sailor's been sunk on her rocks.' Slapping his thigh, Father laughed until the tears came, as he always did at his own jokes.

—

A strange thing happened to my parents after a few days in the hotel: they started to talk over dinner. Perhaps it was because Mother looked so nice in her new clothes, with her hair done, and had gained confidence; perhaps it was the relaxed environment; but she started to laugh and flirt with Father a little. Arguments shifted from domestic and trivial matters into literary debates. There were still skirmishes, and Father lost his temper when he got things wrong or was bettered, but these were more civilised quarrels and didn't stand out against the bright chatter and clatter of the dining room. My mother had given the impression for years that her brain was scattered. She did this, I believe, to let my father, with his limited education, shine above her. Yet Mother had a clutch of degrees, and had studied languages, science, music, and literature. With me taking Gracie off her hands so much, and with Jimmy as her companion, she started ferreting through the secondhand bookshops in the narrow little streets around the British Museum. Before long she was venturing farther afield to the Charing Cross Road, buying anything that caught her eye and taking it back to the hotel where she would read until dawn, devouring book after book instead of sleeping her life away. A casual remark of one of the owners of the bookshops introduced her to the Reading Room at the British Museum, a hushed, insular blue-domed room where scholars and writers worked in companionable silence. At first she delved into familiar tomes, then, gradually, as she idly turned the pages of the big red indexes, she would be drawn by arcane titles and descriptions. After she had read those books, she would sometimes discuss them in the evenings with us. More frequently, she sat and gazed into space and didn't hear when we spoke. She soon began buying fat students' notebooks to take into the Reading Room, where she sat on one of the heavy blue-leather and mahogany chairs at the long curving desks. She had started to write. I only found this out by accident when she sent me to fetch her purse. That's when I discovered the three red notebooks. I took one out and looked at it curiously. Opening the first page, I read: 'The river runs deep through the town . . .' then closed it guiltily. One thing Mother always had impressed on us was privacy. It was something of an obsession with her, though I wasn't to discover why for another year.

Meanwhile, Father continued to house-hunt. With neither time nor money constricting him, he was in no hurry. I think he enjoyed the comfort of the hotel, with service on tap and a large and varied menu from which to choose. In addition to this, he no longer had to worry about Mother being left on her own while he stayed out to all hours. However, Mother was anxious to be settled in a place of her own, with us safely in school instead of roaming the streets of London. When Father announced he had found the ideal family house in Gypsy Hill, a red-brick Victorian villa with five bedrooms, numerous reception rooms, and a long garden with a lawn and fruit trees, she visibly relaxed. After all, Gypsy Hill was a rural suburb with woods and a golf course, and just eight minutes by train from Victoria.

'And you have actually been there, have seen it for yourself?' she asked. 'You haven't taken the word of an estate agent this time, have you?'

'Of course not,' Father said indignantly, even though he had done exactly that more than once before. 'I went over the house with a fine-tooth comb with a surveyor. Well, not the garden of course, it was too cold, but I could see it through the windows and it was nicely maintained. The house was rather full of bookshelves, but I'm having them taken out.'

'Bookshelves!' Mother said. 'Oh, I'd like bookshelves.'

'These fill the rooms like a public library,' Father said. 'They're not only around the walls, but across the centre of every room. There's barely space to move. But' – and here came the clincher – 'I went round to the neighbour, Mrs Gibb, a nice old woman, with a husband who looked half mad to me, and a daughter who's nothing much to look at, an elderly spinster, a schoolteacher,' he added hurriedly. 'And Mrs Gibb told me the fabric was as sound as a bell.

Her father developed the street in 1889 and gave her one of the houses as a wedding present.'

'It sounds ideal,' Mother said. 'When can we move in?'

'It hasn't been decorated since it was built,' Father said. 'I've arranged to have it done up, nothing too fancy, just a lick of fresh paint and some wallpaper. I left the colour scheme and all that to the decorator's wife, a bright woman. It should be ready in two weeks.'

It amazed me that Mother didn't see the insult in that. She wasn't given – nor did she expect – the opportunity to see it for herself, or to be allowed to choose the paper and the colour of the paint. She left it all to my father, who had the most terrible taste in everything except his own clothes, and even there he couldn't go far wrong because he simply asked outfitters and tailors, 'What's your most expensive one?'

We learned that the house's previous owner had been a colonel in the Gurkhas, an eccentric man of ninety-five who practised Buddhism, collecting every book he could find on Eastern religions. He also did yoga outside in all weathers. As a ritual, he would wash under a cold tap in the yard. He got the coalmen to fill the upstairs bathtub with coal, to be used to heat the upper rooms so that his elderly, long-suffering wife wouldn't have to keep carrying scuttles up and down the stairs.

'I hope you've ordered a new tub,' Mother said.

'No, the builders said a little bleach and it will be as good as new. It's only coal dust, it never hurt a miner.'

'Well, I suppose that's what coal tar soap is made from,' Mother mused. 'And Vaseline, which, after all, goes on babies' bottoms – no, that's made from petroleum.'

'Anne, what are you on about?' Father asked, but humorously. He was always in a good mood these days.

Surprising Mother, he suggested that, since we had abandoned all our furniture in Cornwall, they should go shopping for more, so that it could be delivered the day we moved into our new house.

'Shouldn't we wait to measure up?' Mother suggested.

'A table is a table, round or rectangular, a sofa is a sofa, and a bed's a bed, double or single, no matter what size the room,' Father said airily. 'Stop fussing, put on your hat, and let's go to Harrods.'

'Oh no, Harrods is enormously expensive,' Mother said.

'Well, all right, we'll go to Heal's. Anywhere will do, it's all the same, to be sat on and dusted.'

I almost laughed out loud at that, because Mother always said she never wore her glasses so she wouldn't see the dust. Oddly enough, it was true. When our untidy home got too much for her, she used to take off her glasses and bumble around like a short-sighted bat. I always tidied up on Saturday mornings and sometimes between my school-work. From the age of nine, when Mother was laid low, I had cooked simple meals and washed clothes by hand. Looking back, it doesn't seem real that I bought the first washing machine in our family when I grew up and had money of my own. Occasionally Father also cleaned with vim and vigour, especially when he had invited guests. He'd get out the vacuum cleaner, the tin of furniture polish, and a stack of dusters and then attack the house like a military campaign. He particularly took great pride in polishing brass.

At Heal's, Mother wasn't allowed a word in edgeways. My own opinion, as usual, was completely ignored. Faced with acres of confusing choices, Father suddenly made up his mind that we would be bang up to date, asking the brash young salesman to point the way to the future. We ended up with modern, pure 1950s spiky furniture that looked and was uncomfortable, including a grey bouclé sofa bed and three armchairs. Two of the chairs were dark red with grey dashes, and one was peacock blue. I didn't see how they possibly matched. There were also Swedish-inspired G-Plan bookcases, a coffee table, a sideboard, and a square dining table and chairs, all in beech, and bedroom furniture as well. According to the salesman, the G-Plan allowed you to buy a hundred different pieces of furniture from any store in Europe and they would harmonise. When Father had taken care of that, he disposed of us by dropping us off back at the hotel. Then he continued on to Harrods, where he shopped entirely for himself, buying several antique pieces, including a leather-topped desk and a wall of Globe-Wernicke glass-fronted bookcases for his new study. Then, amusing himself with a pun – a 'globe on a Globe' – he purchased a rotating, terrestrial globe that lit up at night like a lamp, to sit upon the bookcases. So, while we were all modern, he remained period. Somehow, he must have thought that the muse of poetry descended only in a more traditional environment.

It snowed the night before we moved to Gypsy Hill. Again we travelled in two taxis, this time with all our shopping, and Mother's books, which by now filled several boxes. Sweeping over Waterloo Bridge with the tide rising high, the river in full flood, predictably Father started proclaiming,

> This City now doth, like a garment, wear
> The beauty of the morning; silent, bare,
> Ships, towers, domes, theatres, and temples lie
> Open unto the fields, and to the sky;
> All bright and glittering in the smokeless air.

'It's Westminster Bridge, not Waterloo,' Mother interrupted.

'It doesn't say that specifically,' Father said.

'Yes it does. The title is "Westminster Bridge", not "Waterloo Bridge".'

'It could be about Westminster Bridge looking at it from Waterloo or from the Embankment, or from anywhere. It could even be a memory, the poet looking back in time.'

'Yes, or looking down from Big Ben, ding-dong,' Mother said sarcastically. 'Of course it's the view from Westminster Bridge. It's written in the present tense.'

'What difference does that make?' Father said. 'It's poetic licence, something you know nothing about.'

As they continued to bicker, we passed the Old Vic, where almost exactly a year earlier I had been so beguiled by Richard Burton in *Under Milk Wood*. It suddenly occurred to me that I could come here to watch plays, perhaps I would see him again, playing the romantic lead that wonderful face was destined for, in *Hamlet* or *Romeo and Juliet*. Lost in happy daydreams, I barely noticed as built-up streets and poor areas close to the river, like an illustration in *Sketches by Boz*, gave way to an almost rural landscape straight out of a Christmas card. An untouched blanket of snow covered playing fields. A church tower stood out among tall conifers brushed with silver frosting, and leafless branches of the bare trees lining the street were garlanded with ice that glittered in the sun. A flock of starlings flew down just then, looking for food. In the bright sunlight, their winter feathers shone green and blue, flecked with amber and red, like jewelled coats.

Mother got out of the taxi and stood looking about her. Then, she sniffed the air.

'Yes,' she said happily. 'This place smells wholesome.'

And so it was. Black iron railings broke the surface of snow like a spiky decoration painted by a child on a continuous landscape that flowed over garden, pavement, and fields. In the morning light, a classically proportioned school building with a clock tower on the far side seemed to float ephemerally in the distance, like a mirage.

We were the first to walk up the garden path that day, our footprints breaking the virgin snow. On the door, in the centre, was a stained-glass picture of a sailing ship on a blue sea. Father had the key. We waited ceremoniously as he put it in the front door and turned it.

'Welcome home!' he said, then quickly stepped in ahead of Mother.

'George, you're uncouth,' she said. She glanced down a hall with rooms off and a staircase rising to vanish around a corner. 'But it all looks very nice.'

We crowded in, our feet clattering on the mottled grey marble floor of the hall. The house smelled of fresh paint. It was clean and cold, the snow reflecting in through the naked windows on to high ceilings and bare pine floor-boards with a bright, white light. The rooms echoed, appearing larger than they were, as we rushed from one to another, our feet thundering on the stairs. I chose my bedroom in a little wing off the main part of the house, with a big square balcony that looked out over all the gardens at the back. Jimmy and Freddy laid claim to the attic. Downstairs again, I was enchanted by old gas mantles everywhere and bell pulls beside the marble fireplaces: black marble in the sitting room, white marble in the dining room. Above the door in the room we decided to use as a breakfast room was a box with numbers that lit up when the bells were pulled. Obviously, it had once been used as a kitchen, in the old days when there were servants about. Mother was less enchanted by a huge cauldron in the scullery, what she called a 'copper'. It rested on a brick pier under which a fire was to be lit, and was where household linen was boiled. She looked critically at the cracked concrete floor and the single cold-water tap above the stone Belfast sink.

'I thought you'd had the place done up?' she said to Father, who was lighting a fire in the adjoining room. 'This scullery is positively Victorian.'

'Well, I thought you'd like to arrange all that yourself,' he said. 'A new stove, choose some tiles for the floor, that kind of thing.'

'Then why did you even bother to have it painted? This particular shade of green on the walls is very gloomy. And brown woodwork? It's ugly, George.'

'It was the original colour, so I just told them to do it the same. It suited somebody once,' Father said. I doubt he had even noticed how dark and poky this made the little scullery seem, even in the snow.

'Well, I don't like it, it's depressing,' Mother said. 'And it's going to be very hard to cook meals while new floors and hot-water pipes are being laid. It isn't as if it's summer, when we can live on salads.' But these were small quibbles; I could tell she liked the house.

Father had finished with the fire, which was curling smoke back into the room. Leaving Freddy to fan some life into it, he went out to the front gate and stood peering up and down the road, waiting for our furniture to arrive. Huddled in her coat, Mother looked pinched.

'Your father should have come ahead of us and got a few fires lit,' she said. 'We can't just stand here in the cold without even a chair to sit on.' She walked through the empty rooms, huddled in her overcoat and fur bootees, a scarf over her face, both arms clasped around Gracie as if hoping to find some warmth somewhere. By now, Father was stamping his feet on the pavement outside, as if on parade, and working up a rage.

'British workmen!' he stormed, for all the neighbours to hear. 'You pay them a king's ransom and they suit themselves. If they were in the Army, I'd have the lot of them clapped in irons.'

Mother stood in the open door and watched him.

'George, are you out of your mind?' she shouted. 'Come back inside. You're making the house even colder. If the furniture doesn't come soon, I'm taking the children back to the hotel before we all catch pneumonia.'

I walked to the window and stood looking out at the snowy garden. Suddenly, I saw a gnarled face, so old it was brown as a walnut shell. It was a woman staring back at me from over the garden fence.

'Coo-ee!' she called. I ran out into the garden to see what she wanted. 'Hello my dear, I'm your neighbour, Mrs Gibb. I've made some pancakes, would you like some?'

'Is your house warm?' I asked hopefully.

'Very cosy,' she said. 'It's Shrove Tuesday. We can't have you children missing that, can we?'

'Mum, it's Pancake Day,' I called, running through the house to the front. 'Mrs Gibb has invited us next door for pancakes.'

'Go on, take your brothers and Gracie,' Mother said. Then, as the removal van came rolling into sight at the end of the street, she added, 'Oh, thank God. When they've had a pancake, Rose, send your brothers back to help. Ask Mrs Gibb if you can keep Gracie there until this icebox warms up.'

While we ate piles of speckled pancakes with lemon and sugar, in front of a hot fire, Mrs Gibb told us how, when she was a girl, our street had been a lane through cornfields. She described a world of horses, and a pond on the village green, now built over, where cows and sheep were watered. She was so old that her eyebrows bristled out over deep-set eyes, more like an old man's. Her face was wrinkled like a tortoise and her iron-grey hair was twisted into a loose bun from which wiry threads exploded in every direction. Her husband, once a big, raw-boned man judging by the clothes that hung from his body, sat at the table in a striped collarless shirt and hummed quietly to himself as he rocked back and forth.

'Do you make toothpaste?' Freddy suddenly asked. The toothpaste we used was called Gibbs. It was pink and smelled of disinfectant. What made it different from other brands sold in tubes was that it came in flat little silver tins with lids in assorted colours, blue, red, yellow, and green. That way, there was one for each of us, which stopped us arguing. My colour was green.

'No, dear, but Mr Gibb's father did.' Mrs Gibb almost twinkled.

Freddy's mouth dropped open. 'I've never met anyone famous before,' he said and raced back home to tell our parents that he'd met a man whose father made toothpaste.

—

Eventually, we settled down in our new house, to our new lives at Gypsy Hill.

School was a dark cloud on the horizon where Jimmy was concerned. He and Father had fallen out over Jimmy's last school report in Cornwall, which said he wasted his time and needed to focus. A master had discovered that Jimmy had been truanting and, even worse, he'd been caught red-handed acting as the lookout for some of the seniors in their love nest in the cricket pavilion. In exchange for his vigilance, Jimmy was given cider and cigarettes. There was a big row over this, and Jimmy was suspended. Such goings-on made him seem more worldly to me, but Father said that Jimmy was wasting his education and that he was taking him out of school.

'He can go to work,' Father had declared. 'No time for hanky-panky, smoking, or boozing. He'll be too busy earning his keep.' Father had left home at fourteen and it had been the making of him, or so he declared.

'You didn't have a home to leave from,' Mother reminded him. 'That boy will leave school over my dead body.'

The row had simmered down during our hectic move to London, but it hadn't gone away. Without discussing it, Father looked around and found Jimmy a job as an apprentice in a tailor's shop, and during one Saturday lunch, while we were seated around the table in the break-fast room, he announced his plans for Jimmy's future. It was so astonishing, so unlikely, that we all stared at him in amazement.

'What?' Jimmy said. 'A tailor?'

'Where on earth did you get such a deranged idea?' Mother asked. 'Nobody in this family has ever been a tailor. Are you mad?'

'I was walking along Knightsbridge,' Father said, 'and saw a notice in a window: Apprentice Wanted. So I went in and fixed it up. It's a good trade. People will always need tailors. He's starting on Monday. He can travel up to town with me each day, and I'll make sure he sticks to it. None of his sliding off.'

To our utter astonishment, Mother picked up the loaf

of bread and hurled it at Father. She was a good shot, for it hit him in the face, knocking his glasses off. We braced ourselves for his response while Gracie got down from the table, picked up his glasses, and held them out to him with her chubby hands. Father snatched them and put them on.

'You'll be sorry for this, Anne,' he threatened. His face as black as thunder, he stormed out of the house, slamming the front door with such a crash that all the stained glass rattled.

Nothing more was said about Jimmy being a tailor's apprentice, but he was moody and barely civil to Father, and there were constant flare-ups, so I wasn't surprised when he told me that he was going away, and I wasn't to tell anyone.

'I've joined the RAF,' he said. 'I hate it at home, Rose. It's been nothing but rows for as long as I remember.'

'Jimmy, you can't!' I exclaimed. 'You're too young.'

Jimmy was not just my big brother, he was my best friend. We were very close, and I couldn't bear the thought of his leaving me.

'My mind's made up,' he said. I knew it was, but I tried anyway.

'You're too young,' I repeated, but I could see the stubborn set of his jaw and knew that nothing would dissuade him.

'I'm going to the RAF training college,' he said, excitedly. 'It'll be like going to boarding school. They sent the forms and Mum filled them in. She forged Dad's signature.'

Father didn't find out until the night before Jimmy left, when Mother sat him down and told him. As predicted, there was a flare-up, a big one, but by then it was too late;

they'd sent a travel warrant and Jimmy's things were packed.

'Why the Air Force?' Father wanted to know when he'd finally calmed down. 'I could have pulled a few strings for him in the Army.'

'My brothers can pull an equal number of strings in the Air Force,' Mother retorted. 'And if he'd joined the Navy instead, Bunty could have pulled strings there. Don't think you're the only person in the world with a big ball of twine.'

Father glowered. 'Don't talk to me about your brothers,' he said shortly.

The truth was, Jimmy had been in the Air Training Corps at school and enjoyed it. Now he wouldn't have joined the Army if they made him a general and paid him in gold dust. He said he loathed Father so much he wanted to sever any connection with him. Although I understood his reasons, I knew that once he left he would be lost to us for ever, and this realisation made me terribly sad.

—

Four doors down from us lived a family of Jewish refugees from Romania, the Schultzes. Mr Schultz had recently died. Clara and Ruth, the two plump, dark-haired, and doe-eyed daughters, came round to introduce themselves to me.

'Where will you be going to school?' Ruth asked. As she did so, she looked around curiously at all our spiky new furniture. The pieces were so lean they scarcely filled rooms designed for solid Victorian pieces.

'I don't know yet,' I said.

'Oh, you must come to our school!' Clara, the elder, said. 'We can all go together. Our Latin mistress, Miss Lemon, lives at Number 95. When we're late, she gives us a lift. She keeps saying we must be in better time, and this is abso-lutely the last time, no favouritism, but we're always late and she's always giving us a lift.'

They looked at each other and burst out laughing. Then, as if by mutual consent, Ruth told me that Number 95 was a hotbed of unusual eroticism since Miss Lemon lived with her lover, Miss Divine. Miss Divine had been the games mistress until rheumatoid arthritis had struck, gnarling her hands and twisting her limbs. Now she was confined to a wheelchair, which the devoted Miss Lemon wheeled everywhere. As her affliction had worsened, Miss Divine had retrained to teach the secretarial sixth shorthand and typing from a book.

'But two women can't, you know . . .' I broke off. Can't what? I wondered. This hadn't been in Miss Cadwallader's lecture.

'Oh, you poor girl,' Ruth said. 'They've been together for thirty years. Miss Divine used to be, um, active, once. She hasn't always been in a wheelchair, you know. You've got a lot to learn, but then, I suppose, you are from the sticks.' Oddly enough, I didn't know what the sticks were either. This was a very fast and sophisticated world I was entering.

And so it was settled. I went to Mary Datchelor, a school founded by a Quaker spinster to educate girls. It took me twenty minutes to bicycle from our house to the 'new' school building dating from 1877, in Grove Lane, Camberwell. This was an elegant, Georgian street where the Prince Regent had kept one of his mistresses. He used to drop in on her during his mad dash to Brighton, to the arms of another mistress. The Empress Josephine of 'not tonight' fame, and one of Napoleon's forgotten daughters, also lived there. After the Russian Revolution, a scattering of Romanovs had congregated in an entire Nash terrace, set back from the road, where they still lived behind tasselled blinds, frugally eking out their days.

A new school meant I had to have a new winter uniform in a different colour from my Cornish green and silver. This wasn't bought from a shop but had to be ordered from the school tailor, who called to fit me with a navy gym slip, blazer, velour hat, and a navy and gold tie.

'What nonsense,' Father said. 'A gym slip doesn't need measuring. It's like a sack.'

Sack or not, I had to have one, as well as all the other paraphernalia, from divided skirts for hockey to a powder-blue Grecian dance tunic.

'Thank God we can afford this,' Mother said, looking at the final bill. She positively glowed, basking in the knowledge that she could pay her way now without quibble.

While I was busy settling down at Datchelor, Father was casting his net wide to find bridge and chess clubs to join. He heard of a good place that had many such activities under its roof and where the standard of the players was high. This was all that interested him, since he was an exceptionally good player. He asked Mother if she'd care to go with him to Morley College in Westminster Bridge Road as his partner. She had always been good at bridge, but had gradually stopped playing with Father because the post-mortems were bitter and accusatory, lasting until dawn. She refused, but he needed a partner to join in and so he persisted. Eventually, off they went one unseasonably warm night in early June, leaving me to baby-sit Gracie.

Ruth was on her own that evening, while Mrs Schultz and Clara were delivering leaflets for the upcoming general election. She soon came round to invite me to watch a film on TV with her. We didn't have a television because Mother was convinced it would ruin our eyes. Back in Cornwall, the parish council had bought a set out of funds, installing it in the parish hall so we could all watch the Coronation. It was so small, and we were so many packed into the place, that those at the back could barely see. Yet, it was still thrilling. This had impressed me and, enthralled with television, I couldn't resist Ruth's invitation.

'Gracie will have to come,' I said. 'It's past her bedtime, so I'll probably get into trouble.'

'She can sleep on the couch,' Ruth decided. 'It won't hurt her. Your parents won't be back till late, you can take her home before they return.'

When we got to Ruth's house that evening a storm was already brewing. The air was stifling, so we left the door open to the conservatory, which was so crowded with tropical plants and ferns they overflowed into the sitting room. I can't remember the film now. Probably it was quite bland, or perhaps it was a science fiction serial like the *Quatermass Xperiment*, but, unused to television as I was, it seemed that much more vivid. The storm broke, lightning filling the room and thunder rolling overhead, coinciding with a storm occurring in the film. The real outdoors and the events we were watching on the screen merged. In the flickering black and white light from the television the tropical plants appeared to come to life, seeking us out. I hadn't noticed that Gracie, who had never seen television before, was sitting bolt upright on the sofa, taking the film in, while Ruth and I huddled together for support in an armchair.

When the characters on the screen shrieked, Ruth and I clutched each other and shrieked in unison. Mrs Schultz and Clara returned home to our hysterical screams and

Gracie's howls, snapping off the set immediately, so we never did see the end of the film. She picked Gracie up, soothing her tearful face with kisses and pats while lecturing us about inflicting nightmares on a child. She told Ruth she could go to bed at once, but, although Freddy was in bed at home, I wouldn't go until my parents returned. When they eventually arrived, some time after midnight, we heard Mother say clearly, 'I will never ever play bridge with you again, George, so help me God. That is the last time.'

'Ach! The bridge, always it causes the divorce,' Mrs Schultz said. 'Never you mind, they will forget it in the morning.'

But they didn't forget it, the argument lingered in the air in hostile remarks and a sense of wretchedness. A few days later, Father told me that he'd agreed to go to a dance at Morley College, but Mother had refused to go with him; would I accompany him as his partner instead?

'Ask your father why I won't go,' Mother said.

I looked helplessly from one to the other.

'Tell your mother she can't dance,' Father said.

'No, tell him that I'm sick of his womanising,' Mother said coldly. 'Even in the middle of a rubber, he is casting his eye about. You go, Rose, he might behave himself if you're there.'

I gave in and went to keep the peace, in my new green taffeta and the fluffy white bolero. I'd learned to dance at school in my Grecian tunic and, in the end, I looked forward to this evening out.

❦

'My daughter,' Father proudly introduced me. 'My daughter, Rose.' I was the only person there of my age, and, although I did look older than a girl who was almost fourteen, I still felt too young to mix with that crowd. I was almost the height – five feet four – that I would be as an adult and had quite mature curves. My hair was wavy, the same chestnut brown as my mother's, my eyes were hazel-green beneath distinct black eyebrows. The one thing everyone always remarked upon was my 'English rose' complexion. The air was hot and choking with the smell of Nuits de Paris, caked face powder, and tobacco. Raddled women screamed with loud laughter, and whiskied men with hungry eyes clasped me close with their hot, moist hands, whispering words into my ear. I felt ashamed that I had put on the lipstick and pressed powder from the compact I had stolen from Mother's dressing table. The red of the lipstick, the only colour that Mother ever wore when she could be bothered, was too bright and adult for me and perhaps encouraged all this attention. Overwhelmed, I told someone to tell my father that I was going home on the bus, knowing if I told him myself there would be a scene. I ran outside where the air was fresh and cool.

The college had been built on the site of a ruined church. All that remained was its solitary spire standing forlornly on the corner of Westminster Bridge Road. As I stood quietly on my own at the crossroads, slowly I got my bearings. On the opposite side of the road was Lower Marsh, which led into The Cut. Almost without thought, I crossed the road and started to walk. In a few minutes I had reached where The Cut crossed Waterloo Bridge Road. The solid grey walls of the Old Vic lay opposite me, like a great ship safely docked in harbour. I knew then that I had been heading there all the time.

Since it was late, the performance on stage would be coming to a conclusion. Soon the crowds would be flocking out, moved in some way, having been transported for a brief moment to the bucolic fields of Illyria or the craggy heath at Dunsinane. I looked at a poster pasted to the wall. The name I was unconsciously looking for wasn't there. Tonight's play was *Romeo and Juliet*, with John Neville and Claire Bloom. Hesitantly, I hovered on the pavement, then decided to walk toward the river, perhaps to stand on Waterloo Bridge and watch the great city at night. I crossed The Cut and continued toward the railway bridge, just a few yards ahead. Under the bridge, it was dark and sour, full of pigeon droppings from birds huddled in the girders overhead, but a small café with an arched plate-glass window looked bright and welcoming. 'The Cave' was written in black script above the door. I hesitated. I had a few coins with me in the clutch purse Mother had lent me, enough for a glass of orange squash. I had never been in a café on my own before. Even while exploring museums, I had always had someone with me, but I quickly pushed the door open and went in.

At the counter, I asked for a glass of squash.

'Not cappuccino, Miss, you don' wanna cup of frothy coffee?' sang out the man serving. He sounded Italian.

'No thank you, I'm thirsty,' I said, counting out the money.

'"Teach me . . . teach me tonight . . ."' he sang, unscrewing the top of the squash bottle. I took the glass and carefully walked to one of the booths. The bench seats were made of yellow plastic, the tables, red Formica. The floor tiles were cracked but clean. On the wall behind me was a long mirror, and on the opposite side posters were casually pinned up. As I slowly sipped my drink, spinning it out, I gained in confidence. I felt a sense of adventure. This was a fine bright night in early June, and I was young and carefree. I could walk to the Houses of Parliament, or I could roam through Trafalgar Square. There was nothing to stop me doing anything I wanted.

'"Take my hand, I'm a stranger in Paradise,"' sang the man behind the bar. I began to feel aware, as animals instinctively are, of a strong, intense gaze. I felt a powerful physical presence and had the overwhelming urge to turn around. Instead, more cautiously, I half turned my head so I could see the interior of the café reflected in the long mirror. I could see his profile just beyond me, in the adjoining booth, a dark-haired man sitting alone and leaning back, quite relaxed, smoke curling from the cigarette between his lips. Perhaps he knew the watched was now watching because he spoke without removing the cigarette.

'It's Amalfi.'

Overhead a train rumbled, the noise and vibration surrounded us, cutting out sound, almost stopping thought. I turned to look at him. There was a moment in the midst of the rumble and rattling of the train, when our eyes met and locked. I felt a shock of recognition, that one moment in time was frozen, imprinted in my memory for ever.

'It's Amalfi,' he repeated. He gestured at a poster. 'In Italy. I noticed you've been studying it. All the posters in every small café in London are of Amalfi or Sorrento. It's to lend an exotic tone of mystery and escape, so people will think they're anywhere else but where they are, drinking badly made coffee from a chipped cup. Have you ever been there, to Amalfi? I recommend it.'

There was warm, lazy laughter in the lilting deep voice, a feeling that any words would do, because whatever they were, he knew the effect they would have. He need not even have spoken; his very presence was a magnet. Blindly, I looked at the poster, pinned my gaze on it yet saw nothing. I clutched my glass with a sense of disbelief. Like Alice, I was falling down a hole, everything spinning round and around. The voice was unmistakable – and the face undeniably belonged to Richard Burton. He was seated a foot away; just a few inches of yellow plastic, the width of the mutual back of our bench seats, divided us. Sculptured bones, taut gilded skin as if he had been in the sun, the casual curls springing around his strong forehead, an intense, amused gaze, as if he were used to that sudden flash of recognition, that moment of confusion while people wondered: Could it be . . . is it . . .?

'No,' I said. 'No, I've never been.'

I wanted to tell him I had seen him in *Under Milk Wood* and would never forget it until the day I died. I wanted to blurt out that I had seen all his films: *My Cousin Rachel* and *The Robe*, *Desert Rats* and *The Prince of Players*. I'd be truthful and say I hated *The Prince of Players*, that it was blown up and overacted, but that I still adored him. I wanted to lose myself in those vividly green eyes, watch that wide and mobile mouth shape words.

Instead, in a voice I barely recognised, I asked, 'Is it far to Waterloo Bridge?'

He pointed overhead to where the trains trundled. The back of his hand, I noticed, grew dark hairs. His fingers were not as I imagined an actor's at all, but blunt and strong. Even in the midst of my confusion, I realised he was making a small joke.

'I mean Waterloo Bridge, the bridge over the river,' I said.

'Oh, that bridge,' he said, his voice still gently mocking. He glanced at his watch. 'I'm going that way, I'll show you. It's about half a mile. You don't mind walking, do you?'

And, as simply as that, was how it all began.

Four

❧

The pavements tilt as I glide along them, cocooned in radiance. He briefly takes my arm as we cross streets, perhaps sensing that I am incapable of paying attention. We say nothing. Sounds and sights vanish. I am adrift, floating away to the stars. There is a condition called 'waking sleep', when one is asleep, but yet sees and experiences things as if awake. This is how I feel, powerless, on this June night. My stiff green taffeta skirt whispers, my mother's Givenchy envelops me in a perfumed cloud, even my legs feel different, clad in sheer stockings as they are.

I have no idea how we have arrived at the slight incline that leads up to Waterloo Bridge, but suddenly, we are there. On our left the Royal Festival Hall, built four years earlier for the Festival of Britain, glows like a luxury liner passing us in the night, its great expanse of lights reflected in the river. People stroll along the promenade below us. There is music on the air. I tell myself he is merely being courteous, seeing a young girl safely on her way, and then he'll be gone, but when I turn to him and hold out my hand to thank him, he takes it and tucks it firmly into the crook of his arm. With no comment, we stroll on toward the centre of the bridge. We lean side by side against the wide granite parapet that is still warm from the sun, and look down at the oily black water flowing fast below us. Eddies in the current swirl around the heavy buttresses and rejoin the flooding tide. I come to his shoulder. I want to lean my head against his jacket, to bury my face in his scent, to feel his arm around me, but this moment is as ephemeral as the water flowing away beneath the bridge. Soon, he'll be gone, leaving me standing there alone.

'Tides are influenced by the moon,' he says. 'It's not really tidal this far up, but it's enough for it to get high like this twice a day, and low twice a day.'

'Twice a day?' I repeat. 'At the same time every day?' He shifts his position, turns toward me.

'Well no, not at the same time,' he answers. 'It varies. See, if it's at ten as it is now, tomorrow, it will be at eleven, and the next day at twelve, or thereabouts. It's relentless. Time and tide wait for no man.' I nod solemnly, not knowing where the quote comes from, not knowing that he has the most astonishing memory and can pluck lines out of ten thousand different sources. I am unable to think of a single thing to say that could possibly interest him, still overwhelmed that he is here at all, that we are standing side by side on this bridge of dreams.

He suddenly laughs. 'What a load of bollocks I'm talking. You don't want to hear about the bloody river being up or down, or in or out.'

'But I do,' I earnestly assure him. 'The tides and cycles of the moon are fascinating. I want to know everything there is to know about everything.'

He stares at me, at first not sure if I am mocking him. I look back, not realising that I am staring as I devour the lines of his classic profile, outlined against the lights behind him, wanting to store this moment in my memory. The last time I saw this face it had been ten feet high on a cinema screen.

'You really mean it, don't you?' he says slowly. 'You know, what drew me to you was your serenity. You didn't look as if you wanted to natter away like most girls, talking about nothing, and here I am, doing just that.'

I think, 'Nothing is all I have to say. I am struck dumb by your presence,' but, of course, I don't say it. I realise that it is my sense of awe that has made me seem remote and inaccessible and, by chance, it is that which appeals to him.

He picks up my purse, which is lying on the wide parapet, and turns it over in his hands, almost as if he is looking for something to do. It is made of raw silk, lime-green outside and lined with that particular shade of translucent pink, like the inside of a shell, fastened with two semiprecious balls of cut crystal sitting on little discs of silver-gilt.

'You could lose this, it could slide into the river,' he says. 'It's very pretty. It looks oriental.' I take it from him.

'It is oriental,' I say.

'I was right then. Alighting in the Cave was an exotic bird blown far off course, not your usual London pigeon.'

'No, only my purse is exotic,' I say demurely. He throws back his head and gives that short bark that is to become so familiar.

'Touché,' he says, and smiles. 'Now, what would you like to know? I'm a good teacher.' I think before I answer.

'This river must have a wonderful history,' I finally say, wanting my words to be mature and clever. 'Tell me about what we can see from this very spot, who passed by, the buildings that used to be.'

'A tall order, but I'll do my best,' he muses. He takes me by the hand and, dodging the light traffic, draws me across the bridge until we stand on the opposite side, looking downstream. He keeps my hand in his big bear's paw as he gestures with the other. 'The river wasn't always built up like it is today. Meadows ran down to the water, which was half a mile wide at this spot. There were quays where boats were tied, but when the tide was out people often had to wade through mud to get on the ferries, or they paid extra for the ferrymen to carry them. A ferry boatman, John Overie, who plied his trade right here where we're looking, worked so hard year after year, he stacked up a fortune, a bit like the doorman at the Ritz, who's probably got more money than the people who tip him. Overie was so miserly, he faked his own death.'

'Why?'

'So his grieving family would eat less.'

'That doesn't make sense!' I protest. 'He couldn't pretend to be dead for ever or they'd inherit his money and spend it.'

'True. I expect he just wanted to save money for a week or two. When you're a miser, every penny counts. But he got his comeuppance. When he decided to come back to life people thought he was a ghost and clubbed him to death – or at least they clubbed what they thought was a ghost to scare it off.'

Then he tells me how John Overie had an heir, his daughter, Mary. As soon as her fiancé heard she had come into a fortune, he rode like the wind to marry her. His horse stumbled and he was thrown off and killed. By now, Mary was so disgusted by all the trouble money caused she pulled down her father's house and built a church and a convent.

'It's called St Mary Overie and it's still there, on Bankside, behind that power station and all those ware-houses,' he says, and points past a wall of buildings along the river frontage. 'Mary, who sounds the kind of woman I would have enjoyed knowing, gave sanctuary to whores. They were called geese and even licensed to be whores by a bishop. There's a tomb, dated fourteen something, with Mother Goose cut with a chisel on it. Mother Goose, den mother of prostitutes, it's quite a thought.' He turns and smiles briefly. 'Am I shocking you?'

'Mother Goose!' I exclaim, fascinated.

'You think she's a kindly old lady who tells children fairy stories, don't you? No chance. Children have been fooled by adults for centuries. And yet, the goose is a magic bird. The great Nile goose created the world by laying a cosmic egg; goddesses ride the back of storms, half geese, half human.'

Feeling worldly beyond my years that he is talking to me like an equal and using grown-up words so freely, I say, 'How do you know so much?' He laughs.

'For an ignorant Welshman from the Valleys? Bawdy old Southwark is in my bones, it's where Shakespeare and Marlowe lived and worked. Can you imagine what it must have been like?' I gaze down the river, absorbing it all, watching the current flowing deep and strong past the old city with all its history. 'Come on, girl,' he says, 'Waterloo Bridge hasn't given up all its secrets.'

He takes me down the steps to the lower level below the bridge, to the Embankment. We stop and look up a narrow street toward the Strand. He tells me it's called that because it used to be the original foreshore of the river.

'Look at the old street names,' he urges. 'They tell a story, they're steeped in history.' The black and white sign of the little lane we're peering into reads Savoy Hill. Almost reverently he says, 'Right here, along the river, stood the most beautiful palace in London. White, pure white limestone, dazzling in the morning sun. Close your eyes and imagine it, turrets and graceful pointed towers with pennants fluttering in the breeze. The Savoy Palace. London residence of John O'Gaunt, most powerful man in the kingdom, married to Blanche of Lancaster, the fair maid of the north, and she the most beautiful woman in England. Bastards. All that lot ever did was put down the Welsh. Well, we got our revenge with the Tudors.'

Without warning, effortlessly, his voice changes and he starts to quote from *Richard III*, the very last speech in which Henry, Earl of Richmond – to become *Henry VII*, the first Tudor king – proclaims his victory at the Battle of Bosworth Field, the place where the hunchback ran around shouting, 'A horse! A horse! My kingdom for a horse!'

Thank God I don't clap or say anything trite. In fact, I am utterly overwhelmed.

'Am I boring you?' he asks. I am so absorbed I almost cannot answer.

'No, it's wonderful,' I say. 'You've made it come alive. Please don't stop.' I remind myself to stop gushing, to keep my head.

'Well, enough of old John of Gaunt. I expect you'd like to converse with Cleopatra now. I'll show you some history that's three and a half thousand years old. The real thing.'

I am mystified as we walk a hundred yards along the Embankment where, outlined against the water, is Cleopatra's Needle, a tall granite pillar, surrounded by winged figures and two solid bronze sphinxes with lions' paws and enigmatic smiles. He doesn't speak and stands by quietly while I read aloud from one of the plaques on its base.

'"This obelisk quarried at Syene was erected at On (Heliopolis) by the Pharaoh Thothmes III in about 1500 b.c. Lateral inscriptions were added nearly two centuries later by Rameses the Great. Removed during the Greek dynasty to Alexandria the Royal City of Cleopatra. It was there erected in the 18th year of Augustus Caesar b.c. 12."'

Then I read that it was abandoned in a storm in the Bay of Biscay. So I tell him of my own storm in the Bay of Biscay, how I was so seasick once that I was fed quartered oranges to suck, though I am careful not to give him any clues to my age.

'I'm sailing to the States soon, on the *Queen Mary*,' he says. 'So far, touch wood, I've never been seasick.'

'Then you won't be appearing at the Old Vic?' I ask, my hopes dashed. It is the first time I have brought up his work. Somehow it seemed as if mentioning his fame would remind him of who he was and underline the wide gulf between us, he the prince and I the humble goose girl.

'Yes, I've signed up for next season,' he says. 'I'll be coming back later.' So he won't see my glowing expression, I turn back to the Needle, which is not so much a needle as a tall, thin pyramid.

'It says six men perished in a bold attempt to succour the crew of the obelisk ship, *Cleopatra*, during the storm October 14th, 1877,' I read. 'But they don't say what happened, or how the Needle was saved. Do you know?'

'No, I have to admit I don't. I'm sure there's a book somewhere you can look it up in, something for you to do.' He pauses. 'What do you do?'

'Do?' I say. This has caught me off guard. 'Why, nothing.'

To my horror, the words slip out. 'I'm still at school.' There is a brief pause, then I hurry to change it. 'Finishing school.' It sounds dreadfully pretentious and I blush, wondering if he has seen through my slip-up, but I can't tell him I'm at college because he'd quickly see through that.

'A posh young lady,' he says. 'You'll be doing the season then, pearl necklaces, feather boas, curtseying to the queen, being a deb and all that?'

'Oh no!' I answer, horrified at where my lie is leading. 'I hate that kind of thing. I'm not sure what I want to do. When I was young, I wanted to be an explorer, but most of the world has already been explored.'

'If you've got any brains you'll go to university,' he tells me. 'I went to Oxford and it opened my eyes. Until then, I hardly knew what a book was. I read voraciously, acquiring knowledge, soaking it up like a sponge. I played rugby and drank a great deal of beer. Be a travel writer. If I didn't do what I do, I'd be a writer. In fact, making films is a bastard of a way to earn a living, almost as bad as performing the same play night after night. I'd never stick it out for a long run, I'd be praying for a flop, I'd get drunk and fall off stage, anything to kill the boredom. If it wasn't for the money, I'd give it all up tomorrow, live in a garret in Paris or Rome, and write.'

'What would you write?'

'Oh, I'd start off with short stories to get the feel. I've already written a few. Then perhaps some kind of a memoir. I don't think I'd be any good at writing fiction.' By now, we are sitting on a bench with cast-iron winged sphinxes at each end. He pats one affectionately. 'Greek chariots had creatures like this with huge curving wings in gold. And a circle of scimitars on the wheels to cut off the legs of the opposition's horses.'

I shudder. 'How horrible.'

'They're buggers to drive. I was hopeless.'

'You've driven a Greek chariot?' I ask, amazed.

'Well, yes, but only in a film. Mostly, they made me ride a horse, which wasn't as bad as the wig they stuck on my head. I was out in Spain this spring for Alexander, ruler of half the known world before the age of thirty.' Jumping up, his voice full of enthusiasm, he starts to describe the V-phalanx that Alexander invented. 'It was shaped like a spear that penetrated their enemies' lines. Until then, they always stood in a long line and hurled themselves at each other. It was brutal bloody murder. Under Alexander, the Macedonians learned to form a circle right in the heart of their enemy, shields up in a solid wall, the men in the middle with their shields over their heads, see, it was like a bloody tank, the enemy couldn't get at them. A magnificently controlled tactic.'

I want to know more about filming, who was there, what it was like, but dare not ask in case I sound too curious. In any case, he is still marching up and down on the wide pavement, reliving military tactics of the ancient world. He sits down again next to me.

'You have plenty of time to kill while filming,' he says. 'The makeup takes hours, the setups take half a day. All you do is hang about the set, waiting to be called to say two lines. I devour books, mostly biographies, history, that kind of thing. I beg people to bring them from London. And crosswords. Do you do crosswords?'

Shamefaced, I have to admit that I don't. I feel very young and very ignorant. Why don't I do crosswords? Why don't I read more? I sit there and think about the time I've wasted and vow to do better. I don't tell him that my parents do the *Telegraph* crossword each morning, snapping and snarling over the clues like two dogs. Mother, whose knowledge of music and literature was far wider, always guessed them first. It drove Father so wild he often grabbed the paper and screwed it up. After he had gone, Mother would retrieve it, and carefully smooth it out. 'Now, where was I?' she would say. Later, and with malicious glee, she would leave the paper carefully folded at the crossword page on the hall table, there to greet Father when he came home. Sometimes, if he was in a good mood, he would look at it and even comment cheerfully on some particular answer that had baffled him. If he was in a bad mood, he would snatch the paper up and stalk outside the front door, where he would throw it in the dustbin in the side alley, clanging the lid down hard. Mother would glance up and say casually, 'Oh dear, your father's had a bad day.' If the front door was also banged, she would raise her eyebrows and add, 'A very bad day.'

'What are you thinking?' he asks. 'You look sad. A penny for your thoughts.' He holds out a coin. For a moment, I almost reach out to take it.

'My thoughts are worth more than a penny, Richard,' I tease.

Richard. All night I've avoided using his name, for fear I might call him 'Mr Burton'. Now, I've said the word.

'My friends call me Rich,' he says, as if there's nothing at all wrong with my calling him by his first name. Then he quickly adds, 'When I was a young man, I always said I would marry the first girl who took my penny, but I never met one who would. You women always say the same thing: "My thoughts are worth more than that." Try asking a man, you'd get a straight answer.'

'Men are the biggest liars on earth.' I say. 'Men will lie

to conceal, they will lie to look good, and they will lie to keep the peace.'

Before I can turn my opinion into a proper debate, a lone magpie flies down from the plane tree above our heads and lands on the embankment wall.

'Your opinion of men has shocked the birds from the trees,' he says. I glance up.

'I wonder what's alarmed it; only owls and nightjars fly at night.'

'And nightingales,' he says.

The magpie hops along the river wall and looks at us brightly, his crisp black and white feathers clean and bright in the glow from the golden orbs that hang in pairs in their decorative cast-iron stands. I half-chant the old doggerel verse, 'One for sorrow, two for joy; three for a girl, and four for a boy. Five for silver, six for gold, and seven for a secret that's never been told.' Richard looks up into the dense foliage.

'There must be another one hiding there,' he says. 'One for sorrow's no use. I demand two, two for joy.'

Still the bird stares at us. I wonder if it thinks we will feed it; or perhaps we're disturbing its nest. Then, I tell him that I'm very keen on birds and their habits, have been since we lived in Cornwall.

'Magpies gather in spring,' I say, 'but no one knows why. Huge gatherings up to a hundred birds. Country people say they congregate for what they call crow marriages, where single birds pair off, but lots of pairs are there, so that doesn't make sense.'

'Oh, they're all the matchmakers,' he says. 'You always have to have busybody matchmakers making a fuss where mating is concerned. Now, what does it say in your rhyme about a hundred birds?'

'Nothing. It stops at seven.'

'Tell me again.' Obligingly, I repeat it.

'"Seven for a secret that's never been told." I have a secret.' he says. 'A secret that's worth seven magpies.'

'There's someone,' he starts, 'been in love with me for years and I knew it. I played him like a fish on a hook to get what I wanted. Oh, he got something out of it, but I was the manipulator, in control. It was a dangerous game and cruel. I could have destroyed us both.' He stopped. 'There, that's my secret, all you'll get out of me.

I hear Big Ben strike midnight. My heart begins to beat. Father will be furious with me. Like Cinderella, who finally must admit that her gown is nothing but rags, her footmen only scrawny mice, her sparkling coach just a farmer's pumpkin, I have been sitting here, lying about who I really am. And I am still naïve enough to think that maybe my parents would notice, perhaps even care, if I am not home when expected. Are they out looking for me now, my mother nervous and wringing her hands? After all, I have never, ever stayed out so late before. Will a taxi pull up with Father in the backseat, spitting with anger because I had run away from his boring dance, and telling Richard the truth, finally, that I am just a foolish school-girl? I grab my little oriental purse and stand.

'Where are you going?' he asks.

'It's so late,' I say. 'I have to go home.'

'When shall we two meet again?' he asks. 'In thunder, lightning, or in rain?'

I know it's *Macbeth* – and three witches at that – but I am too embarrassed to reply. What must he think of a girl so young she has to rush home at the stroke of midnight? I run across the pavement and flag down a cruising taxi. In a flash, I am inside.

'Gypsy Hill,' I tell the driver.

Richard is still there, standing on the pavement, staring at the taxi. I almost think he isn't real but a ghost. The taxi speeds up and he is left behind. I sink back into the seat. I suddenly realise that I don't have enough money to pay the fare. I tell the driver this and he half turns his head.

'Man bothering you, was he, Miss? Don't worry, I've taken many young ladies home for nothing when they've been in trouble. That's what London cabbies are, knights in shining armour.'

Five

In July, before the end of the school year, our class went to Regent's Park for an open-air performance of *A Midsummer-Night's Dream* with, I think, Dorothy Tutin playing Titania. We went early, straight from school on the bus, carrying little picnics that had been specially prepared by Caroline, our school chef. An unusual woman with sausage curls and always wearing a white, overall coat, Caroline stood over six feet tall. She took great pride in giving us the kind of wholesome food that was good for us, and she lectured if we demanded too many chips. She often said things like: 'Young ladies don't need stodge, you need to be able to feel the pea under the mattress to win the prince.' I'm sure it's thanks to Caroline that so many of us were healthily slim and not covered with spots or puppy fat in our teens, despite the fact that our morning break included a third of a pint of milk in a small bottle with a straw and Chelsea buns sprinkled with sugar.

That evening in Regent's Park I can remember unpacking from grease-proof lined boxes little cheese and tomato tartlets sprinkled with fresh chives, finger salad, cucumber sticks, celery and carrots, with a grease-proof twist of salt and pepper, and boxes of strawberries, with another twist of castor sugar to dip them into. It was a lovely evening, the sun still warm, casting a golden light across the park as we sprawled on the grass under massive trees, some of which had been there for hundreds of years. Perhaps they were not there when this had been part of the vast north forest that stretched from Soho, where William the Conqueror had his hunting lodge, to Epping Forest, where Boudicca arrived at the head of her hopeful army to do battle with the Romans, but certainly some of the trees were casting their shade in 1811 when the Prince Regent commanded his hobgoblin little Welsh architect, John Nash, to design the park and the elegant white stuccoed houses that curved in long terraces around its perimeter. He did a wonderful job; I think of all the London parks, Regent's Park is the most beautiful.

In our flared linen frocks of five different pastel colours – lilac, blue, pink, yellow, or apple-green – we looked like flower petals scattered on the grass beneath the trees. While we bit into the moist and flaky little tarts and dipped our strawberries in sugar, we could hear the elephants trumpeting from the zoo, and parrots screeching. An occasional disembodied giraffe's head would float by above the high fence. Replete, I lay on my back, eyes half closed, and gazed up through the lacy green canopy of arched branches overhead. As I had done every single waking moment since, I remembered the night – just a month earlier – when I had walked with Richard along the river. I relived every word, every gesture, all of which I had carefully written in a soft-covered exercise book with wide-ruled lines. Up until that time, I had been scribbling poetry and the usual schoolgirl complaints about teachers and parents, especially parents, especially complaints about Father's spendthrift ways and bullying habits, but now, my meeting with Richard seemed the only part worth rereading. I had hidden the exercise book with a few other treasures in a shoe box placed under a loose floorboard in the corner of my bedroom. The hiding place was further concealed by a carpet. For the past month, just before bedtime, I got the book out to read again what I'd written. In my mind, I tried to interpret the expression on his face when he looked at me. In my adolescent daydreams I would imagine what might have happened if I hadn't run off as I did. What if he had waved a taxi down and we both had got in? I imagined myself leaning back and resting my head on his shoulder. He would put his arm around me and tenderly kiss my brow. 'The Ritz!' he would tell the cabbie. No, not the Ritz. The Savoy, of course, where else but the site of John O'Gaunt's dazzling dream palace? We would dine in the terrace room overlooking the river. We would have champagne and eat – what? Oh, food didn't matter. You can't taste food in daydreams – but you can dream of fruit, which is so erotic. So, while stretched on the soft grass in Regent's Park, I imagined Richard feeding me small sweet lychees, with their delicately scented white flesh. I saw myself feed him one back and as I did, he kissed the tips of my fingers. Then, we danced and he held me in his arms. On a carousel we kept on dancing. And dancing.

That was where my dream always came to a full stop. The next step was too big for me to take, even in my fantasies.

———

When we got up to walk to the Rose Garden, where the play was to be staged, we noticed that the back of Mary Hamilton's blue frock was stained with blood. Three or four of us took her off to the public toilets, where we clustered round her like midwives, trying to wash it out. The machine that sold sanitary towels was empty, and we were too embarrassed to ask for help from Miss Wilton, the English mistress who had escorted us that evening. Tall and willowy, Miss Wilton had deep blue eyes and glowing copper hair in a bun that coiled low on her neck. Ah, dear Miss Wilton. How I yearned to narrate Chaucer as she did, with delicacy and grace: 'Whan that Aprill with his shoures soote The droghte of March hath perced to the roote . . .'

Instead, we donated our flimsy ladylike handkerchiefs and helped Mary drape her sweater around her hips like a sarong.

'Can you see anything?' she kept asking, as we walked back to the group. Unlike most of us, Mary had started her periods very late, brought on or kept back, I can't remember which, by the shock of her parents' recent divorce. Now she and her mother were living in disreputable lodgings above a rowdy pub, while her father had kept the family home as a love nest for himself and his girlfriend. Mary told us that with few married women at work, her mother had got a raw deal in the divorce. Judges had decided that men owned all marital property by right and doled out a pittance to ex-wives.

One of us – I can't remember who – commented that now Mary had started, the entire class was menstruating. This meant that every day several of us would be bleeding. I wondered why it should be, why nature had designed us to suffer the indignity and discomfort of stomach aches and the fears of odour and bulky pads showing with loops and hooks and uncomfortable elasticated belts. These were the days before Tampax and deodorants. On top of this, we had to sit out swimming, while boys could dive clean-limbed into a pool and run and be strong the entire day long, never having to worry.

—

The play was magical in its setting of a leafy glade, surrounded by rose trellises and lit by lanterns. There was Titania, Queen of the Fairies, in her silver coach drawn by Peaseblossom, Cobweb, Moth, and Mustardseed in their gauzy gowns, and Puck, mischievous in red and green, with a tall feather in his cap. Oberon, splendid in his wizard's robes sparkling with stars, came in from a concealed entrance in the high-curving hedge. The spring-loaded clowns, Quince, Snug, Bottom, Flute, Snout, and Starveling, tumbled across the grass from behind us. Toward the end, a sudden storm with thunder and torrential rain had us all running for shelter under the trees and brought the performance to an abrupt close. As I stood with the others, waiting for the storm to abate, drinking in the strong scent of rain-washed roses and wet grass, aching with unrequited longings, I dreamily incanted Theseus's lines to myself: 'But earthlier happy is the rose distill'd than that which, withering on the virgin thorn, grows, lives, and dies in single blessedness.'

—

Shakespearean romance filled my head until the following Saturday when I woke early to the sound of the vacuum cleaner banging about. It was my father, hoovering, a sure indication that he had guests coming. By the time I got dressed and came downstairs he had already polished the furniture and produced a bottle of Scotch for the men and a bottle of sherry for the women. As he cheerfully bustled about, he informed me that he had invited seven members of his Morley College bridge club to make up two tables that night, a bridge party to which Mother wasn't invited.

'She can't play, and we only fight over it,' he chuckled, in a remarkably good mood.

My father's interest in Morley College had baffled me ever since the night I went to his ghastly dance and saw the place, and what he called 'the night people', for myself. I knew instantly that this scene simply wasn't stylish enough for him, but my mother had no doubt at all about what had drawn my father to the place.

'There's a woman behind it,' Mother said to me, grimly. 'There always is.' Then, she took herself off to bed with a book, before the first guests arrived.

And so it was. At some stage that night, woken by a drunken rumpus downstairs, I got up and went down for a glass of milk. In the kitchen I bumped into a young woman from Maryland who was reeling around, looking for ice from a refrigerator we didn't possess. She wore blue Capri pants and lacquered Japanese sticks in her hair.

'Hi,' she said. 'I'm Amy. I guess you must be the daughter?'

'Yes,' I said shortly, resenting being called 'the daughter'. When she passed me on her way to the sink, I caught a whiff of a pungent sort of animal stink.

'Your dad got the ladies sherry, with cutesy little glasses to drink it from,' she giggled. 'He's a doll, but someone should tell him we ladies prefer Scotch like the men.' She then told me that she was a student. 'A mature old student,' she added with a laugh, 'but everyone is very kind to me.'

I couldn't understand how she could float about the kitchen and be so smelly, and yet be so oblivious to it. Looking back, perhaps the stench was garlic, something at that stage I don't think we ever had in the house. It was just something read about in Transylvanian epics to scare off werewolves.

I didn't realise how unwittingly kind I had been to her until next morning, when my green Raleigh bicycle was gone. So was the blue carpet from the first flight of stairs. My father had given both to Amy, the student from Maryland – the bicycle, he said, because she was very broke and it would save her money by helping her to get to her classes, but the carpet was a puzzle because my father had quite literally torn it from its moorings. So what on earth did she want with it? Faced with strangely bare stairs and our wrath, Father became a mixture of sheepishness and aggression. He tried to say he didn't think I wanted my bicycle any more, that it was just lying there in the conservatory taking up space. As for the stair carpet, he said Mother had complained that she didn't like the colour.

'Plain blue shows the dirt, you said so yourself,' he insisted. 'I thought we could get a nice floral Axminster.'

'I don't want a floral Axminster!' Mother snapped, her dander up. 'Thanks to you and the decorator's wife, we've got floral wallpaper already, which I loathe. You can't just give our things away!' Suddenly, she stopped. A look of utter disgust crossed her face. 'You're having an affair with her, aren't you?' she asked.

'Who?' Father blustered. 'I don't know what you're talking about.'

'Whoever you gave Rose's bicycle and the stair carpet to. A woman is behind this, with you a woman always is. Well, I want them back in this house today, our stair carpet and Rose's bicycle. They are not your love tokens to hand around. They belong to us.'

'Yes,' I echoed. 'I do use my bike, you know I do! How will I get to school?'

Of course we didn't get either back. Mother said it probably had a lot to do with the amount of Scotch Father had poured down his throat, judging by the empties.

'Your father's a stupid drunk, Rose, but at least he has the sense not to drink too often. He must have got over-excited, like a dog in heat.' But I could tell she was shocked, even though she had found more courage to stand up to him since we had moved to London.

When the short-lived affair with the woman from Maryland was over, Father also gave up Morley College and hastened toward his preferred stamping grounds in town. As with nature, his emotional life abhorred a vacuum, and within a few weeks he had started another affair, this time a serious one. All came to a head early one morning after a sleepless night when, hollow-eyed and exhausted, he woke up Mother to tell her he had packed a case and was leaving immediately. He was so loud I could hear him from behind my closed bedroom door, so I got up, in case Mother needed me. I had always felt more mother to her than daughter, even back then. Father was, as usual, histrionic. Wanting to get it all off his chest before he left, he said the affair had started when he had written a play for the office dramatics society – she was his leading lady. One scene involved a passionate kiss which had to be rehearsed a number of times and it was those rehearsed kisses that had revealed beyond doubt that Barbara was madly in love with him. Almost gabbling, he poured it all out. Normally, he said, he tried to keep his relationships secret, but this one was bigger than him. He simply had to confess it before he went out of his mind.

'Anne, you will never understand what it is to love like this,' he cried. 'It's like a mania, a disease! I can think of nothing else!' He was so on fire with love he had sat up all night writing poetry.

I heard my mother finally reply.

'You woke me up to tell me this?'

'This time, she's the love of my life. I couldn't just sneak off like a thief in the night without telling you.'

From my balcony room, which faced down the stairs, I saw the drama continue to unfold. I saw Father carrying his case and Mother running after him in her nightgown.

'I'll be back later for the rest of my things,' he said. By this time, Mother was fighting for his case, trying to prevent him from leaving. Then, she stood in front of the door.

'You can't do this to us, George,' she pleaded. 'Can't we talk about it?'

'No,' Father told her. 'It's too big to fight.'

To my horror, Mother then fell to her knees and wrapped her arms about his legs as she begged him to stay.

'I'll do anything, I'll change,' she moaned.

'For God's sake, Anne, stop it!' he shouted. 'Let me go! I don't love you and never did.' With a lunge, half kicking, half pulling his legs free, he snatched up his case and his hat from the hall table and forced his way through the door, leaving her weeping on the floor. I ran down the stairs, closed the door, and knelt beside her.

'Mummy, please stop,' I begged. 'Get up, come back to bed, you're cold.'

'What am I going to do?' she sobbed. 'How will I live without him?' I hated being a witness to her raw emotion, but most of all I hated my father for doing this to her.

Somehow, I dragged her up and took her back to bed. Dawn was already inching in over the treetops. I made a sweet cup of tea, which was supposed to be good for shock, and sat with her while she drank it. She fell back on her pillow and continued to cry hopelessly while I dressed Gracie and made breakfast. That afternoon, alone in my room, I wrote a long letter to Mary Grant, the agony aunt of a woman's magazine. I said my father had abandoned us, my mother had collapsed into bed, and I was the oldest child remaining at home. What should I do? I sealed and addressed it and hid it under my pillow to post later.

The next day, a Sunday, after Mother had spent a tormented night, Father reappeared. He strolled in blithely with his case and told Mother that his conscience had pricked him, that he realised we all meant too much to him. Mother, of course, was overjoyed and cooed around him for a brief honeymoon period, until things got back to their normal state of friction.

Father's remorse was all an act of course, as I discovered many years later. When Barbara came to the door of her flat in her robe and saw him standing there with a suitcase, she was bewildered. She invited him in and introduced him to her fiancé. 'I sat there on her sofa and wept, my dreams in tatters,' Father recalled in his self-deprecating way, laughing ruefully at the memory. 'I felt too much of a fool to come running home at once, so I spent the night in a hotel. Besides, I really thought my heart had broken and wanted to be alone in my misery. However, I got over it.'

My father was a man of extreme moods, he could be in utter despair one moment, but he would visibly straighten his shoulders, utter the word 'However', and look around beaming, as if to say, 'All is well, I'm better now.' That always caught at my heartstrings and made me forgive him, whatever selfish, foolish thing he had done. In that quick, unconscious gesture of his, I always thought of the cruelly treated and unwanted child he had been, made to sleep under the stairs, or shoved in a dark cellar for some misdeed. In my mind I saw the child squaring his shoulders, trying to be brave in the face of daunting adversity and unhappiness.

—

That summer I spent days lying in the garden and dreaming of Richard. I had a secret place beneath the pear tree at the back, hidden behind a long rose trellis that divided the garden between a more formal area and an orchardy wilderness. This was where the unmowed grass was soft and sweet to lie on, and wild apple mint grew in great aromatic drifts. On warm nights I would often sleep outside. At dusk, a barn owl from the bombed church at the end of the road came sweeping low beneath the trees. Later, I would hear a strange grunting noise, which heralded the arrival of a family of hedgehogs, rooting about for slugs. If I lay still some of the babies with their soft pale bristles and shiny black button noses fearlessly tumbled over my sleeping bag. Later still, a fox crossed from one garden to the next, running beneath the trees like a grey ghost, its tail held low, its eyes intent. In predawn's pearly light, the first blackbird sang from the top of the pear tree, replies echoing from treetop to roof ridge throughout the gardens. Then came the smaller birds, tits and finches, wrens and robins, and last, the big birds, the crows and ravens, jays with their harsh cries and vivid blue wing feathers, and my beloved laughing yaffles, sometimes called rain birds because their ringing cry sounded clearer just before it rained.

One morning, when I went back to the house early from the garden, I caught my father red-handed in the kitchen. He had the kettle boiling away full blast as he steamed open a small pile of letters. Astonished, I stood unseen outside the window, where I had been about to drape my sleeping bag on the washing line, and watched him. Carefully, he peeled back the loosened flaps and extracted the contents, which he quickly scanned. While the glue was still sticky he returned the letters to the envelopes and pressed the flap down. He kept two letters, slipping them into his dressing gown pocket. I made a deliberate noise hanging up the sleeping bag and came in.

'You're just in time for a hot cup of tea,' he said, pouring the boiling water into the waiting pot. 'Are you cold?'

I shook my head. 'No, it was a lovely night.' I glanced at the remaining letters, spread carefully out on the table. 'Anything for me?' I asked casually.

'No, just bills and a letter for your mother,' he replied, not batting an eyelid. But when I said, 'Shall I take Mother her letter?' he hesitated for a fraction and said, 'No, she's still asleep, have your tea first.' Aha! I thought. You mean, wait until the glue is dry.

When I told Mother what I had seen, she just shrugged. 'He's been doing it for years,' she said. 'He has no shame. Sometimes he gives me my letters still damp and if I ask, he says the postman must have dropped them in a puddle. It goes back to his childhood, when he had to know what was going on in order to survive.'

We all knew how awful Father's upbringing had been. In ways, we were all prisoner to it as much as he was, if not more, for it meant that we were to forgive him everything in perpetuity. His mother had been a refugee from Russia and had somehow become separated from her family. She was forced by poverty to give my father up and, after a series of foster parents, he ended up being sold at the age of three, to a wretched family in the Midlands, for nine golden guineas. He was intended to work in their green-grocery business, slave labour, which started when he was four or five years old. Their home had two rooms, one upstairs, one downstairs. The downstairs room, open to the elements, was both sitting room and shop. My father's bed was a pile of blankets beneath the stairs. When he objected, he was put in the coal cellar with no food, often for days on end, his shrieks ignored.

The stories broke my heart, but still, he was now an adult, and he was reading our private letters!

'I call it sheer nosiness,' I said crossly. 'What if he keeps your letters back and you never see them?'

Mother gave me an apologetic little smile.

'I always check his dressing gown pocket after he's gone to work, to see if there's anything,' she admitted. 'I usually put them back of course, after I've read them, so he's none the wiser.'

'I wouldn't let him read my letters,' I burst out.

'But he does read your letters, Rose. You wrote to a magazine over that nonsense when he left and I found the reply in his pocket.'

I was horrified and blushed a fiery red. 'How could he! Why don't you say something?'

'Because some of the letters he hides are addressed to him and this way, I know what he's up to. Sometimes, a little deceit is the only way.'

'Can't you see, he's made you as bad as he is?' I said.

'I know that's how it must seem to you,' she replied, 'but I've made my bed and must lie in it. I married him. He's your father. He does his best.'

'No he doesn't!' I said. 'He does whatever he wants to do. He's selfish. Look how he is about his own private things.'

Father was like a character out of the *Boy's Own Paper*. He hadn't quite grown up. He had taught himself shorthand when he was only seven years old and loved tricks and puzzles. He had even devised a difficult code during the war. In many ways, he was contradictory, gathering secrets to himself – often in a dangerous way – because he wasn't averse to blackmail, but also as a kind of protection against giving away too much of himself, a hangover from his dreadful childhood. During my growing-up years, I remember how he would spend long hours making fake drawers or secret panels in his desk, or even in a built-in wardrobe in the corner of his bedroom. In one bureau, he had installed a long rod that held the top drawer closed from the drawer beneath, so that even if you had found where he had hidden the key, you still couldn't get in. His booby traps were many and would catch the most innocent of us off guard. He screwed a hook into the back of his 'socks and collars' drawer, from which he ran a cord through the back of the tallboy, up the wall behind the mirror, to a bookshelf on which he placed a silver mug filled with water. If an unsuspecting person opened the drawer, the mug tipped over and she or he was soaked. Mother discovered this when she went to put his socks away one day, and it scared her badly. She screamed and clutched her heart and almost fainted.

'I clipped his wings by having you children,' Mother said now, sadly. 'He wanted to fly, to write, to be something. I tied him down with responsibilities.'

I wanted to say, don't you realise that you are the bright, creative one, you're the one who should fly? Not only were Father's feet bedded in clay, they were of clay. I said nothing, however, because, suddenly, it seemed a pointless argument. I think my mother's rigid upbringing had made her one of nature's natural martyrs.

One of the morning's still-damp letters that Father had

handed over to Mother, as if fresh from the post instead of the kettle, was from my grandmother. As Mother read it, she said, 'Oh dear. Granny's been very ill. The doctor says she can no longer live alone. She wants to come here; how will we manage? You know how she and your father just don't get on.'

'Can't she live with Uncle Bunty?' I asked. It seemed to me Uncle Bunty and Aunt Vera were very capable, financially, of taking her in.

'No, I think Vera is suffering from postpartum depression,' Mother said.

So much for Uncle Bunty and Vera being of help.

———

As long as I could remember, there had been tension between my father's and mother's families. After we had left India for good, late in 1948 we had expected to stay with both our grandparents in Mayfield, the big castellated house in South Wales with its central dome and corner turrets where we had stayed on previous furloughs, but we soon learned that Granddad now lived there alone. Granny had moved to the cottage they owned in a small village on the rolling chalk hills of the Downs. The mystery of our grandparents' separation was kept from us children; it was only much later, in the middle of yet another family row, that I discovered the secret of Grandfather and the plump Welsh maids. So, instead of the spooky house in Wales, for a few blissful months we stayed with Granny, in Patcham, near Brighton. Father was not with us at first. He had remained in India for a while, and then stopped off in the Middle East for some 'secret' work involving espionage, before finally flying on to London. I was not yet eight years old, but I remember this as a peaceful time in our lives. Granny's small, two-bedroom cottage had a huge aviary in the garden, filled with chickens and canaries in different shades of yellow and orange. In the colder weather she brought the canaries indoors and they lived in cages among her geraniums on the circular, black ebony table in the big bay window of her sitting room, from which you could view the sea.

I remember that the weather grew warmer, the sky was often blue, and the Downs were covered with huge drifts of golden cowslips. All we had to do to reach all that space and freedom was walk through a small wicker gate at the end of the back garden beyond the aviary, then cross a sunken lane. At other times, I enjoyed going into Brighton on the open-air bus, passing the Prince Regent's fantasy palace with its domes and fretwork carvings. While it rained often that summer, I mostly remember those hot days when we would play on the steeply sloping beach that had no sand, just big round pebbles that Jimmy said were fossilised dinosaur eggs. On colder days we promenaded along the pier, half a mile long and filled with entertainments, and booths that sold ice cream and candy floss.

Everything changed when Father arrived some six months later. He resented having to give up his easy bachelor life in India, where he could have stayed indefinitely, to find work in an overcrowded market to support us. He went up to London job hunting and through contacts was offered a position in the Commonwealth Relations Office. Although it was a 'cushy number', as he described it, it wasn't well paid and he started to cast his net about for other ventures. With houses still in short supply after the Blitz, he decided that we should remain at Granny's. Mother moved out of the big attic room with its adjoining box room she had shared with us – we loved it because we would pile into her bed while she told us stories – and into the dining room, which was converted into a bedroom, with Father.

Granny's cottage, despite heavily carved ebony furniture, Benares brasses, and a black bearskin rug complete with gaping jaws before the fire, had seemed spacious. Now it felt crowded and constantly reverberated with arguments that rose and fell at night from our parents' room. Granny bristled, directing sarcastic little barbs at my father and snapping at my brothers and me. Before Father came, Granny had told us lovely stories and I had helped her weed the strawberry patch. She and I would pick baskets of golden yellow gooseberries and make redcurrant jelly that shone like a row of jewels on the shelf in the pantry.

It was to get worse. Uncle Bunty came home, still wearing his smart Navy uniform with two rows of brass buttons down the front, and carrying a sausage-like duffel bag filled with lengths of silk from Hong Kong, bars of Hershey's chocolate from the United States, and South American coffee. He'd been a submarine officer in the Royal Navy, torpedoed a record three times on the dreaded Archangel run in the bitterly cold North Atlantic. He had then met a Wren and they were going to be married soon, but meanwhile, he demanded his old room back – our attic. Jimmy, Freddy, and I were shoehorned into the dining room with our parents. I slept on a brown corduroy reclining chair and the boys on a mattress on the floor, crammed between my parents' bed and the window. The first night Uncle Bunty was home, as we got ready for bed, without comment he marched into the dining room with lengths of rope and several blankets and covered the oak sideboard so we wouldn't scratch it.

Worn out with the adult arguments, I slept deeply and

one morning I woke with cold, wet sheets. I got up out of the dampness, convinced that someone had played a trick on me, and stood by the chair-bed, whining, until Father, who was already up and trying to dress for the office in that cramped space where all our clothes hung from hangers on the picture rails, lost his temper, reached for a bristle hairbrush, dragged up my wet nightgown, and beat me on my bare bottom. Outraged, I screamed that I hated him. Granny's two dogs started to bark and Uncle Bunty banged on the floor overhead. White-faced with a mixture of anger and exhaustion, Mother got us up and propelled us into the panelled front hall that now served as a dining room.

From the kitchen, Granny said, 'I knew nothing good would come of it when you married that man.' She came in with the porridge that was always cooked in a porringer the night before, and banged it into our bowls. Subdued, we ate nervously, glancing up when Uncle Bunty came out of his room, hair tousled and wearing pyjamas. He stopped on the stairs and jerked a thumb at Father, who by now had joined us at the table, looking his usual dapper self in a blue pinstripe suit and crisp white shirt.

'You,' Bunty said. 'Get out of this house and take your brats with you.'

Splashing his tea everywhere, Father jumped to his feet and raced up the stairs.

'Oh God,' Mother said faintly, as my father and Uncle Bunty threw punches at each other. She covered up her face with her napkin. 'I can't take any more of this.'

'You married him,' Granny said. 'We did warn you.'

Indignantly, I said, 'Uncle Bunty is horrible.'

'Hush, child,' Granny said. 'Don't interfere.'

The fight ended when Father and Uncle Bunty tumbled

on to the half-landing, and into a grandfather clock that stood there. Granny collected clocks and the house was alive with chimes, bongs, and dongs, but this one, with its mahogany pagoda top and etched brass face, was her pride and joy. She grasped the heavy stick with a gnarled knob that she used to separate her dogs when they scrapped and started to whack Father and Uncle Bunty hard across their backs.

'Stop that!' Granny shouted, her voice thick with anger. 'Stop it now before you wreck my house!'

Father clambered to his feet and pushed past her down the stairs. In the hall he put on his hat, picked up his brief-case, without a word, left for work, slamming the front door behind him. Mother looked scared.

'Don't worry,' said Granny grimly. 'He'll be back.'

'More's the pity,' said Uncle Bunty, coming downstairs to the table, where he helped himself to a piece of toast. Mother didn't say anything, but her hands shook, her cup rattling against its saucer.

In his lunch hour, Father bought a sandwich to eat on the way and caught a train from Victoria down the line, timing the ride for exactly twenty minutes. When the train stopped at Wimbledon, he walked out of the station and into an estate agent's across the street. He said, 'I want a house immediately. What have you got?'

The agent got up and walked to the filing cabinet. 'How much money do you have?' he asked, pulling out some particulars.

Father didn't even bother to inspect the property. He signed a contract, handed over a cheque, and told the agent to sort it out with his solicitor, then he returned to work, having bought a house he hadn't seen, all within the space of an hour.

When Mother learned what he had done, she looked stunned.

'What kind of a house?' she asked faintly.

'One with three bedrooms, a bathroom, and a garden,' Father said.

'I'm not sharing with Freddy,' Jimmy said.

'You'll do as you're told,' Father said.

'It doesn't seem very big. Are the rooms large?' Mother asked.

Father shrugged impatiently. 'It's a house. We're moving in on Monday.'

'Next week!' Mother exclaimed.

'I'd move in tomorrow if I could,' Father said, with a glance at Granny, 'but that's the soonest we can exchange contracts.'

Granny gave my father a measured look and said, 'Well Anne, Lord help you, but it sounds to me as though George has not inspected this new house he intends you all to live in.'

Uncle Bunty laughed to hear this. Then, whistling, he went for a walk on the Downs with the dogs.

The house was poky and too small for the money it had cost. The worst part of it, as far as Mother was concerned, was the disused bomb shelter, full of rainwater, just outside the kitchen door. Father quickly planted gladioli atop it, as if that would take care of the problem, but Mother remained terrified that one of us would fall in and drown, and so she forbade us to play in the garden, locking the back door with a key that she hung on a piece of string around her neck. Instead, she took us for walks over Wimbledon Common. Once the haunt of highwaymen on an old coach road out of London, it was now a wilderness of broad-leafed woodland, gorse scrub, and wild grasses surrounded by new suburban housing, and it was there that Jimmy and I found the dead baby and Mother truly began her downhill spiral. So, we moved from Wimbledon to Downside, and then again and again, until, finally, we landed in Gypsy Hill.

One might think matters couldn't get worse for our family, but one would be wrong. Now Granny, who loathed my father, wanted to live with us. Things were coming around full circle.

Six

My grandmother was a feisty, forthright woman who, before she got ill and frail, had reminded me of Queen Mary with her pearl eardrops, silver curls piled on top of her head, and clear blue eyes that seemed to see right through you. Scottish born, her early years in England had softened her accent although there were occasional hints of her Highland roots, such as the way she rolled her rs. My mother, an unwanted girl in a sea of tall, clever brothers, had always been a bit afraid of her, as had all the family, including Granddad. 'She was just so good at everything, she put everyone in the shade,' Mother often said. 'It gave her the kind of confident arrogance that turned her into a virago who ruled the roost with a rod of iron. People jumped when she issued orders.'

During the week that I turned fourteen, Granny arrived with her dog, Jaffa, an arthritic, orange-roan spaniel, hence his name – after Jaffa oranges from Israel, just coming into the country for the first time. Once lively and vibrant, Granny was now tired and slow. Her hair was unkempt and her clothes were covered with dog hair. Her face, once almost classically beautiful with a glowing peaches-and-cream complexion and those magnetic blue eyes from her Scottish heritage, was now white and sunken, her eyes hooded and ringed with circles. We learned that the dramatic change in her appearance was caused by a medical condition that prevented her from digesting protein. No matter how much she ate, she was actually starving, her body feeding on its own muscles, including her heart. As if this weren't enough, her sight had deteriorated. She was not yet blind, but she would be within a few years.

Mother had planned on going down to Patcham to help Granny with the move, to arrange the sale of her house and to pack up everything but, in insulting terms, Bunty insisted that he would do it.

'He suggests we're not capable of helping his mother move from her home,' Father had said, 'yet he won't accommodate her himself. Why can't she live with them, closer to her friends and everything familiar?'

'We've been through that,' Mother had replied. 'You know it's impossible with Vera the way she is.'

'That isn't it,' Father had sneered. 'Bunty simply wants to help himself to anything worth having.'

It seemed that whatever Bunty wanted, Bunty got, but Mother excused him, as she always did because he was her youngest brother whom she was in the habit of defending.

'He's had a dreadful time with Vera. He has to watch her like a hawk.'

In anticipation of Granny's arrival, we emptied our dining room of furniture so that we could turn it into a bed-sitter for her. The tiny breakfast parlour, with its own table and chairs, was now to become our new dining room. Into that small room went our dining table and chairs, a sideboard, and the enormous, old-fashioned walnut harmonium that Father had bought in an auction for Mother. (Mother had refused to play it, informing him that she was not 'a performing seal'.) When Granny arrived, she took one look into the breakfast room and demanded that her things replace most of ours, since hers were far superior. After much quibbling, she got her way. So there, wedged in along with the harmonium, were Granny's too-long table and heavy leather-covered chairs with brass studs, and, ironically, there too was the precious Tudor sideboard that Bunty had once covered with blankets to protect it from us savages.

When it came to her own bedroom, Granny seemed to have only one plan in mind, and that was to push as many of her possessions as possible into the room. At one end was her walnut bedroom suite consisting of her big bed, dressing table, two wardrobes, and two chests of drawers. On the floor beside the bed lay the skin of a tiger she had shot herself. At the other end of the room were a sofa, two armchairs, several small tables, and a circular brass tray on folding legs, which stood on her bearskin before the fire. Whoever sat in one of the armchairs had a foot stuck in the bear's wide-open mouth. Into every other inch of the room were squeezed Granny's clocks, which spilled out into the adjoining conservatory, among her pots of geraniums and the empty canary cages.

The rest of her pieces – and there were a great many of them – were incongruously added to the spiky modern mishmash of our existing furniture, which by now everyone thoroughly despised. And it wasn't as if Granny's 'far superior' additions helped the matter. Her things had fallen into great disrepair. The exotic influx of richly carved ebony furniture that used to gleam like satin when Granddad had cared for it with a toothbrush and a tin of beeswax, was now neglected and dirty. The lot had been won in an epic card game between Granddad and some maharaja, and it was said to be worth several lakh of rupees, a vast sum. It was a full matching suite and consisted of the great round table with a pink marble top, and cut-out panels with carved foxes eating grapes, and curving legs with elephants' heads. Back at Patcham, Granny had had it in the bay window where it had been very elegant. With it were six or seven small matching occasional tables with pink marble tops, and tall stands on which Granny's giant blue and white Chinese urns stood. These were placed in the corners of the landings, where they were barged into by Freddy and Gracie until eventually not one urn remained.

My favourite piece was a whatnot, a kind of tall display unit made of black ebony, with randomly placed shelves surrounded with filigree carving and cupboards with inlaid doors and ivory handles. On the shelves sat little soapstone and jade and brass ornaments, including a pair of coiled python candlesticks with ruby eyes. I also liked the large ebony elephants, perhaps because I was impressed with the story of how they had survived an earthquake.

'Remember, Girlie, how we would have been crushed to death if it hadn't been for Ebenezer?' Granny asked my mother.

'What happened?' I asked.

'An earthquake,' said Mother. 'My dog, Ebenezer, an Irish terrier, barked and dragged at our nightclothes until we all woke up and left the bungalow. Five minutes later, the whole building was flattened. The only things that survived were the elephants, minus a couple of ears and their tusks.' She glanced sideways at my father, who she thought was too busy ordering the removal men around to hear what she said. 'Poor old Ebbie. Your father hated him. I'm sure he strayed him, although he always denied it.'

But Father had heard. 'It was fireworks at Diwali,' he said impatiently. This was the Hindu Festival of Lights. 'The stupid dog ran off. If I'd strayed him why would I have spent two days touring the bazaars looking for him? Why would I have offered a reward?'

'I offered the reward,' Mother said.

'Yes, and we had every rabid mongrel in India arrive on the veranda,' Father said. 'Hordes and hordes of beggars who camped there and wouldn't leave. I had to get the gardener to turn the hose on them.'

'He was a lovely dog, we should never have left him with you,' Granny said, bending down to pat Jaffa as if he were suddenly at risk of being strayed too.

By the time the furniture was in place, everyone's nerves were frayed, so much so that Granny collapsed, worn out with the strain of moving. She had to be taken by ambulance to hospital, where she was given a blood transfusion and would remain for some weeks. At the end of the day, I sat quietly in her crowded room with her clothes piled on the bed waiting to be put away, and felt sad that her entire life, large homes, servants, horses, carriages and grand balls, was now reduced to this. In my hand I held the gold chain and large, green jade heart with pearls set at intervals that Granny had pressed into my hands shortly after her arrival that morning.

'It's for your birthday, Rose,' she had whispered. 'It's spinach jade, a rare colour, very sought after.'

I had thought she had forgotten my birthday. I bent to give her a kiss. Her skin was soft and smelled of flowers.

'It's beautiful, Granny. I'll look after it,' I promised.

It was while Granny was in hospital that I learned about the reason for the old rifts in the family – and it seemed that new rifts were being created as well, for she had not yet spent a single night in her crowded bedroom and already Father had begun to niggle and bitch about her living with us. For one thing, he seemed to realise suddenly how much less space there would be with someone else living in the house. Granny's dog needed looking after, too. My father refused to let Jaffa into the rest of the house; in fact, he loathed the poor fat thing. Most of all, it was a matter of revenge: Granny had come to him for help, and he'd make her pay for that incident in Patcham, when she had whacked him and Uncle Bunty with the heavy stick. He also had another worry, which he mentioned to me often.

'Now I'll have mother and daughter ganging up on me together,' he'd say.

So, with Granny not even there, but her room waiting almost in an ominous way, tensions were building.

This was a difficult time for my mother, too. It was as if the unpleasantries of her past had packed up and moved to London with Granny. She was very worried about her and visited her in hospital often, taking the bus to and fro. I'm not sure what they spoke of when they were alone, but Mother began to open up to me about those family feuds, finally bringing answers to questions I had had since a child. Also, Granny was in King's College Hospital, which was very close to my school, so I was able to pop in often for a visit. In this way, and from both of them, I slowly began to learn the vast and sometimes sensational family history. At the core of the biggest rift was Mayfield.

Mayfield had been a problem between my grandparents right from the beginning. Huge and turreted on its hill in

South Wales, and with its massive central dome, Mayfield had been in the family for years until my grandfather finally inherited it. Granny wasn't very fond of the place. She wanted something smaller and more compact. Granddad, on the other hand, loved Mayfield, and he couldn't wait to get back to it when he retired in 1937, and they left India for good. Granny eventually won out, however, and they bought the cottage in Patcham as well. When the war came in 1939, everything was retrenched. Rationing was the order of the day, and people who kept a few hens and had a vegetable patch had to give up their eggs and vegetables for redistribution. They were also expected to put up troops, in Granny's case two naval officers, who stayed at the small cottage in Patcham. Then Mayfield itself was requisitioned as a boys' Borstal. The huge bedrooms were filled with low iron cots with stretched springs and thin mattresses, makeshift dormitories where the boys would sleep. They had been evacuated from some big Midland city that was being bombed, so Mayfield must have seemed quite pastoral by comparison. Granddad went to South Wales to run the place, and Granny went with him. They were both very well suited, with their strict military background, and Granddad had always been a disciplinarian.

The first time I saw Mayfield was when we visited just after the war, during our first trip home from India. The Borstal boys were still there, and still sleeping in their long lines of cots in the huge bedrooms. We children were forbidden to mix with them, though we never did learn exactly what they had done wrong. I don't know what the room beneath the small dome had been before, but when we were there it was a bathroom. In the middle of the floor sat a high-backed copper tub that the maids filled from tall copper jugs. I remember one unforgettable bath I received while at Mayfield. I had already been warned that I was never to glance up at the dome, and obediently I always sat in the tub with my head down as the maids washed me and soaped my hair, pouring water from the jugs over me to rinse. One night, unable to contain myself any longer, I gazed upward. My eyes locked in wonder on the painted ceiling. There were naked men and women, nymphs and shepherds, gods and goddesses, Pans with pipes and horns, and satyrs with huge erections. The maids instantly reported me to my grandfather.

Still wet and wriggly as an eel, I had just enough time to jump from the tub and pull on a white flannel nightgown before Granddad flew into the room in a rage, a razor strop in his hand. To my astonishment he whacked me harder than I had ever believed possible. Still smarting, and furious at having been beaten, I flew down the long echoing corridor and straight into one of the dorms. I have a very clear memory of jumping from cot to cot, the boys tucked under grey blankets in neat rows, all laughing to see me flying over their heads. Some even chased after me as I went, my long white nightgown inching up higher and higher, showing off my little legs. Behind us came Granddad, as furious as he could possibly be, razor strop still in hand, and behind him came the two pretty maids. I can still see the great, leaded bay windows straight ahead of me at the end of one corridor, filled with bright summer light as the sunset flooded in. When Granddad finally caught me, I was stropped again, and the Borstal boys, though innocent, were all lined up and thrashed as well.

Shrieking, I fled to my mother, and told her all that had happened.

'The bastard,' she said. 'He used to beat the hell out of

me and my brothers, but I'm damned if he'll do it to my daughter.'

That said, Mother stormed off and got the strop herself. She found it right where Granddad always kept it, alongside a linen roller towel on the back of the door in his own monk's bathroom. It was probably still warm from use. It was the very same strop he had used on her when she was a child; Mother told me years later that she recognised some kind of coat of arms stamped in the top, and that's how she knew. Snatching it up, she then marched to her father, who was in the study, and hit him across his back.

'This is for a lifetime of pain and indignity,' she shouted. 'It's a pity you're not naked as you deserve to be, the better to feel it.'

That was my first real memory of Mayfield, but I had sweeter memories too. When all the may trees on the hill came to bloom, it looked like a hillside of white snow. I also remember Father loudly singing, during that first visit, a madrigal called 'Early One Morning'.

Early one morning, just as the sun was rising,
I heard a maid sing in the valley below:
Oh don't deceive me;
Oh never leave me!
How could you use a poor maiden so?
Remember the vows that you made to your Mary?
Remember the bower where you vowed to be true.
Oh how could you grieve me?
How could you leave me?
How could you leave me in the valley below . . .'

I thought it was a lovely song, even though it seemed to

upset my grandfather terribly each time Father sang it, which was often.

⎯

It was later in 1948, when my own family finally returned from India, that we learned Granny had packed up and left Mayfield for good. When Mother and we children arrived at the Liverpool docks, we went straight to Granny's cottage near Brighton. Then Mother took us to Mayfield again, so that we could all visit Granddad. Some days after we returned to Granny's cottage, one of the maids, Mary, telephoned Granny's house and broke the sad news. Grandfather was dead. Mary had found him when she went in with his morning tea. He was lying on the floor next to his bed, in a sea of blood that had gushed from his mouth and nose. Granny then flew into hysterics and blamed my mother for the death. Her reasoning was not only superstitious, it was quite ridiculous. During our quick visit to Mayfield, Mother had picked a big bunch of may blossom out on the hill, not knowing that it was bad luck to bring it into the house. One of the maids threw it out. Then, the day after, Mother found a wounded robin and brought it into the kitchen to treat. It died. That was the nail in my grandfather's coffin, so to speak, for it had set the tone for a death to follow soon. Mary had blurted out about the may blossom and the robin to Granny, when she phoned to tell her Grandfather was gone.

'You killed him!' Granny screamed at my horrified mother. 'It's all your fault!'

To this day I can remember the cadence of the shriek.

There was a big powwow about what to do with the body. Granny wanted Granddad brought back to Patcham, to be nearer her now that they'd never get the chance to make up.

'We'll bury him in the graveyard at the bottom of the hill in Patcham church,' she said tearfully. She had his body brought to Brighton on the train, bizarrely accompanied by my father and Uncle Bunty, two of the most incompatible travelling mates. They sat and insulted each other all the way.

—

Now, with Granny in the hospital and Mother upset over the tension Father was already causing, I began to get answers, finally, to so many questions. Granny had left Mayfield because she found out that Granddad was having an affair with each of the maids. I remember these girls well, Peggy and Mary. They were both from the village, Abertillery. I remember that they had wonderful voices, real Welsh voices, and were forever singing some song. I also remember their cute little uniforms, with frilly white aprons. They were the ones who bathed me in the big copper tub and then told Granddad that I'd sneaked a look up at the ceiling. When Granny found out what was going on, she promptly packed up and moved to the cottage in Patcham.

Later, Granny revealed to me yet another part of the story: it was my own father who first told her of Granddad and the maids. I simply couldn't accept this. I went home from the hospital and asked Mother for verification.

'Oh yes,' Mother said. 'It was your father spilled the beans. First of all, he was jealous, for he fancied Mary and she'd spurned him, and then, he wanted to pay my father back for slighting him over his marriage to me.'

That was when I remembered how upset Granddad would get, every time he heard my father going about Mayfield, singing 'Early One Morning' at the top of his lungs: 'Remember the vows that you made to your Mary? Remember the bower where you vowed to be true.'

—

When Granny returned from hospital, rejuvenated and alert, our lives gradually settled down into a routine almost imperceptibly established by her. She got up early before anyone else, and in her blue wool dressing gown – it grew more ragged over the passing years – she would fetch the cold milk in the little carrying crate from the front doorstep. It was Channel Island milk from Jersey cows with a gold foil top under which lay a thick layer of rich golden cream that blue tits had learned to get into. Carefully, so that the cream wasn't disturbed, Granny would set one bottle on the table and put the rest on the cool stone of the pantry floor. She would make a pot of tea and ladle the piping hot porridge she had made the night before into a bowl and sprinkle salt on it. Then she would carefully pour some of the cream from the top of the milk into her first cup of tea and pour the balance into another bowl. She would dip her spoon first into the hot salty porridge, then into the cold cream. A spoonful of porridge, a dip of cream. A spoonful of porridge, a dip of cream. When I once asked her why she didn't just pour the cream on to the porridge, she replied as if it were transparently obvious, 'Because porridge must be eaten hot.'

When Father realised what she was doing, how much she enjoyed the little morning ritual of the top of the milk, he saw an opportunity for revenge. Wanting to spoil her simple pleasure, he took to getting up earlier and earlier to beat Granny to the front door. He would pick up the crate and walk along the hall, vigorously shaking the bottles one at a time, mixing up the cream.

I would wake to the sound of thunder on the stairs as

147

Father galloped down to get to the front door before Granny, while she scooted along the hall from her room. On many a morning there was an unseemly tussle on the front step as they collided and squabbled about who would pick up the milk. They reminded me of two children in the playground. Granny said she would order her own milk from the milkman, but my father hurled the offer back in her teeth with a sneer. 'This isn't a common lodging house,' he said. Then, he would retreat to the bathroom, with its stained-glass windows with paintings of little birds in roundels. He was always careful to leave the door wide open as he stood at the basin, his little shaving brush whipping up tons of lather, the foam scarlet in the morning sun that shone in through the coloured glass.

'Early one morning, just as the sun was rising, I heard a maid sing in the valley below . . .' The bathroom ceiling was so high that his voice echoed all through the house. My grandmother would finally slam her door very loudly. No one was better at psychological warfare than my father. Finally, to keep the peace over the milk, Mother ordered an extra pint for Granny, but Father was incensed when he saw six bottles instead of five on the doorstep. Thus, the battle of the cream continued unabated.

Family stories became a part of the Sunday morning apple tart and coffee sessions, a little ritual that Granny and I started. Everything surprised me. I learned that Granny was a wonderful pastry cook, trained in Switzerland. This was unbelievable.

'You trained as a cook?' I said, amazed.

'When I was seventeen my parents sent me to stay with my uncle and aunt for the London season. I came out, you know.' I shook my head. I didn't know. 'They lived in

Chelsea,' Granny continued. 'His money came from high-class patisseries.'

Interrupting her, I said, 'I didn't think people in trade did the season.'

'Oh, all that snobbish nonsense stopped with the Victorians,' Granny snorted. 'Trade made Britain great. The Victorians worshipped money and honoured those who made plenty of it. My Uncle Andrew was very wealthy, a highly respected member of society.'

'Who were you presented to?' I asked. 'Queen Mary?'

'No, Victoria's son Edward the Seventh, and Queen Alexandra,' said Granny, as if suddenly seeing it all again. 'In 1907. I was born when Victoria was on the throne, but she died in 1901. It would have been something to remember, curtseying to her, the old witch. Though, from all accounts, she gave up on most things after Albert died. Yes, I did the season, but I wasn't happy. I didn't enjoy all those dances, all those introductions to young men whose mothers only wanted to know how much money a girl would inherit. I started to ask Uncle Andrew about his business and instead of sleeping off a ball, I would get up early and go with him on his rounds of the shops. I was fascinated. I told him I wanted to learn the business. He said in that case I had to learn how to make cakes with the best patissiers in the world – and that's the Swiss.'

'Not the French?'

'No,' Granny said firmly. 'The Swiss. They understand chocolate. I was dispatched to Switzerland for a year. I loved it, not just the lessons, but the whole *belle époque* thing. Switzerland was so romantic then. Everyone came in the summer for the walking and climbing, that was the real season, not this modern craze for winter sports. I climbed in the Alps, I walked to Italy, I went to Vienna in the spring. It was all glorious.'

'Did you join your uncle in his business?' I asked.

'No,' Granny said, shortly. 'I met and married your grandfather when I was nineteen. He was a very handsome and dashing man in his youth and carried me off to India with his regiment.'

The first thing Granny taught me was how to make pastry: to mix it lightly with just the tips of my fingers, and add the merest drop of water to help it bind together.

'Too many housewives are lazy,' she said. 'They can't be bothered to deal with a difficult crumbly texture and throw in half a cup of water. Then they wonder why it ends up cement. And always use fresh butter, Rose, none of this shortening. Would you eat a mouthful of that muck with a spoon?' I made a face. 'Exactly,' she said. 'And yet that's what you're doing when you eat pastry made with shortening.'

The purpose of these lessons was to enable me to make a perfect covered apple tart, decorated on the top with little pastry leaves, glazed with egg yolk and milk, sprinkled with sugar, and filled with the tart sweetness of tender Bramley apples.

'Use a sweet eating apple for an open tarte Tatin,' Granny instructed, 'but nothing but a Bramley will do for covered tarts and pies.'

I became so adept that while Granny put on her hat and went to morning service in the church across the road, I could make the tarts on my own. When she returned, she would take off her gloves, but not her hat. Then, companionably, we would sit and talk at the table with a slice of warm tart, a big dollop of whipped cream, and a splash of aromatic, very strong fresh coffee in a big cup of hot milk. Until then, I had never appreciated that coffee could taste as good as it smelled.

I will always remember the special feel of those languorous Sunday mornings, which developed a resonance of their own. After her snack, Granny would retire to her room to take off her tight church clothes before walking Gracie and Jaffa around the park, wearing a wide-brimmed straw to keep off the sun, one of her legendary flower-bedecked titfers. Once there, she would meet and chat with a few cronies while I prepared lunch. As I peeled potatoes and washed vegetables, I listened to *Family Favourites*, which was broadcast on Sundays from noon until two p.m. on the Light Programme. It linked families at home with our armed forces serving around the world, particularly in Germany and Cyprus. The theme tune, 'With a Song in My Heart', was followed by the memorable words: 'The time in Britain is twelve noon, in Germany it's one o'clock, but home and away it's time for Two-Way Family Favourites.' After a little friendly banter between Jean Metcalfe in London and whoever was presenting from Germany that week, the first letter would be read out: 'For Corporal John Grady in BFPO 99, from Mum and the twins, who say, Hello John, hope to see you soon and don't forget to write, here's Bill Hayes with "The Ballad of Davy Crockett",' That's when the big hit of the year dropped on the turntable '. . . Born on a mountain top in Tennessee, greenest state in the land of the free.' Sixteen million listeners in Britain alone would sit back and relax, feeling that all was well with their world, at least for one more week.

After an all-night bridge session, Father would be upstairs still unshaven, writing in his dressing gown. Mother would be pottering about in the garden, and I would be sprawled on the lawn while lunch cooked, the windows wide open, the radio turned up. I knew all the hits: 'Love Is a Many-Splendoured Thing', 'Rock Around the Clock', 'Unchained Melody', and 'The Yellow Rose of Texas', which became one of the most requested songs on *Family Favourites*. 'The yellow rose of Texas is the only gal for me . . .' I sang along, eyes half-closed, watching swallows dip and soar across the high, blue sky. Whatever else happened that summer, it was a time of daydreams. Thoughts of Richard floated into my mind like drifting clouds. By now I had pictures of him, those Hollywood beefcake images from magazines such as *Picturegoer* and *Photoplay*. Whatever songs were played on the radio, somehow I associated them with him: 'Oh my love, my darling, I hunger for your touch . . .' I echoed softly, wondering where he was, what he was doing.

Three months were to pass before he came back into my life.

Seven

❦

On afternoons, when I should have been on the muddy sports fields playing hockey, I would sneak off after lunch, in my school uniform, and catch the bus up to the Old Vic in time for the two-thirty matinée show. As I remember, three of Shakespeare's plays were performed in rotation that autumn at the start of the 1955–1956 season: *The Winter's Tale*, *The Merry Wives of Windsor*, and *Julius Caesar*. I saw them all more than once, spending my entire weekly pocket money allowance of half a crown. It cost two shillings to sit on the backless, hard benches high up in the balcony, 'in the Gods', in a crush of students and tourists on a shoestring. The bus fare, which was thruppence each way, meant I couldn't afford a programme, which was sixpence, or a drink in the interval. Sometimes, to stretch my legs, I would walk as far as the Cave and casually peer in the window, knowing that he wouldn't be there, and prepared to flee if he were. More often I would sip some water from the cold taps in the ladies' room and then return to my seat in the Gods where, in the dismal light, I would strain to read some literary book, hoping someone would notice the title and be impressed. (Having done this myself, as I grew up I came to recognise how the earnest brigade carried difficult books or obscure newspapers such as *Pravda*, like accessories, placing them very visibly on tables in left-wing cafés, like the Partisan, where they came to play chess and argue over bowls of soup.)

I wasn't the only one who bunked off games. My expeditions were brought to a halt when half the form was missing from the playing fields one afternoon and there were not enough girls standing there in the biting wind in navy divided skirts and raw red knees to make up a hockey game. Next morning at register we were asked to do the decent thing and own up. In all innocence, I went along to the headmistress's study, not realising that I was the only one who was doing 'the decent thing'. Quailing before Miss Pearce's gimlet gaze, I shuffled on the Chinese rug before her desk, trying to think up a good excuse. With *Julius Caesar* being on the syllabus, I said I needed to catch up with the theatre because I had missed so much in Cornwall and felt left behind.

'London is so wonderful,' I gushed. 'You're so lucky.'

'Exercise is important, too,' Miss Pearce said, looking over the top of her gold-rimmed spectacles with a steady gaze. 'Healthy mind, healthy body. But, this time, since your motives were good, we won't make an issue of it. However, did it not occur to you that Miss Wilton has already booked a class visit to *Julius Caesar* as well as *Henry the Fifth*?'

'No, Miss Pearce,' I murmured.

'Well, it won't hurt you to see it twice,' she smiled, warming visibly. As she walked me to her study door – a rare honour – she dropped a kindly hand on my shoulder. 'I am very proud of you, Rose,' she said, 'for having the courage to own up to your breach of trust.'

Feeling like a rat, I slunk off back to the classroom, where the other girls crowded around, some in disgust that I'd been a goody two-shoes and some in awe that I had braved the lion's den.

'What did she say?' they asked. 'Are you going to be expelled?'

'She said I could cut games for the rest of the term,' I said, flippantly. 'And she's telling my father to double my pocket money so I can go to the theatre more often.'

After that I threw myself into hockey and reached the second eleven. Instead of weekdays, I switched to going to matinées on Saturday afternoons, though I seem to remember that it cost more. Sometimes, I would just drop in at the Cave and tuck myself into a corner at the back with a book – a book I actually read – and a glass of squash, which was cheap and which I could spin out for a long time.

One afternoon in November, when a damp mist swirled around Waterloo Road and turned the dark area beneath the bridge into a frightening place, I was huddled in my usual spot and thinking about leaving when a shadow fell across my table. I froze when the voice that had haunted my dreams for so long said, 'Hello. May I join you?'

My heart actually leapt; I felt it thump unevenly and I thought I would be sick. If I looked like a frightened rabbit, he didn't comment. Without waiting for a reply, he put his cup of tea on the table, the contents splashing into the saucer, and sat down. Leaning toward me, he kissed me on the cheek. He smelled of whisky, soap and tobacco. He smelled like my father, and it was strangely reassuring.

'Well, what have you been up to, Cinderella?' he asked. 'Still at finishing school?' I was shocked that he had remembered my lie.

'No,' I blurted. In my head I repeated, Thank you, God, that I'm not in school uniform. Thank you, God, I'm wearing nice clothes – stockings and not socks, a ribbed jersey with a nicely cut flared skirt and matching coat, which lay on the bench seat on the other side of me. Thank you, God, yes, thank you dear, dear God, that my guardian angel has prompted me this day of all days to slip a tube of lipstick into my shoulder bag before I left the house, which I applied on the bus. Unable to think of anything that made sense, I said, 'At the moment I'm keeping my grandmother company. She's been ill.'

'Very laudable,' he said, 'but you can't hide yourself away behind lace curtains for ever. You need to go to University, widen your horizons.' He picked up my book. '*Pride and Prejudice*? No, no, don't read prissy English novels like this, all fingers crooked and tea with lemon. "Dear Miss Bennet – Yes, oh yes, Mr Darcy!"' he mocked, picking up his tea with a crooked finger and daintily sipping with an exaggerated air. '"It is a truth universally acknowledged, that a single man in possession of a good fortune, must be in want of a wife." God, what a pill Jane Austen is! What did she know of life? Read history, biography. Get your head around reality.'

'Reality!' I exclaimed. 'Jane Austen wrote about everything she saw around her, she brings Regency England to life. But acting –'

'But what? What were you going to say?' he jumped in when I broke off.

'Well, acting is not real, is it? You create an illusion.'

'Life's an illusion, a bloody great big illusion.' He stopped. 'You're right. Acting isn't real man's work. It's a sissy job. God knows why I'm a bloody actor. I should be down the mines like my da, shovelling coal in one of

Masefield's dirty British coasters, rolling steel in a fiery mill down in Port Talbot. And Jesus, what do I do? Mince about a bloody stage in poofters' clothes, slap all over my face.'

I was riveted. He exuded raw magnetism; I was being pulled toward him, slowly, then faster and faster. It was an alarming sensation, like looking over a bridge and having that irresistible urge to jump. I wanted to fling myself against him like the other half of a magnet.

Abruptly, he said, 'Let's get out of here, fancy a drink?'

I shook my head. 'No, I have to go.'

'Where do you have to go? To look after your bloody granny?' From his pocket he took a flat bottle and poured a splash into his tea. He offered the bottle to me and I realised he had been drinking. I shook my head. 'Rehearsals, bloody rehearsals,' he said, drinking from the bottle.

'What are you rehearsing?' I asked, mesmerised as the level in the bottle went down.

'The great, the glorious Henry the bloody Fifth,' he sighed. 'The quintessential Englishman and me a quintessential bloody Welshman.' He jumped up, banging the table and spilling his tea as he started to declaim, '"The game's afoot: Follow your spirit; and, upon this charge cry 'God for Harry, England, and Saint George!'" English, see? I've sold out, left my homeland, it's all bloody England every step of the way down the slippery slope that leads to the primrose path of ease and comfort and my damnation,' he said, stretching the metaphors. He came round to my side of the table and picked up my coat, holding it out like a matador to the bull. 'Well, Miss Austen, are we going, or not?'

'Not to a pub,' I said primly, slipping into my coat and putting my book into my bag.

'Well then, what? Your wish is my command.'

'Can we walk, like we did before?' I asked.

'Very well. It's cold, it's foggy, it's Christmas Day in the workhouse, but if the girl wants to walk, we'll walk.'

The man behind the bar glanced up and shook his head, tut-tutting. 'Hey, Rich,' he called out. 'Nice to have you back.'

'Bugger off,' Richard replied.

The man grinned at this. As we left, I heard the bartender singing, flamboyantly, like an opera singer: '"Earth angel, earth angel, will you be mine?"'

The foggy November darkness closed around us. He took my arm, pulling me close. My shoulder fitted snugly into the angle of his shoulder. It felt comfortable walking alongside him, retracing our steps of the summer as far as Waterloo Bridge. Instead of crossing it, he led me down to the South Bank. In the fog, the round orbs of the lights cast fuzzy haloes that formed circles in green and gold, like Van Gogh's suns swirling about a riotous sky. The entire feel was like being inside an Impressionist painting with shadowy dark figures, some of whom were holding black umbrellas. As if reading my mind, he said, 'Vincent Van Gogh and Camille Pissarro lived in South London. They painted scenes like this, almost interchangeable in this light with the Seine of the eighteen seventies or eighties.'

'I've never seen them. Are they in the Tate?' I asked.

'I don't know where they are. I get my education from books,' he said, 'but there's something about this light that appeals to me.'

'It's like being on stage,' I said.

'Bugger me, Miss Austen is right, why didn't I realise that?' he mocked. He pulled me around to face him and tipped my face up beneath a light. 'Tell me, Miss Austen, what is your name?'

'Rose,' I said.

'How suitably old-fashioned. Among all Miss Austen's Emmas, Lizzies, Janes, and Harriets, is there a Rose?' he asked, quoting, ' "Mr Collins had only to change from Jane to Elizabeth – and it was soon done – done while Mrs Bennet was stirring the fire." No, I don't believe she mentions a Rose.'

'So you do read her!' I exclaimed.

'It's part of every Englishman and woman's education,' he said, 'and I am working on being an educated Englishman much as a Welsh wolf practises how to be a sheep in sheep's clothing.'

Perhaps I have not remembered everything exactly as he said it; forty-five years is a long time to look back; but my memory has always been good, so good that later I worked as a court reporter and was often able to recall entire judgments almost verbatim or with the help of a few quick notes. My meetings with Richard affected me so deeply that after each meeting with him, I would relive it, reciting to myself, over and over again, each word that he spoke, each gesture, all so important to a young girl in love for the first time. Then, I would carefully record the words in my exercise book, hidden beneath the floorboard in my bedroom, for future reading. It's strange how, when I start to immerse myself in these memories, more and more floods back with such clarity. I remember the empty white flagpoles along the river wall, the smell of the river itself. It was ebbing and a strip of exposed sand cast up a rank, oozy smell. When I recall that, I remember him talking about Dickens, and mudlarks who used to dig in the shores for flotsam and jetsam and golden guineas if they were lucky, washed down by the sewers which used to empty into the river. He said he preferred mud honey. He wouldn't say what that was and later I looked it up. It wasn't in the dictionary but I tracked it down in my father's *Brewer's*, a big edition with a varnished brown cloth cover. It said, 'Mud-honey. So Tennyson calls the dirty pleasures of men–about–town.'

In the gloom, we leaned against the stone parapet beneath one of the globe lamps. Cold mist swirled up, sharp with the taste of river water in it. He felt me shiver. He put an arm around my shoulders, drew me close.

'All history has been here, Rose. Traitors, kings, emperors. When the river froze, they held ice fairs on the ice. Peter the Great – imagine him in his bearskin hat and wolf furs – skated a full mile from the Houses of Parliament down to the Tower of London, passing this spot. Bran's head is buried under the White Tower itself.'

'Who is Bran?'

'Have you never read *The Mabinogion*?'

I admitted that I had never heard of it, and so he began reciting in Welsh. I was electrified.

'You haven't a clue what I've just said, have you?' he asked, when he stopped.

'No,' I admitted. 'I know it's Welsh because the maids in my grandparents' house used to speak to each other in Welsh.'

'My lovely Welsh! The language of the people, not of the gentry. Like gold and coal, it comes from the land.'

He told me that *The Mabinogion* was a collection of Welsh mythological stories. Little remained, most having been destroyed by the Norman and English overlords, so it was doubly precious to the Welsh, who had fought hard to preserve their difficult language. Bran was Welsh, the giant king of Britain. When he died, his head continued to speak, entertaining his lords at a feast that lasted for eighty years. At the end of the feast, he ordered his head to be cut off and carried to London, where it would be buried under the White Tower. As long as it remained there, guarded by his familiars, Celtic ravens, Britain would be safe from invasion.

'Did you know that at the end of the war, we were down to just one raven? A bit like Gibraltar losing all its apes, only perhaps a little closer to home. Winston Churchill ordered more young ravens to be brought here from Wales and Scotland. A garrison of ravens, no less. They have ranks, Sergeant Raven and Corporal Raven, and they even have pay books. Five bob a week each they get. And a Beefeater in all his knickerbocker glory to look after them.'

I laughed. 'You're joking.'

'It's true. He's known as the Keeper of Bran's Birds. I'll take you there one day, you can see them for yourself. You'd have to knock down the Tower to get to see Bran's head. The entire collection of the crown jewels, crowns, orbs, and sceptres, is sitting right on top of it.' His lips grazed my hair. Suddenly he said, 'Let me take you to a place you've never been, it's quite close.'

'How do you know where I've been?'

'I know you've not been there,' he said mysteriously. 'Come on, are you game for an adventure?'

'Are we leaving London?' I asked.

'Good grief, girl, I'd be arrested as a white slave trafficker. In the States you can get the electric chair if you carry sweet young things across state lines. All I'm going to do is carry you across the river to Paradise.'

'In a boat? It sounds more like Lethe than Paradise.'

'No, on shank's pony. Come on, Miss Austen, stop asking questions or the moment will be lost. Let's go.'

We walked the length of the South Bank, passing the diffused lights of the Festival Hall. Few people were about, yet when I glanced up at the vast windows above the entrance, I could see movement, people sitting at tables, drinking and eating, laughing. They could have been in a spaceship. At the end of the promenade, we reached the iron railway bridge that carried trains across the river to Charing Cross Station. He pointed.

'Up there.'

'On the railway bridge?'

'Yes. It was originally built three hundred years ago so people on this side of the river could walk across to Hungerford Market. The old bridge is gone. They've left us an iron tightrope, its soul destroyed when the market was knocked down to build Charing Cross Station.'

We climbed the narrow steep stairs, like those on a ship. At the top the pedestrian bridge stretched ahead like a narrow alley beside the railway lines. There was just room for two people walking side by side. Someone with a fear of heights would easily be scared, looking down through the ironwork to the dark river far below. In the middle of the bridge, as trains rattled and vibrated mere feet away, he stopped, put his fingers to his lips.

'Look, see the people teeming by,' he whispered, 'with their baskets of fresh fruit and vegetables from the fields of Kent. Hear the chickens cluck in their wicker cages, and the greenfinches, who still find the voice to sing even though caught this morning with sticky lime. Look, at the stalls with striped canvas awnings, jugglers, muffin men and fire-eaters, dancing bears and braziers. Put your hands out, feel the heat, warm your hand on this cornet of hot chestnuts.' His mesmerising voice brought it vividly alive.

When he finally stopped, I sighed. 'How do you do that?'

He knew what I meant.

'It's a trick,' he said. 'I can show off better than anyone.'

'No, it's a gift. I saw you once, at a reading of *Under Milk Wood*. It was the first time I realised how words alone can make things so real you actually do see them.'

'Dylan Thomas was a genius, and I let him down,' he said.

'How?'

'One day, I'll tell you. It pains me to think about it.' His voice and mood had changed. He was suddenly depressed. 'And it pains me to be without a drink so long. I need to wash this smog out of my throat.'

He was striding off, his shoes resounding on the iron plates. The bridge continued on, but where it hit the Embankment was another steep staircase, curving, and wider this time, of granite and not iron. He took my hand and we ran down to the bottom. Without stopping he turned away from the river up into Villiers Street, named after the first Duke of Buckingham, he said, while I trailed breathless in his wake. He seemed preoccupied and tense, as if a darkness had descended on him, and I, having almost lost my will, was in another skin, looking at myself walking up that hill. This other self saw the big round ball of the Coliseum on the skyline, like a stone moon come to land on the rooftops along the Strand, and tramps, many of them in the tattered rags of old military uniforms, lying under the arches beneath the station.

Just before we turned into the Griffin, a dive where he said they sold Murphy's, he said, 'You won't mind if I hide you in a dark corner, will you? Sometimes I'm recognised and there's always a lot of curiosity if I'm seen with a girl.' He seated me in the privacy of a high-backed booth in the corner by the door while he went off to the bar to get the drinks. It was one of those places where everything was so varnished with the patina of age and tobacco smoke it looked different shades of waxy brown. Hanging lights cast a poor light, not helped by reflecting off a ceiling the colour of amber. It was cosy, with a coke fire burning in the grate and a mahogany bar, black as treacle and shiny with the handling of centuries.

He returned with a tray of drinks, two pints and two whisky chasers for himself, a half-pint and a chaser for me, and two cheese sandwiches with a dish of pickled onions.

'I ordered for you, is this all right?' he asked. Dumbly I nodded, and took a tentative sip of the strong ale. It was pleasant, bitter and nutty sweet at the same time, like malt, the kind my mother used to give me to disguise the taste of cod liver oil. Steadily, one after another, he sank two pints and tossed back the whisky after each before sitting back and sighing. 'Bloody rehearsals,' he said.

I nodded at the glasses. 'Is that what this is all about?'

'No, I like to drink.' He looked at my half-finished glass and the whisky I hadn't touched. 'Now, Miss Austen, this will never do. Drink up, keep me company.'

'I could never keep you company where drinking is concerned,' I said. Quickly, I lifted the stubby glass and tossed it back, choking as the fire hit the back of my throat.

'The first time?' he asked.

'I told you, I don't drink – but tonight, well, tonight's an adventure, you said so yourself.' He put a hand out and covered one of mine.

'You don't talk a lot. I like that in a girl. But, now I want to be amused. Tell me about yourself.'

His touch had sent a warmth shooting into my hand. I almost gasped with the strength of the sensation.

'What are you, Scottish, Irish, Welsh, or bloody English?' he prompted.

'I'm a bloody Scot,' I said. 'At least, on my mother's side. My father, I'm not sure about, he's a dark horse, but I'm an honourary member of the Welsh tribe. My great-grandmother was born during a shooting party at Henry Morgan's house.'

'Morgan the Welsh pirate?'

'Yes, at Tredegar. My grandparents had a house in Abertillery, in Monmouthshire, where I used to stay when I was very young.'

'Ah, yesterday then.'

I looked at him, confused. Had he guessed my age? I decided not to test it. Perhaps he did know and this was all a game to a bored man. Trying to keep calm, I described Mayfield, how it was such a wonderful house, with its towers and domes. Then I told him about the night I gazed upward at the ceiling.

'Naked men and women, nymphs and shepherds, gods and goddesses,' I told him, 'and Pans with pipes and horns. There were even satyrs with huge erections.'

Richard roared when he heard the story.

'So my people down in the coal valleys were the gypsies at the gate while yours were the rich mine owners in the castle being horny.'

'It wasn't a castle,' I said. 'It was a large house on a hill with a wall all around and a lodge. Looking back, it probably seemed bigger than it was.'

'But maids,' he said, 'you had bloody Welsh maids.'

'No,' I said. 'They had maids. Peggy and Mary. *They* reported me to my grandfather and he chased me around the house with a razor strop. My mother stood up to him over it.' And then I told him what my mother had said to her father, as she laid the strap across his own back: 'This is for a lifetime of pain and indignity. It's a pity you're not naked as you deserve to be, the better to feel it.'

Richard sat up and looked at me when I reached that part of the story.

'Take me to your mother, let me shake her hand,' he said.

'They had a huge fight and Granddad told us to leave, but my father had something on him. He said if Granddad didn't behave he would tell my grandmother that he was having an affair with both the maids.'

'Both of them? Was he?'

'Apparently he was. I didn't know anything about it, not then. Not for years. I only found out the other day.'

I sat quietly, sipping my beer while I thought about it.

'And your grandfather, is he still living it up, droit du seigneur and all that, with the maids?'

'No, he died. His heart exploded. Granny blamed my mother, and it was all because of a robin and some may blossom.'

Richard nodded as if in complete understanding.

'We Welsh are a superstitious race,' he said. 'Like all Celts, we believe in magic.'

By now our glasses were empty.

'Want another?' he asked. I shook my head. I knew then what would happen next.

He said, 'Right, let's go.'

We walked back out into the night and turned into John Adam Street. About fifty yards on was Buckingham Street, where the Duke of Buckingham's great mansion had stood until it was pulled down for the development of Charing Cross.

'I have a friend who has a flat here, he lets me use it sometimes,' Richard said. 'I thought we could listen to some music, have a pot of tea. We can't go anywhere more public. Is that all right?'

He even had a key. I didn't ask how many times he'd been there, how many times he had used the flat for this purpose. Such questions didn't even enter my mind. To myself, in my youth and innocence, I was the only one. Perhaps, in a naïve and girlish way, I felt honoured to be with him, but overall, I think I just wanted to get as close to him as I could possibly get – and I was not so naïve that I didn't already know some of the feminine tricks, the tossing of my head, the sideways glance, the fluttering eyelashes.

Inside was a white-painted hall with decorative cornices and rooms off. A staircase went straight up. Richard led the way upward and opened the door to the flat. Beyond a small vestibule was a long room across the front of the house, carpeted in a kind of mossy green. I can never see that colour now without thinking back to that carpet and that room. There were some deep chairs and a sofa in oatmeal linen, gilt mirrors on the wall, and a big oil painting of a naked woman lying on a tousled white bed. Her skin was painted in bold blocks of colour.

He moved about, putting on low lights, and then switched the main light off. He chose an LP and put it on the turntable, Mozart, I think, though I also remember some Chopin piano pieces, so perhaps he put a stack on, so low it was more background music than something to listen to. I had taken off my coat and was walking around the room, looking at the painting, picking up a small bronze of a ballet dancer, and a high-stepping Chinese horse, in a kind of grey glaze, with a wonderful, tossing mane and tail. There were some big photographic books on China and the Swiss Alps, and a white kidskin copy of Shakespeare's sonnets. It looked like a presentation copy. When I opened it, there was no message inside.

'Will your friend come back tonight?' I asked. He seemed amused.

'No, not tonight.' He said it in such a way, I suddenly wondered if this flat were his. I never knew. In all the months I would go there, I never saw the owner, never saw the neighbours. Richard said the lower floors were let out as offices and they were always empty during the night.

'Would you like a drink?' He held up a bottle of Scotch. I made a face.

'Can I have tea?'

'There's no milk,' he said. He hadn't been in the kitchen, so I knew he must have been there recently. Or perhaps there never was any milk. He poured a large splash of whisky into a glass for himself. Inspired, he said, 'How about some drinking chocolate?'

'Drinking chocolate?' I queried. 'It sounds lovely.'

'Have you never had any before?'

'We drink cocoa sometimes and Ovaltine.' Now it was his turn to make a face.

'It's American,' he said. 'You'll like it, girls do. While I put the kettle on, have a look round. There's a bathroom through there.' He pointed to the back beyond the vestibule.

The minutiae of the conversation might have been different, but I can recall the room clearly. I know that that was where I tasted hot chocolate for the very first time, although I am vague about the make. I can visualise him pouring the Scotch and taking a big mouthful that he held in his cheeks for a moment before swilling it down with a little grimace, baring his teeth. I can still see him shaking his head as it hit the back of his throat, and a lock of hair falling forward. He was so handsome in that light, the planes and shadows of his face accented, his eyes a glittering, intense green.

When I returned from the bathroom, where I had dried my hands on white towels that were a lot softer than the ones we had at home, my drink was ready, on a small table next to the sofa. I took it and sipped it, curious.

'How is it?' he asked.

'It's sweet and lovely,' I said. 'Thank you.'

'Come here,' he said, his voice roughening a little.

He was seated in a chair by the window, the curtains still open. Blindly, I got up, went across to his chair, and stood there, not sure what to do next. He took one of my hands and pulled me down on to his lap. We kissed, but not for long. He pulled off my sweater in a fluid movement, which was far more expert than if I had done it myself. I was suddenly sitting there in my petticoat, bra and skirt.

'You should wear a waist slip,' he said. 'These full-length things are a fiddle.'

When I think back to this, it makes me smile. I personally don't remember waist slips until later, in the late 1950s or early 1960s, when crinolines were all the rage. Perhaps they had just passed me by, but it was obvious that Richard was an expert in women's clothes. It never once occurred to me that he might be married.

He drew the curtains, then pulled me down to the white sheepskin that lay on the floor. He quickly took my skirt off, then my slip, then everything else. My clothes lay in a circle around the sheepskin. Who was this girl lying there, naked? Who was this girl whose breasts were being kissed and then teased with teeth and lips? Who was this girl who felt strong fingers rubbing, drawing out deep juices? Who was this girl who should have been horrified to feel a tongue in her most secret places? I arched and screamed out when I felt its pointed tip. To permit the breaking down of all my most intimate taboos, all my modesty, everything I'd built as a wall to hedge about my innocence, was an incredible and terrifying feeling.

He was gentle and sensitive that first time. I don't remember how or when his clothing came off, but I opened my eyes and saw his erect penis outlined, a huge shadow on the wall. I recalled seeing Greek paintings on vases, silhouettes of muscular demonic satyrs with ambiguous curving smiles, and little horns, and huge organs that stood out proudly. I remembered the drawings on the domed ceiling at Mayfield. I turned my head and gazed upon the real, massive, thing. It was unbelievable that it had materialised from nowhere. Miss Cadwallader's biology lessons went out of the window; this was like a conjuring trick.

'I can't – it's too big – it won't fit,' I said, trying to get up, beginning to panic. He held me down, gently. I was no longer standing outside myself. I was dealing with myself, and I was frightened. This wasn't a game, this was something that adults did. And yet, why didn't I get up? Why didn't I run into the bathroom and lock the door? No doubt about it, I was prepared, ready. I arched my back and lifted my buttocks.

Kneeling between my legs, he moved in closer. I could see the angle of his powerful torso above me, the matted hairs on his chest and shoulders. Until then, I knew only my smooth-skinned brothers and other boys at the lido, or larking about in the river on a summer's day. There was something animal-like, bestial, about his naked body that both fascinated and repulsed me. I kept my eyes on the angles of the strong face looking down at me, the wide mouth, the flaring nostrils, the glittering green eyes, the lock of hair falling over his brow. He was leaning back so he could see, watching the path his penis was penetrating, watching for the exact moment when the hymen gave way. I held my breath. A sudden push, and I felt such a sharp sting that I cried out. He stopped for a moment.

'Is it all right?' he asked. I nodded. 'Lift your legs over my back,' he said. I did so as he reached for a cushion from a chair and slipped it under me. When I screamed, he put his hand over my mouth. The surge of pleasure overtook and astonished me. It was as if everything suddenly exploded. It hurt but I didn't care. We were slick and slippery together, moving in harmony, moving as one. Suddenly he stopped.

'I've got to pull out,' he groaned. I wrapped my legs tighter about him and held him.

'No, don't,' I whispered, my eyes shut, chanting the words like a prayer. I could feel a rising rush, an incredible surge, and then it was over. I collapsed back on the white rug and lay gasping as he fell across me. After a few moments, he pulled away.

'I shouldn't have done that,' he said.

'It's all right,' I assured him. 'I wanted it to happen.'

'I shouldn't have come inside you,' he said. 'What a mess.'

I sat up, coming back to earth as I realised what he meant.

'You can't get pregnant the first time,' I said nervously. I almost added, 'The girls at school told me so,' but I snatched back the words.

'I hope you're right,' he said. He wiped himself on my flimsy white panties, then glanced down ruefully at the red he had left on them. The white of the sheepskin was also stained with a small patch of scarlet blood. I went naked into the kitchen to get a damp cloth.

As I wiped the mark away, he watched me closely.

'This is very medieval,' he said. 'I feel I should be hanging the sheepskin out of the window, the knight who has won the lady, to say, look what I've done. She's mine now.'

I laughed. I felt relaxed, confident, lithe, and lazy. I felt a woman.

'Well, Miss Austen,' Richard said, as he helped himself to another Scotch, 'you're not a virgin any more.'

—

When we leave the building, the white fog that had hung over the river earlier has already turned into choking, yellow smog. I huddle into my coat, turning the collar up. He walks me to the end of the street, his hands stuffed into his pockets, shoulders hunched. He seems remote as he flags down a passing taxi. Handing over a fiver, he says to the cabbie, 'Look after my niece, will you? She'll give you the address.' With a quick nod to me, he walks away. Perhaps I should feel used by the deceit, bereft that he makes no attempt to touch me, or say when we should meet again, but I know he has to be cautious.

'Gypsy Hill? In this pea-souper? You've got to be joking,' the driver says. 'It's always worse, south of the river.' But when he sees my young, flushed face, as if perhaps about to panic, he changes his mind. 'You've talked me into it, love,' he winks, 'but don't blame me if we get lost.'

He starts the meter and we drive slowly up into the

Strand. People hurry along the streets, the brims of their hats pulled low and scarves up to their mouths to protect themselves from the smog. I sink back in the seat and close my eyes, already desperately wanting to relive the past few hours, like a miser counting coins. The farther the taxi spins me south of the river toward home, the more unreal it all seems. Conscious of the damp panties crammed into my bag next to Jane Austen, mentally I retrace our steps: over the footbridge, to the pub and along John Adam Street, to Buckingham Street, up the stairs, and into the flat. Step by step, moment by moment, I relive it all: the amber glow of the shaded lamps, the electric fire. Then, I almost force myself to remember the satiny sheen of the hood, the length and breadth of the engorged penis that he held in one hand as he directed it toward me. In the back of the taxi, my face and body burn with remembered desire. I expel a long breath I hadn't realised I was holding.

'All right, love?' says the disembodied voice of the cabbie.

My eyes fly open. Shocked, I gaze at him in the mirror as he stares back at me. I feel exposed, as if he has seen everything, shared my passion. I suddenly feel faint.

'I'm a bit carsick,' I murmur.

'Gordon Bennet,' he says, screeching to a halt that jerks me forward to my knees. 'Sorry about that. Are you all right, Miss?'

'Yes, fine, I just need some air,' I say, as I pull down the window and stick my head out. 'I'm all right now.'

We move off. The foggy autumn air cools my burning face. The back of the cab fills with mist and I am surrounded by a cloud, spookily phantasmagoric, unreal. We complete the last half mile at a snail's pace, dropping down into the almost solid wall of fog held in the valley where I live, as if entering into a strangely hushed other world. I get out at the bottom of our road and stand in a daze on the pavement, watching as the taxi turns and drives away. It is like a ship sailing off, a link to a previous life, leaving me abandoned on the far shore.

I walk up the road, following the line of fences, until I reach our house. From the gate, I can't even see the front door. The clammy wet shrubs reach out to grab me. I stumble on the dark path as I creep around to the kitchen door that is never locked. I am ravenous. In the cold, dark kitchen I feel my way about as, cat-like, my eyes adjust to the faint light thrown from the hall lamp. Feeling by touch for the icy bottle on the stone floor of the pantry, I find it and pour milk into a glass. There is some Madeira cake in the tin. Carrying my shoes and bag, I pad quietly along the hall. Granny is in her room, her radio murmuring. Taking a bite of cake, I pause to listen. It sounds like a play, perhaps *Armchair Theatre*, which always absorbs her. I hear Jaffa snuffling close under the door as he smells my presence. Can he smell anything strange and different about me? Tonight, I don't go in to see Granny.

Safely in my room, I strip off my clothes and slip into my dressing gown. I don't know why I had rushed. It is a ghost house, everyone shut away in their own rooms. I know no one has missed me, or even wondered where I was. Father won't be back for another hour or more. As long as I am in bed by then, no one will be any wiser. Just to make sure I haven't been dreaming, I open my bag and pull out my white panties. They are almost dry, still streaked and stained with my own blood. I sniff them. There is a faint odour, but nothing significant or memorable.

In the icy bathroom, I run an inch of hot water, kneel in the tub, and sponge myself. I am sore. I pat myself with a towel and examine it, but there is nothing to see. I rub in some cold cream, slip my nightgown over my head, and go to bed. I feel like the little leprechaun who learns a secret he is dying to tell. In the end, he whispers the secret into a pot and buries it in the ground, not knowing that the wind has heard him and tells everyone. I have a secret, and can't tell a soul, not even the wind. Just before I drift off to sleep, I whisper my secret to myself.

'Well, Miss Austen, you're not a virgin any more.'

Eight

❦

The next morning I rose early and peered out of my window to see if the world around me had changed as much as I had. There was the village, a thousand years old, and looking the same as I had come to know it. It had somehow survived in all its quaint and leafy charm when neighbouring areas were swallowed up and made ugly by the sprawl of London. We still had rambling woods where gypsies had camped as recently as twenty years earlier, and where Queen Elizabeth I used to hunt. Her favoured tree, beneath which she enjoyed picnics while looking out over the whole of London to Hampstead Heath on the distant horizon, was known as the Honour Oak. There were spacious parks and golf courses and, until recently, there had been windmills. By the millpond on the Common there was a toll gate that still charged cars sixpence for going through. The old black and white noticeboard said that geese, ducks, and chickens could pass for one penny; cows, sheep, and pigs, thruppence. The main village road had wide green verges with spiky black iron chains looped from low white posts. Huge chestnut trees almost met across the street, casting a delicious shade in the summer.

Now, the leaves were gone and a network of bare branches looked stiff with cold. On the corner were high iron railings that surrounded the ancient plague pit. In the spring, daffodils and crocuses grew thickly on the short grass between gravestones. Someone tended it and cut the grass, but it must have been elves, for I had never seen anyone at work.

Beyond the plague pit, handsome Georgian houses were set back from the road, then came the solid Victorian pub, where Charles Dickens and John Ruskin used to meet weekly at a luncheon club, and where Father belonged to an upstairs poetry group. This was the kind of society where earnest men in big round glasses and women in droopy skirts and sandals put the world to rights over a half-pint of shandy. Next to the pub was a dusty post office-cum-haberdashery, run by two twittering old maids from whom Granny bought knitting wool and lisle stockings, always stopping for a long gossip. The news-agent's was opposite, in a row of eighteenth-century shops and cottages with small windows and an almost topsy-turvy jumble of red-tiled roofs.

The old village was still the same.

I left the window and went slowly down to breakfast, as I had for so many mornings in the past, presenting what I hoped would be my usual face to the others. But this morning was different. I was different. Last night, Richard had happened. As I sat there, consuming tea and toast and bacon and eggs with fried tomatoes, I wondered what they would all say if they knew that I had gone to a strange flat with a near-stranger and had made love for the first time. Couldn't they see that I was no longer a child? But not a single person in that house seemed any the wiser. In fact, nobody in the world knew, except Richard and me. I should have been glowing, stars should have been circling, yet I sat at the same old table in a state of numb shock, chatting to Granny, joking with Father, cutting up Gracie's bacon, ignoring Freddy, who was reading a comic.

Granny, with her fey ways, suddenly seemed to sense something. She glanced intently at me.

'What's the matter?'

'Nothing,' I said, feeling the start of a blush. I got up and went into the kitchen on the pretext we needed more milk.

I spent the rest of that day in bed, in a state of languor. Alternately, I dozed and dreamed, my thoughts muddled as I relived the excitement of the night before. Once, I even broke into tears, clutching my pillow to me, my face hot and wet. My mood swung wildly from delirium to exhaustion. Looking back, I suppose this was just what nature had intended, with her mysterious hormones and primitive emotions, but I knew nothing about what was happening, only that I felt so different from just the day before. I didn't go down for tea or supper. Toward midnight, I crept to the kitchen for some milk, then drank it standing by the stone sink, staring out of the window, seeing only my reflection against the dark glass. I looked like a ghost, my eyes huge, dark shadows beneath my cheekbones. As I rinsed my glass, all the romantic clichés, all the dreams, seemed to bounce off it and into the sink: girls who did it were ruined for ever. I stared at the water swirling away and saw my future swirling with it.

At school the next day, I was still in a daze, mooning from lesson to lesson, taking nothing in, looking blankly at the mistresses when they snapped at me to pay attention or asked why I hadn't done my homework that weekend. Of all the girls who were in my year, I was sure I was the only one who had done it. Memories of Cornwall and those mad, laughter-filled days when we whispered about Mr Nash and Mam'selle and Auntie Moo came back to haunt me. Now I was the fallen angel.

One evening, I arrived home from school to discover a family row in the making. As I came in through the back door, I found Mother sitting at the table, clutching a bank statement. She appeared to have been waiting for me because she thrust the letter at me and, without preamble, said, 'He's spent all the money!'

I didn't even have to ask who he was. I knew it could only be my father.

'He's left us destitute,' Mother continued. 'We're without a penny. What are we going to do, Rose?'

'Left? You mean he's gone?' I asked, my stomach sinking. Part of me had always hoped that one day Father would go; even though it was a scary prospect, but at least we'd have some peace.

'No, of course not,' Mother said. 'Why should he leave? He's got it made here, hasn't he? Three women to wait on him, while he takes his pleasures elsewhere.'

I knew we were in for a dramatic few hours. Sighing, I sat down and waited for the full story. Mother pushed the bank statement across the table to me.

'Read it!' she commanded. 'See for yourself what the bastard's done.'

I stared down at the rows of words and figures. They didn't mean very much to me so Mother jabbed at the balance on the last page: £49 15s 2d.

'That's all we have left between us and the workhouse,' she said. 'He's taken over a thousand pounds. He thought I wouldn't find out, wouldn't bother with the post, leave it to him as I always do, but he's been very shifty lately, shiftier than usual, I thought. Something felt wrong. I was right. No doubt he's spent it on women and gambling, not to mention his fine clothes.'

We heard Granny's key in the front door. She had returned from her afternoon painting class. Mother sat up straighter.

'Wait until your grandmother hears of this,' she said. 'She'll have something to say to him.'

And so, over innumerable cups of tea, like three witches we chewed over the bank statements and discussed the options. Granny suggested that Mother give piano lessons to make ends meet. Mother reared back in alarm, saying she would rather die. She countered that, instead, Granny could bake some of her fabulous cakes and sell them in the baker's. Granny preened over the compliment. The piano lessons didn't take fire, but the idea of cakes did. For a while, Mother and Granny grew almost animated as they progressed from a postcard in the newsagent's window to a full-fledged industry with a little van to do the delivering.

'It's no good,' Granny finally pronounced. 'I'd need some help, and you're a hopeless cook, Girlie. Better to take in lodgers.'

'I'm not going to have strangers roaming about the house,' Mother protested. 'They'll steal all the silver. Lodgers are notorious for that.'

I was amazed. 'But we don't have any silver,' I said.

'No, not now, thanks to that bastard,' Mother sighed. 'Other women can depend on their husbands. I can depend on nothing.' Then, she remembered anew all her grievances and listed them in detail: loose women, gambling, selfishness, conceit. This list of Father's faults was long enough, but then Granny added to them, stoking the flames: liar, ignoramus, weak as dishwater, Lothario.

When Father finally came in, it was to an inquisition. Mother flung the statements at him, and then, as a final coup de grâce, she pulled out of her pocket an old letter that she had found and saved for years, waiting for just such a moment.

'I found this,' she pronounced. 'It shows only too clearly that you were a rat when I married you, and you're still a rat.'

'What is it?' Father asked, bristling.

'It's a letter I wrote to you when we lived in Simla. You were in Delhi.' Mother then proceeded to read from the letter: 'I'm stretching the money out as best I can, but you know it doesn't go very far with so many expenses. I've pulled down some of my old garments to knit baby clothes.' She stopped, dramatically, and looked at me. 'Those were for you, Rose,' she said. Then she continued reading. 'But by next week I won't be able to pay the servants. Please, I beg of you, don't gamble everything away again. George, I miss you. Little Jimmy and the baby miss you too. When will you be back in Simla again?'

When she finished, she looked up at him, the letter trembling in her hand.

'I've been struggling to make ends meet for nearly twenty years,' she said, 'and it's worn me out, George.'

Granny snorted. 'Much of this is your fault, Girlie. You should have packed your trunk immediately and come home. Not gone on to have two more children with an inveterate gambler.'

Father was incensed. 'Keep out of this,' he snarled. 'In fact, go to your room!'

'Nonsense,' said Granny. 'I'll do no such thing.'

Father leaned across the table to snatch at the letter, but Mother stuffed it back into her pocket. For a moment, I thought he was going to hit her. 'Where did you get that?' he demanded.

'I found it in your box.' She was referring to the black tin box he kept under his bed. The admission that she had actually got hold of the key and looked through his sacred box in which he kept his personal papers started another row in which he listed all her faults: no dress sense, can't dance, thick ankles, bad manager, poor housekeeper, terrible cook, moans and complains, no fun, doesn't understand him.

Suddenly, I couldn't listen any more. I ran from the kitchen and up the stairs to my freezing bedroom, where I sat listening to the distant screams, which ended only when Father crammed a few garments into a case and stormed out of the house. The front door banged, the windows rattled, then all was quiet.

Mother came into my room and perched on the end of my bed.

'Well, he's gone,' she said.

'He'll be back,' I replied. 'I wish you didn't fight so much.'

'It's not me, it's him,' she said. Anger still bolstered her up but I knew that soon she would be reduced to depression and tears.

Father stayed away for two days, where, I have no idea, but I came down on the third morning and, once again, the familiar black bowler was on the hall table, next to the neatly folded canary-yellow gloves I had knitted for him. I knew that he must have sauntered back home in the night. Fetching the milk from the porch, Granny nodded at the hat.

'Well, he didn't stay away long, more's the pity,' she remarked. 'It's peaceful when he's not around.'

'But Mother misses him,' I said. It was true. She hated him when he was there, but she fretted when he was not. Although I thought she would be better off without him, it was obvious that, deep down, she cared for him. If he hadn't made her feel so inferior and so constantly under-mined her confidence, things would have been better between them – but I knew the truth of the matter. Her fault was that she was better educated than he was, that the poets whom he struggled so hard to master were completely comprehensible to her. Her fault was that she wasn't a geisha, who would wait on his every whim. Her fault was that she wasn't a dizzy blonde or a redhead who wore lipstick and drank gin-and-tonics and waved a cigarette about in a long holder, a sociable woman who could kick up her shapely legs in the Charleston, or dance the waltz without stepping on his toes. Her faults were legion.

'Your mother is the clumsiest woman I have ever met,' Father liked to say on the few occasions when they had danced together. 'My toes are bruised and my shoes ruined.' In answer, Mother once displayed the ripped hem of her evening gown. It was a garment she was to drag out many times, during similar arguments over the years, symbol of a torn marriage.

'You tore that,' Father would say, with an air of com-plete disdain. 'You tripped over it.'

'No, you tore it,' Mother would insist. This would inspire Father to show us marks on his ankles, which were dainty and white, with blue veins.

'See where she kicked me?' he'd whine.

'I kicked you because you were ogling other women,' Mother would say in her defence.

Ginger Rogers and Fred Astaire, they were not.

Depressed over this latest squabble, and perhaps seeking comfort, my resolve crumbled and again I sought out Richard. Hating myself for looking obvious, after school the next day I caught the bus up to Waterloo and sat in the Cave, on the off chance that he would come in after rehearsals. I waited and waited, my nose buried in a book, calm on the outside but shaking inwardly. I kept glancing up every time the door opened, then looking down quickly. I saw him at once when he came in and felt almost sick to my stomach. I desperately wished I hadn't come, but there was no escape from my corner seat even if I did wish to sneak out.

He ordered a cup of tea and a doughnut, then came over to my table and sat down.

'The Queen of Sheba, no less,' he said. 'How are you?'

'All right,' I mumbled. He sipped his tea, took a bite of the doughnut.

'What's the book?' he asked. I showed him. It was Milton's *Paradise Lost*. It was a set book at school, but I didn't tell him that.

'Poor old blind John,' he said.

I wanted to say something clever, but couldn't think of a thing. Suddenly, I realised that the school bookplate was inside the slim volume and quickly put it away inside my bag.

'Well, Miss Austen,' he said, taking me by surprise. 'Do you want another cup of tea, or do you want to spend an hour in *Paradise*?'

'I want another cup of tea,' I said, and he laughed.

'I bet you do. My brother will be here in a minute to collect me in my car. I'll send him away and then we'll go.'

His brother was an older, thinner-on-the-top version of Richard. When he came as far as the door, Richard spotted him and went over. Then, they both disappeared outside. I saw them through the window as they walked around the corner. After four or five minutes, Richard returned, though he remained on the pavement. From there, he glanced through the big window of the café. When he saw I was looking at him, he jerked his head toward the river. Obediently, like a puppy on a length of string, I got up and left. Outside, Richard flagged down a taxi and we got in. I don't think we said a single word all the way to the flat. We sat on opposite corners of the backseat and I suddenly felt estranged and ashamed. This was all wrong. Prince Charming had become a total stranger.

In the flat, he switched on the fire. The warmth and instant heat from those electric bars was pure luxury, one I had not seen before in our home, where the only source of heat had always been coal fires. I waited for the magic to return. He was too quiet, it was too clinical. He poured himself a large drink and one for me, something green in a small glass.

'What is it?' I asked.

'Crème de menthe. Peppermint. You'll like it. Girls do.' I remembered that he had said the same thing about the chocolate. He seemed to know well what girls liked to drink, especially while visiting that flat. I sipped it, and the warm, sticky sweetness flooded through me like green fire.

'It's nice,' I said, licking my lips.

'I told you.' He swallowed his drink fast and then poured another. He drank this one in a single gulp and then, visibly, seemed to relax. 'Bloody Ifor,' he said. 'He gave me a hard time.'

'Who is Ifor?'

'My bloody caretaker of a brother. He's too much of a busybody for his own good. Or for my good, I should say.'

'Was it about me?' He looked at me and smiled mockingly.

'Oh, he doesn't even know about you. He thinks I've got some other bird on the go, a girl he likes and thinks needs protecting from a wolf like me.'

I can remember a flare of jealousy. In a small voice, I asked, 'Do you have another girl on the go?'

'Does it look like it? I'm here with you, aren't I?' Pulling me to him, he kissed me lightly on the mouth and tasted my lips. The liqueur had relaxed me, made me feel good. I leaned in to him, allowed myself to melt into his arms. He nuzzled my ears and my neck, tasted my mouth again. Leaning back, I swallowed some more liqueur, emptying my glass, savouring the last drop.

'Here,' he said, filling the glass again, so that it over-flowed on to my fingers. 'You don't have to eat the glass, there's a full bottle.' I suddenly wondered who he had bought it for. Then I didn't care. I was the one drinking it. I drank the second glass in a single greedy gulp, choking as it hit the back of my throat. My eyes filled with water and I started to laugh.

'I'll get the hiccups.'

'Well, then you'll have to drink some more to stop them, won't you?' he said. He licked my sticky fingers, one by one, then the inside of my palm.

While we were talking, while we were drinking, while he was pouring out a constant flow of whisky and crème de menthe, he had managed to remove all my clothes. It was a giddy, tipsy little pas de deux, until, for the second time in my life, I was about to make love. When he entered me, our frantic motion soon approached a climax. I was arching my back when, even as I cried out and clung fiercely to him, he wrenched himself away. He collapsed and lay panting on top of me before rolling off. As we lay side by side, he took my slip and wiped himself, then my belly.

'Coitus bloody interruptus,' he said.

'What's that?' I asked.

'A system devised to ruin good sex. It's in the Bible. The sin of Onan. But it's better than a Johnny.' I hadn't the faintest idea what he was talking about. This was something else I would have to look up when I got home. These were the days long before birth control pills, and I don't ever remember Richard using a condom. The preferred method of birth control, I was soon to learn, was simply to pull out.

He dragged the quilt off the bed, and we lay on the carpet before the fire, where we made love repeatedly throughout the night. The levels in both bottles went down until I felt so sick I thought I would never be able to face crème de menthe again. We talked, or, he talked and I listened. I could have listened to him for ever. I wish I could remember all he said, but with time, many things fade and all I can remember is the essence. Oh, a few things remain, some things jog the memory – like a rounded, emerald-green bottle and the taste of crème de menthe, like a dusky pink, satin eiderdown – but it's like a dream one tries to capture in the morning, or a handful of ashes left from the leaping flames of a once bright fire. I crept home in the early hours, thrilled over another evening with Richard, and with a terrible hangover already beginning.

The following day I decided to apply at the newsagent's for a job delivering newspapers before school each morning. It seemed the only way I would be able to come up with pocket money. To my surprise, Freddy said he would go with me.

'I could do with some extra money,' he said. 'Dick has a notice in the window asking for paper boys. The pay is seven and six a week.' That was three times my pocket money, which, with our newly restored poverty, I was no longer getting. It seemed a fortune. I could afford new stockings and perhaps a frock in the sales. Then I considered what it would be like, delivering newspapers to our neighbours, and lost my nerve.

'You can do this kind of thing, Freddy. You're a boy,' I said. 'I'll feel stupid asking for a paper round. Besides, I don't have a bike.'

'Don't be such a sissy,' Freddy said. 'Come on, before someone else gets it.'

Grumbling and complaining, my head throbbing, still feeling terribly ill, I wrapped one of Mother's long knitted scarves around my neck, pulled on my mittens, and walked down the road with Freddy. His fair hair shone in the morning sun, his cheeks and nose were pink with the cold, and his skinny knees looked chapped and raw. Although we fought and argued so much, I was very fond of my little brother. He was small for his age, having been born with weak lungs. He had almost died on several occasions with viral double pneumonia and several bouts of severe bronchitis, for which there were no effective drugs. At those times, my mother had struggled day and night with Friar's Balsam steam baths and sheer will-power to pull him through. She loved him more than any of us; but at that moment I forgave him for being her favourite.

At the newsagent's, I reluctantly hung back as the bell pinged above the door. Freddy turned and grabbed my sleeve.

'Come on, Rose!' he said, 'seven and six a week!'

Dick, who ran the shop, was a rugby player gone to seed. His belly hung over his sagging grey flannels, but his arms in rolled-up shirtsleeves were muscular and strong. He could swing a bale of newspapers with no effort. His hair was long and swept back off his brow, except for a lock that kept falling forward. His face was rugged and friendly, but he had a glint in his eye whenever he looked at girls that was too bold and too appraising. He looked me up and down.

'Think you can do it?' he asked. He said 'do it' so suggestively that I stepped back a pace. He grinned.

'Yes, I can manage. You put the numbers on the newspapers and I put them through the correct letter boxes, right?'

'The bag is heavy. On Tuesdays and Wednesdays, when the old biddies have their weekly mags, *Woman* and *Woman's Own*, it's bloody heavy. Sundays, it's fucking heavy.' He gazed arrogantly into my eyes, to see if he had shocked me.

'I can manage,' I repeated.

He hadn't asked Freddy, who was smaller and slighter than I was, if he could manage, but you could see that Freddy was a tough little thing, all sinew and determination.

'Okay, you can both start tomorrow, seven and six a week each.'

'No, it's extra on Sundays, the rounds are longer,' Freddy piped up.

'Does it say so on the window?' Dick demanded.

'No, but that's right, isn't it? On Sundays it's an extra half crown each round. The other boys at school told me so.' Dick laughed and took a swipe at Freddy's head.

'Okay, Mr Know-all. Extra for Sundays.'

Dick asked if we had bicycles. Freddy had one, but mine had been given away, by Father, to the woman from Baltimore.

'I'll manage,' I repeated stubbornly.

'The village is all spread out,' Dick said. 'I don't want you being late for school and some council busybody turning up here to check the ages of my boys.'

'I'll get a bike,' I said with more conviction than I felt. I knew Mother couldn't buy me one. With only £49 15s 2d left in the bank – there would be even less by now – how could she? Even though Father's pay was still coming in, it wasn't enough.

That evening at home, with no debate, Granny quickly came to the rescue.

'If you need a bicycle, then you shall have one,' she decided.

As a paper girl, zooming along on my regular round, I got to know the village people very quickly. I would meet the shopkeepers on their way to work, or while they were opening up for the morning. Now that I was almost one of them, or at least on the same side of the counter, I felt an affinity to and familiarity with them that I hadn't felt as a customer. They were a tightly knit group, always looking out for each other, and they were particularly fond of their young paper boys and, now, a solitary girl. They seemed convinced that we were all about to die of pneumonia, and were always inviting us in for a hot drink. By the end of my round, I was always awash and running late for school, but with the tea, we would have a good gossip.

My favourite shopkeeper was the lady who ran the sweet shop, a tiny creature with the highest heels and the tallest dyed-black beehive I had ever seen. She had scarlet lips and false eyelashes that batted fast as she spoke. She was working to put her two sons through private school. I remember watching her, with her arched insteps and bulging calves, and thinking, 'Here you are, standing on four-inch heels every day to educate your sons. I wonder if they will ever appreciate it?'

The Village Dairy originally sold cream and milk from the cows that used to roam the village until the war, but by the 1950s, it had become a grocery store only. In memory of its former days, it still had a large brown china cow in the window, with a milkmaid in a full powder-blue gown and white apron. With brown ringlets cascading down the front of one shoulder, and a mob cap, she looked rural and sweetly innocent, and in marked contrast to the living grocer and his wife. They resembled dead ghouls from another world. Like the lady in the sweet shop, the wife's hair was dyed black, but it lay flat and tightly waved against her skull. Her round face was often powdery, as if she dusted it with flour from one of the bags on the shelf, and her lipstick was always melted, seeped into the lines around her mouth. He had a high, domed head, wispy white hair, and waxen skin glistening whiter than the lard he sliced up with a palette knife and laid into neatly folded squares of greaseproof paper. He would peer through thick glasses, and his pale blue eyes seemed to bulge out on stalks, giving me the creeps when I was caught alone with him in the back room. She would come in and snap something in a low angry voice that would send him shuffling back to his position behind the counter. Then, she would quickly smile and show me where the biscuits were to dunk in our tea. I hated drinking tea with the grocer and his wife, but I was far too polite to refuse a cup when offered.

I whirled through the village, did my rounds, and rushed home for a wash. Then, I would jump on my bike again and go spinning off to school, pedalling like the wind straight up steep Dog Kennel Hill, where King Charles I's big hunting dogs had once been kept in some long-ago deer forest. By the time I got to school, I'd be exhausted; all I wanted to do was put my head down on my desk and sleep.

After our second meeting at the flat, my relationship with Richard became almost regular. Before we parted company for the evening, he would say, 'See you on Thursday at six,' or 'See you Monday at five.' The day and time were always under his control, but I didn't mind. I no longer went to the Cave, but made my way straight to the flat. If he wasn't there yet, I would wait patiently in the Griffin, and check every ten minutes or so. When I told him I couldn't drink crème de menthe any more, he laughed.

'So, what is Miss Austen's preferred tipple?' he asked. 'Champagne?'

Champagne seemed a wonderful idea.

'Of course, champagne,' I said grandly, and, after that, he always got in a couple of good bottles and had them waiting in the refrigerator. That was another thing that set the flat apart from my normal life. We didn't have a refrigerator at home. I had never experienced the joys of really cold milk, and ice when I wanted it in a glass of water. The chilled champagne was sparkly and easy to drink and made me giggly and happy. Richard would watch in amusement as I sipped it to start with, then, as I got more excitable, downed it in flamboyant gulps. Once, I dared to throw the glass over my shoulder to shatter against a wall, but I didn't repeat it because I had to clean up the mess in a drunken state and I cut my finger.

'Here,' he said, sucking my finger clean. Even that small action he made erotic.

Those nights in the flat with Richard and champagne, lying naked on the pink satin quilt before the electric fire, became a kind of haven to me, the most stability I could find in a world of adults gone mad. When he held me close against the warmth of his body, cradling me in his arms, his legs entwined around mine, I felt special. I felt loved. It was as if we belonged together, in that cosy yet elegant room with its thick green carpet, the music softly playing, the lights low, and the heavy white curtains closed against the dark night. Home and school seemed not just far away, but irrelevant.

My life seemed schizophrenic, split between making love with Richard half the night, and being a schoolgirl with a paper round by day. Because we were so hard up again Mother, who was unable to find her degree qualifications, got work as a ward orderly at the local hospital. Since she was always tired, extra chores fell on my shoulders. I felt aggrieved, but I should have seen how hard it was on her. It was the last day of Christmas term when I thought that she might crack with the strain.

Although it was barely four o'clock, it was nearly dark when I came home from school, my bag filled with cards and little gifts from all my friends. I wheeled my bike around the back and leaned it up against the wall. Granny had done the washing up and put the things to drain on the wooden board. I put the kettle on and started to put the crockery away. In the adjoining room, I riddled out the cold ashes of the fire and laid a fresh one. The flames quickly caught the screwed-up balls of paper and fire-lighters. While it was blazing up, I studied Mother's scribbled note, which was propped up on the high mantel-piece in the dining room: 'Don't forget to change the sheets. The laundryman comes in the morning. Granny said she would get some chops for supper. Peel the potatoes. There are carrots or cabbage or some tinned peas.'

Often, she didn't tell me what to prepare for the evening meal, leaving it up to me to rummage for whatever I could find. Granny would pick up fresh meat or fish from the village, but Mother hated the routine of shopping and trying to think up creative meals on a tight budget. She solved this problem by not bothering to change her weekly order with the grocer. She was both threatened and repulsed by the snobbery of the village shopkeepers and had come across 'a nice little man who keeps his prices down' in a nearby but poor, cosmopolitan district where she felt comfortable. Weekly, he would deliver exactly the same items to our door. Father was always exploding when he opened the store cupboard in the hall to find fifty-six pounds of sugar or twelve pots of marmalade, but Mother never seemed to find the time to call through an amended order, and this continued to be a bone of contention between them.

As the kettle boiled, I heard Granny's key in the front door. She came into the kitchen with a small package of lamb chops tied up with string.

'I'll just let Jaffa out, then join you for a cup of tea,' she said. 'Is there any gingerbread left?'

I gazed out through the window in the kitchen door as, followed by Granny, Jaffa hobbled up one side of the lawn, then rather shakily lifted his leg against a shrub. Father had started complaining about that, now. 'The garden is not a dog's lavatory,' he'd say.

'I take him out around the block every morning and evening,' Granny snapped, but that didn't satisfy my father. It was another thorn of many. The three of them were always arguing and bickering about something, with Father always starting the rows instead of just letting things be.

Granny and I sat down to a cup of tea before the blazing fire. When I had come in half an hour earlier, the room had been cold and bleak; now it was cheerful, the flames reflecting points of light off the brass candlesticks and the Staffordshire vegetable tureens on the sideboard. Granny lavished butter thickly on her slice of gingerbread and bit into it.

'It needs a little more ginger,' she observed.

We heard Mother's key in the lock.

'She's home early,' I said.

Mother came along the hall, still wearing her coat, and sat down heavily at the table. In the winters, she rarely took her coat off indoors. I had often seen her wear it to bed and once, when I took her up a cup of tea and she threw back the blankets to go to the bathroom, I was astonished to see that she still had her fleece-lined bootees on, her stockings wrinkled and torn. 'I can't abide these winters,' she would say. 'This house is like a mausoleum. I swear the cold will kill me.'

Now, seated at the table, she looked white and exhausted, so pale and downcast that I was filled with fear. She seemed to feel too deeply for the sick or the dying patients in her ward, often sitting holding their hand long after her shift was over. One lonely old woman, who had come back from India like we had, especially affected her. She had no one, except for a son in Canada, who never came, so Mother talked to her for long hours, chatting about all the old familiar places and a way of life that was long gone.

Seeing Mother's tension as the old woman lay dying worried me; I had seen that look about my mother's face before, when she'd had a nervous breakdown. It was when we moved to the small Surrey village of Downside. Rather than helping things, the move had only served to make Mother feel even more estranged from the world. When she discovered that my father was having an affair with the vicar's wife, she finally cracked. She had been shopping with my brother Freddy in the little basket seat on the back of her bicycle, when she suddenly felt giddy and fell off. She had been taking a shortcut across a common and landed in a bog, breaking her ankle. She crawled for a mile to the main road before she was found, with Freddy, who was only six at the time, doing his best to help her along. When people came to her aid, she began to scream. She continued screaming while she was being rescued, and she screamed all the way to the hospital. She screamed for a full day and nothing would dissuade her. Then she stopped, and for weeks lay in a daze, her eyes closed, neither speaking nor eating.

'Of course she can't eat or speak,' my father said. 'She's got a sore throat from all that yelling.'

But the doctor told him that Mother was very ill with her nerves and might not get well for a very long time. The doctor said that having another baby would cure her 'hysteria', as he called it and that's when Mother got pregnant with Gracie. I could never forget how ill she was during those years, and now, sitting before me at the kitchen table, she had the same gaunt look about her.

'She died,' Mother said, referring to the old lady from India. 'We were so sure she would make it, but she died.' And then, Mother started to shiver violently. 'This job is getting to me. I can't bear it any more.'

Granny looked at me. 'Take your mother up to bed,' she said. 'I'll open a tin of chicken consommé.'

Chicken consommé or calf's-foot jelly were Granny's answers to all weaknesses of the body or spirit. I ushered Mother upstairs and quickly straightened the sheets and the hard nuns' blankets on her tangled, unmade bed. Then I plumped up a pillow, while she took off some of her clothes.

'A bath?' I suggested tentatively. 'It will warm you up and help you to sleep.'

'I'm too tired,' Mother said. 'Leave me alone now, Rose. I just want to sleep.'

'Granny's heating some consommé,' I told her.

Mother didn't reply. She got into bed and pulled the blankets right over her head, disappearing from sight like a burrowing mole. For a moment or two I hovered, staring at the silent mound, at this woman who managed to take herself off into a world of dreams between one sighing breath and the next. At times, I thought that Mother's life had really ended when she was a girl, before she met my father. All her best achievements and happiness seemed to lie with studying, with music and books. The years since, of having four children and bringing up a family, were something that seemed to be happening to someone else. I often felt that the real 'Girlie' was locked away inside this woman who had grown increasingly tired and beaten down. Is that who she found again during the long hours she slept like an unmoving log? The real Girlie?

I heard Father come in and ran downstairs to greet him. There was the habitual spring in his step, a jovial smile on his face. He dangled some keys in the air.

'I've passed my driving test,' he announced. 'Come see, come see!'

'See what?'

'I've bought a car,' he said gleefully.

I was stunned. All thoughts of my mother, that silent grey shape beneath the harsh blankets, left me. My father had been able to drive for a long time, but, like many men of his generation, had never taken a test. It didn't much matter, since he had not been able to afford a car, but in the twinkling of an eye, all that had changed. Here were the keys and outside was the car. It wasn't long before Freddy materialised and then Gracie came running. Granny walked along the hall carrying a steaming soup cup. We all trekked outside to the cold pavement to stare at the black Austin motor, gleaming beneath the street light.

'This spells trouble,' Granny said cryptically.

Ignoring her, Father beamed and asked, 'Who wants to go for a spin?' He unlocked the door and then gestured for us to get in. In a flash, Gracie scrambled on to the front passenger seat. Freddy hesitated, then got into the back. He punched Gracie on the shoulder.

'You should be in the back,' Freddy said. 'I'm older than you.'

'Mother? Rose? Are you coming?' Father asked, getting into the driving seat. Granny's lip curled as it always did when he referred to her as mother.

'No thank you, George,' she said. 'I value my life.' She glanced at the cup she held. Little tendrils of steam blew away in the chill wind. 'You'd better take this up to your mother before it gets any colder,' she said to me.

'Leave it, leave it,' Father said impatiently. 'Whatever foul brew you have there, it will keep. Come on, Rose, hop in.' I hesitated, then, feeling disloyal, I took the cup of consommé from Granny.

'I'll go next time,' I said. 'Have you really bought it? It's ours?' I wondered where on earth the money had come from.

'All ours,' Father said. 'It's an early Christmas present. Toot, toot! Off we go.'

With a jerk he let in the clutch and the car lurched away from the pavement and into the path of a passing van. Loud hoots were exchanged, an angry sound that was to remain a permanent part of Father's driving experience down the years ahead. Then the new car disappeared up the road into the dark night. I wondered why, if Father could afford a car, Mother had to do a poorly paid job she found exhausting. Nothing they did made much sense.

'Wonders will never cease,' Granny said. 'Now come on in, Rose, before you catch your death. I'd better heat that consommé up again.'

Nine

With Christmas approaching, Granny was all secrets and plans for the presents she intended to make for us. She and my mother were very different personalities. Granny was pure 'Empire stock', the kind of brave, ladylike, even beautiful woman who marched across the world with her husband and picked up all the broken pieces as she went. Mother was remarkable for her own talents, but she suffered badly from nerves. Granny, on the other hand, had a youthful curiosity and zest for life that allowed her to make friends easily. She had her little round in the village, pausing for a chat here, a gossip there, buying a skein of embroidery thread from the post office, a quarter of barley sugar from the sweet shop, or sixpence-worth of a white fish called coley for the stray cat she'd taken in, a companion for Jaffa. The fishmonger, attired in a long white coat and green Wellingtons, summer and winter, whatever the weather, stood guard over his enormous white marble slab, which was covered with fish from every sea, all glistening with a fine spray of iced mist from a silver fountain at one end. In those days before tinned cat food, the daily trip to the fishmonger was almost obligatory.

Every elderly biddy seemed possessed of a cat, and Granny knew that if she stood there gossiping long enough, sooner or later she would make the acquaintance of everyone in her age group. In fact, she gossiped so well, at such length and so entertainingly, that many shopkeepers provided her with a chair on which to preside like a queen over her miniature court.

After a while, she noticed that a few women from church, whom she knew well enough to nod to, seemed to have no time to pause for a satisfying chat. With busy and eager expressions, they trotted by on their way to classes at the local institution, baskets filled with books or art materials. It had never occurred to my grandmother that this might be something she could enjoy, but after making a few discreet enquiries, eventually she took a stroll along to the institution with one of her cronies, Mrs Goodrich, where she discovered a fascinating world of courses and classes available to her, free of charge. Soon, she had signed up for French and German, painting, millinery, and basket making. Now, with every morning taken with shopping and gossiping, and every afternoon with a class, her days became happy and fulfilled.

'What do you think of my bonnet?' she asked with a twinkle one evening, as she turned around sedately before Gracie and me. She was wearing one of her creations, a glazed green straw hat decorated with a beguiling bunch of orange silk nasturtiums. She took the hat off and showed us how she had lined the inside with cream-coloured silk.

'It's really lovely,' I exclaimed. 'It looks so professional.'

'This one's for the summer,' Granny said, taking it from my hands. 'I started with a straw because it's fairly easy to work with. Now I'm learning felt blocking, which is much harder with all that steaming and stretching. I've got a marvellous shape on the go for church. Wait till you see it! I never thought I would come to enjoy my dotage so much.'

'You're not old, Granny,' I said gallantly.

'Oh, but I am, my dear. I'm getting on.'

'How old are you?' Gracie asked. 'A hundred?'

'Horrible child,' Granny replied. 'A hundred indeed.' Then, in a confiding tone, she asked, 'Do you think your mother would like a hat for Christmas, Rose? A warm fur? I'm thinking of letting an acquaintance in the fur class shorten my squirrel coat. There'll be plenty left over for a hat and a muff.'

'People don't use muffs these days,' I said, 'and Mother's careless. She'll only leave it on a bus. I think she would prefer a basket.'

'Good! Yes, a basket of split willow. I'll fill it with nice soaps and bath salts and I'll order two flannelette nightgowns from the post office. What do you think?'

'Yes, she'd like that,' I said, wondering if Mother would wear the nightgowns over or under her clothing.

'What are you giving me?' Gracie demanded.

'Nothing,' Granny said. 'Don't you know that it's rude to ask for presents?'

Gracie flounced off, but the conversation stuck in her mind.

Shortly after, when I came in from school one afternoon, I heard sounds coming from Granny's room. I knew that my grandmother was still at one of her classes, so I thought it might be Jaffa scratching to be let out. I went in and found Gracie submerged in the big black shipping trunk that stood under one of the windows. I knew this heavy pine box had been carried in buffalo carts, on the backs of mules and elephants, and even by coolies –

although its great weight when filled seemed far more than even six coolies could manage – from one end of India to the other.

'What on earth are you up to?' I said. 'You shouldn't be in here.'

'Looking for Christmas presents,' Gracie said sulkily. 'I've looked in Mummy's wardrobe and under the beds. They must have hidden my presents here.'

'What makes you think you're going to get anything?' I said. 'Anyway, Father Christmas keeps little children's presents at the North Pole.'

'No he doesn't,' Gracie said. 'Jimmy told me there was no such person.'

'Look at this mess. Granny will have a fit. Help me tidy it,' I ordered.

Instead, Gracie stuck out her tongue – she had learned this gesture from Father – and went to sit in one of the green moquette armchairs over by the fire, where Granny's matted bearskin rug lay. Idly, she put her little white-stockinged foot into the bear's gaping mouth, wriggling her toes on the red felt tongue that flopped sideways from between his big white teeth.

'Bear is biting my foot!' she squealed in mock panic.

'Gracie, stop messing about and shut up,' I retorted, trying to refold the damask tablecloths and napkins, the piles of antique lace and silk kimonos, the feather boas and the ivory fans she had dragged out of the big chest.

Forgetting about the bear, Gracie got down on to the rug and started to torment Jaffa. He thumped his tail a few times, then settled down to sleep again. Suddenly, all the clocks lining the walls, and on every surface of furniture, started to bong and chime. Cogs whirred and weights went up or down to a chorus of the hour being struck. We could always hear the sound around the house, but it was from a distance, and muted. In Granny's room itself it sounded almost frenzied. I wondered how Granny was able to sleep through it all. Or how Jaffa could stand it, come to that. For a dog's sensitive hearing, it must have been torture.

Gracie put her hands to her ears and started to run about the room, laughing. I shouted at her to sit down again, as I took hold of a rough-textured shirt and laid it out on the bed in order to fold it neatly. The shirt, which had once been a greyish white, had narrow navy-blue stripes. It looked almost like a prison garment worn by convicts. I remembered that my brothers once had similar shirts, made of Welsh wool, but they were so prickly that the boys refused to wear them. The entire front of this shirt lying on the bed before me was marked with a big brown stain. I wondered what it was.

Without warning, Granny walked in. She wasn't at all pleased to find her room occupied. Jaffa lumbered to his feet and went across to greet her. She put down her white bag and bent to pat him, but her eyes were fixed on the shirt.

'What are you doing with that?' she asked abruptly.

'Folding it,' I said.

'I can see that. But what's it doing out of the trunk in the first place?'

'Gracie was looking for Christmas presents,' I said, not wanting to give her away but having no choice. We were both caught red-handed. 'I'm putting everything back.'

Granny reached over and lifted up the shirt, handling it gently.

'Your grandfather was wearing this when he died,' she said. 'It's stained with his blood.'

I think my mouth must have dropped open with shock

because Granny said, 'It's all right, it's old blood. It won't hurt you.'

'How could you keep it?' I blurted.

'Don't be so squeamish, child. If you had nursed wounded men, as I have, men who have been hacked to pieces or tortured to within an inch of their lives by Pathans, a little blood wouldn't worry you. Besides, we're filled with blood.' She held out an arm, showing me the blue veins in her wrist as proof. 'I wasn't with your grandfather when he died. Perhaps if I had been there . . .' She broke off then, and started to fold the shirt in its original creases, taking great care.

Quickly, to change the subject, I picked up a lumpy pillowcase that was yellow with age. I peered inside. It looked like a dead animal. I shook it and leapt backward as a heavy hank of hair fell out. I fully expected to see it attached to a wizened scalp and I must have squealed or made some other silly sound because Gracie jumped up from the armchair where she had been pretending to hide.

'What is it? Let me see!' she cried. Granny laughed.

'The contents of my trunk seem to strike you more like Pandora's Box than Aladdin's cave, Rose,' she said. 'I haven't seen that for years. Don't worry, it's not some witch doctor's trophy. It's my hair.'

'Your hair!' I exclaimed.

Gracie said, 'Ugh,' and backed away histrionically.

'Gracie, don't act the giddy goat,' Granny said. 'It's only hair. They cut it off when I was so ill with malaria. The fever wouldn't break and they thought I was going to die. Cutting it off was a bit like throwing everything overboard to prevent a boat from sinking. In fact, it did cool me down and probably saved my life.'

Once I got over my revulsion, I picked the hank of hair

up. Age had faded it a little, decayed the sheen, but once it must have been a glorious shade of reddish gold. It seemed unbelievable that Granny's silvery hair had once been as thick as this, and this bright colour. On one of the tables was a photograph in a silver frame of a beautiful young woman with a heart-shaped face in a long flowing gown, her hair falling long and loose about her shoulders. Granny saw me glance at it, and she said, 'Yes, that was what I looked like when I was sixteen. I could have wept when I got better and I saw what they had done. It grew back in salt and pepper. I turned into a middle-aged woman overnight.'

I looked down at the hank I still held. 'Cutting off your hair wouldn't have made the rest go grey, would it?'

'No, I don't suppose it did. It was being so ill. India had a dreadful climate for Europeans. That's why we would go to the mountains for the summers, and why so many children went home to England to be educated. Their mothers would go too and whole families would be split up for years. I refused to allow that. My place was with your grandfather.'

I knew that my mother and uncles had been educated at schools in the Himalayas because Mother had told me many stories about what it had been like. Just the mention of India by Granny or my parents could bring back my own memories in an instant. I had gone to a convent too, and could remember riding there each day on a little white hill pony through scented pine forests with my bearer. The rocky path lay between the trunks of the pines on the upper slopes. Then, as we plunged downward, it wound through great stands of rhododendrons that tumbled down the sides of the hills in a riot of deep pink and red blossom. I remember riding beneath their arched branches, our ponies' hooves muffled on the thick litter of the forest floor, until we emerged into a wide belt of flame and yellow azaleas. Beyond stood the convent, in the path of a constant wind that blew the length of the valley. Perhaps this is why I loved the scent of pine and the cold smell of snow so much more than the heat of the sun. I remember an apricot tree that grew over the veranda of our childhood playroom in our summer home at Simla. Just thinking of it, I can taste the warm, golden fruit. I remember my brother Jimmy running along the length of the playroom, chasing a peacock butterfly, which he caught and then placed in my cupped hands. I can still feel the fluttering wings. I remember hearing a leopard coughing in the pines at night, and how I would cough like it, laughing as my ayah pretended to be scared.

'I wish we lived in the mountains,' I said to Granny. 'I wonder if there are still leopards in the pines.'

'We tracked a snow leopard in Sikkim once,' Granny said.

'What's a snow leopard?' I asked.

'Like a leopard,' Granny said, 'but far more rare, with a thicker coat.'

'What happened to it?' Gracie asked.

'I shot it,' said Granny. 'I was the best shot in our group. In fact, I was the champion woman shot in India. And I won all those trophies for fishing.'

She pointed to the mantelpiece where – muddled in with her black ebony elephants, framed photographs, and the cobra candlesticks with ruby eyes – sat a row of tarnished silver trophies for shooting and fishing. The ones for shooting were like chalices, engraved with images of rifles, but my favourites were the fishing mugs because they were Chinese, with deeply chased images of fish swimming through seaweed, and handles shaped like leaping salmon. Granny rummaged about in her trunk to emerge with another lumpy-looking pillowcase, which she upended on to the bed. A pelt of thick creamy-coloured fur splashed with brown splodges fell out. I picked it up and nestled my face against it. It smelled of mothballs and lavender.

'Sometimes they call it the cloud leopard because it lives high above the cloud line,' Granny said softly. I held the fur up and saw that it had been styled into a short cape with the fashionable square shoulders of the early 1930s. 'Their eyes are more blue than green. It's said snow leopards are the spirits of the ancients, shaman and lamas, who rode into the clouds on their backs.'

Enthralled, Gracie and I sat down with our feet buried in the bearskin as Granny told us stories of treks into a land of glittering blue glaciers, of valleys filled with strange forests hung with grey lichen, of paths that sometimes cut through dripping ferns, and at other times clung to the sides of sheer drops, with always the sight of the high snow peaks floating far above them in the clouds. Even in the days before they were so rare, snow leopards had seemed like the ghostly spirits of another world, elusive and astonishingly beautiful.

I sighed. 'How could you bear to shoot them?' I said.

'It was a sport that tested the fittest and the strongest,' Granny replied. 'We looked on it as a challenge, as an adventure. It was so long ago that now it doesn't seem possible that I could climb fifteen or sixteen thousand feet and march for a week over the most dangerous mountains in the world.'

Gracie got bored with all these reminiscences and wandered off to find Mother, but I was so captivated by

Granny's stories that I sat on, listening as she talked about a world that I was rapidly forgetting. It seemed that another one of Granny's hobbies, if you could describe it as such, had been to seek out the various British cemeteries in India. Some, in the more remote areas, had been almost absorbed back into the forest, like the old temples, home to monkeys, snakes, and bats.

'You could read our history in those gravestones,' Granny said. 'Each one told a story, a story of heroism and heartbreak.' She pointed at a large, delicately tinted photograph in a gold frame hanging on the wall above the fireplace. It was of a small boy in a floral silk kimono, squinting into the sun.

'That's Baby,' she said.

'Who?'

'My son, Donald.' This was a new name, one I had never heard.

'You mean, one of Mother's brothers?' I asked. Granny nodded, sadly.

'He died when he was just two years and two months old.' She gazed at the photograph for a long time. Finally, she looked at me and sighed. 'Baby and Girlie, your mother, both got typhoid fever at the same time. It was in Jubbulpore, in 1917. We didn't have antibiotics then. Your mother survived, I daresay because she was older and stronger, but Baby died. I didn't think I'd ever get over the heartbreak of it. For a long time, I even wished that your mother had died instead of him.'

I knew that the arrival of the new car would cause dispute between my parents, as quickly proved to be the case. Mother's reaction for days was to ignore the subject completely when Father proudly mentioned it. She would gaze at him expressionlessly, with that flat, unfocused stare of hers that could make me feel instantly uncomfortable when she did it to me. It wasn't a penetrating look, but rather as if I weren't even there, as if she could see through and beyond me, a blank stare that spoke volumes. Her cool, myopic gaze didn't seem to bother my father, however. Perhaps he never even noticed.

'Come and see the car, Anne!' he kept pestering her. 'I could take you shopping. You could cancel that money-grubbing grocer of yours who sends you whatever he fancies.'

Finally, one morning, Mother stopped him in his tracks.

'No!' she said, very distinctly.

'No? No what?' Father blustered.

'No, George, I will not go outside to ogle your car. I have no interest in your car beyond wondering how you paid for it. I dread to think how you must have mortgaged your soul to the devil.'

'It's none of your business,' Father said, flushing angrily. 'You buy your pots of marmalade and I'll buy my car.'

Mother merely flicked a glance at him as she picked up the crossword. What she probably already realised was what the rest of us would find out later: the car would give Father more mobility, which was something he didn't need, at least where women were concerned.

I was sick of hearing about the car, so I quickly slunk out of the back door. It was a Saturday and I had arranged to go up to town with Betty Padsmere on the train from Herne Hill, where she lived, to the Victoria and Albert Museum. I was wheeling my bicycle out of the gate when Father emerged through the front door with a sprightly gambol, the kind of little hop-skip-and-jump which suggested that he had managed to best Mother with a final barb.

'I'll take you to Herne Hill, Rose,' he said cheerily. 'It's too cold to cycle.'

'I'm used to it,' I said, 'and Betty lives only five minutes away.'

'Leave your bicycle,' he commanded. 'I want to take you.'

Reluctantly, I returned my bicycle and ran out on to the pavement where Father was walking up and down, swinging the keys and glancing at our neighbours' windows to see who was watching, obviously hoping they all were. There were two other cars in the street at that time: Miss Lemon, the Latin mistress, had one, an immaculately kept Morris Oxford, and Simon Schultz owned the other, a little black prewar sit-up-and-beg Austin that had cost £5. Now, my father had a car, and his was newer and smarter than the others. He was cock of the walk as he opened the car door for me, bowed me in with an air of exaggerated courtesy, and then nimbly jumped in himself. Like Toad in *The Wind in the Willows*, almost predictably he cried, 'Toot-toot! Toot-toot! Off we go!' He revved the engine and let out the clutch, and we shot away from the kerb to the inevitable accompaniment of the scream of brakes from a passing car.

'Oh fiddlesticks!' Father said, glancing in the rearview mirror. 'Couldn't he see I was pulling out?'

'Shouldn't you have indicated?' I asked.

'In this weather? It's far too cold to wind the window down.'

I sank low into my seat and closed my eyes, hoping that none of the neighbours had seen his getaway. 'Well, what do you think?' he asked almost immediately, as he launched himself into a dangerous three-point turn.

'About what?'

'The car, of course. What do you think?' He didn't wait for me to reply. 'I thought it was about time we had one. Waiting at bus stops in all weathers is ridiculous. Last week I waited for nearly an hour for the Number 37 and then five came along together, like a bunch of bananas.'

'Bananas are yellow, not red,' I said.

'Oh, you know what I mean. A convoy, then, a convoy of ships through the freezing North Atlantic,' he said grandiosely. 'We were all frozen by then. The idea of a car was suddenly very appealing.'

'Where did you get the money?' I asked, audaciously.

With a secretive smile, and that familiar little moue that played about his lips, he said, 'I borrowed it from a lady friend.'

I was startled into silence. I had thought he was going to say he got it from the bank. This admission floored me. This was one tidbit of information I didn't want to pass on to Mother. Now I wished I hadn't asked at all.

In a book I had been given for my birthday earlier that year, the Victorian writer and artist John Ruskin described walking southward from London to Herne Hill, along the ridge above Dulwich, through a mile of glorious chestnut trees, with lilacs and apple trees in full blossom hanging over the wooden palings of cottages on each side of the lane: 'Suddenly the trees stopped on the left, and out one came on the top of a field sloping down to the south into Dulwich valley. This open field was animate with cow and buttercup and below the beautiful meadows and high avenues of Dulwich, and beyond, all that crescent of the Norwood hills.' The Norwood hills were the last remnant of the great North Wood that once had filled the whole of that corner of England from Dover to the River Thames. Gypsy Hill was a part of that broad sweep, closest to the village. It always thrilled me that the name of the road we were driving along, Croxted Road, which I normally bicycled, was derived from a medieval word, Crokestrete, or crooked lane. It had been a part of the Pilgrim's Way that took fourteenth- and fifteenth-century pilgrims to visit the tomb of Saint Thomas à Becket in Canterbury Cathedral. Reliving the past like this fascinated me and was far less worrying than wondering who had lent my father the money for his new car. It took only a few moments to reach Herne Hill. The name was pretty, a cross between 'heron' and 'fern', and the place had been pretty once when a stream ran through it, where John Ruskin had gathered watercress and fished for tiddlers as a child. Now it was built over and the stream surfaced only in a pond in the grounds of a large park, before diving below ground again.

Betty's house was in an area known as Poets' Corner, where the streets were named after great writers who were connected with that area, men like Ruskin, Chaucer, Shakespeare, Spenser, and Milton. Predictably, as we drove by them, my father chanted out the names. He always did, whenever I mentioned Betty. We drew up before her house and I got out of the car.

'Thank you. I'll walk back,' I said. 'I'll be late. I'm staying to supper.'

But Father was getting out of the car as well. I was amazed when he raced me to the front door and rang the bell. 'Thank you,' I repeated. 'There's no need for you to see me right inside.'

Betty's mother, Mrs Padsmere, came to the front door. She was as exotic as a flamenco gypsy, with black curls, gold earrings, and jammy pink lipstick. Her matching pink satin trousers clung to her voluptuous curves. Betty told me that as a girl her mother had gone to our school and had married a boy from the school opposite our house when they were only eighteen. 'They were expecting me,' Betty had said. 'It was a shotgun wedding.' I couldn't imagine them being joyous teenage lovers, not this woman who was so lush and foolish and her husband who resembled Colonel Blimp, with his twirling RAF moustaches and giant beer belly.

'Hello, Georgie-boy!' Mrs Padsmere exclaimed. Almost as an afterthought, she added, 'Good morning, Rose. Betty's still having breakfast. Come on in.'

I was surprised by this familiarity with my father. As far as I knew, my parents and the Padsmeres didn't know each other.

'Any coffee left, Peggy?' Father asked as the two of them walked along the hall ahead of me. 'Your coffee is delicious. Anne has no idea how to make coffee.'

'Scorch the beans a little in an iron pan and add a grind of black pepper,' Mrs Padsmere instructed. 'And a pinch of dry Colman's mustard, too, if you like. Like this!' With that, she laughingly gave Father a little pinch on his bottom. Then she swished past him in the narrow space, on into the kitchen, her pink satin legs rubbing together like a cricket singing in the grass. 'I'll just put on some fresh coffee, Georgie,' she said. 'You can froth the milk. I've got one of those gaga gadgets from Italy.'

I went into the dining room where Betty was on her own, eating cereal and reading one of her brother's comics. Her brown hair was in a high ponytail and she was wearing new glasses with little flyaway wings that didn't suit her, but I admired them because she looked self-conscious and kept twiddling.

'Mummy insisted on these,' she said miserably. 'I know I look silly in them.'

'No you don't,' I assured her. 'They're very avant-garde.' We both burst out laughing, but I was still upset and grumpy about my father's infiltration of the Padsmere home. When he and Mrs Padsmere came in with the coffee they suggested that they should accompany Betty and me to the museum. That's when I almost decided to go home; this was time I wanted to spend with my friend, two girls on their own in town. I had already realised that he had only foisted himself on me so that he could flirt with Mrs Padsmere, and I was fed up with being used like a chaperone.

In the end, however, it turned out well. Mrs Padsmere had been to art school and she was exactly the right person to talk to us about the exhibits, telling us far more about them than was written on the little cards. She combined information with an entertaining take on history and art. Afterwards, Father treated us all to a late lunch in an Italian restaurant in Knightsbridge, a cellar with candles, near Harrods. I felt very grown up and sophisticated when the waiter came with a dish of fresh Parmesan cheese and a pepper mill nearly two feet tall. We had red wine and profiteroles and then we went to see a film, *The Ladykillers*, in Leicester Square. Father laughed so hard he had to go and stand in the foyer. When he returned with choc ices for us all, he blithely pushed his way into the row, treading on toes, banging into knees, and dripping ice cream down the necks of people who sat in the row in front of us. Then, of course, he had to be updated on the story, but Betty and Mrs Padsmere thought he was great fun. Later, when we drove down Charing Cross Road toward Trafalgar Square, I glanced up as we passed the Coliseum and was electrified to see the great shining globe soaring above me in the night sky, the very same globe I could see like a moon over the chimney tops from Villiers Street, when I walked up from the Embankment to my rendezvous with Richard.

At our previous meeting, Richard had asked, 'Have you ever been to an opening night?' I shook my head as I dressed, hating the idea of going out into the cold air from the warm and relaxing cradle of the room. 'Here's a ticket,' he had said casually, reaching for his coat on the back of a chair and fishing into the inside pocket. 'It's for the second night of *Henry*. Is that all right? We're given comps according to our degree of importance. My first-night seats have all been allocated to family, you know how it is.' I nodded dutifully, not sure what he was talking about. 'But you might find yourself near some of my friends,' he had continued. 'You won't let me down, will you, love?' I knew exactly what he meant; 'Keep your mouth shut, Rose,' was what he was saying. I knew that was the deal, but I wished he hadn't said it. I took the ticket and looked at it – it was a seat toward the front, though not in the front row. Despite his cautionary words and the fact that this wasn't for the actual opening night itself, I glowed. He was opening a tiny window on to his life, he was allowing me to dip my toe into a corner of the big pool he inhabited. It seemed to make our affair real. He was doing something special for me.

The ticket had burned a hole in my hand each time I lifted the floorboard and reached into my secret place to look at it. *Henry V*. Wednesday, 14th December 1955. I didn't want to wear my ubiquitous green taffeta with the fluffy bolero again, but there simply wasn't enough money for anything new. It suddenly occurred to me that Granny had some lovely clothes crammed into her wardrobes that hadn't seen the light of day for decades, but that had been models in their time. I waited until she was at church on Sunday morning and then I crept quietly into her room. Feeling like a burglar, I whispered to Jaffa to be quiet.

Just as I was about to open the wardrobe door, I caught sight of Donald staring at me from his photograph that hung on the wall. Was he watching me, with his lost, sad eyes? Next to the photograph hung a sampler that Granny had embroidered as a child. A border of flowers was divided at the top by two perky little wrens. The message, in neat brown stitches, read: Patience and diligence, like faith, remove mountains. I wondered why Granny had placed this next to the photograph of the baby she missed so much. Despite losing him, she hadn't lost her faith. Was going to church so diligently her way of keeping in touch with Baby Donald? I had no time to dwell on such lofty matters as I selected a gown, wrapped in a white sheet, from the wardrobe. I didn't think Granny would miss it since she hadn't worn it for thirty years, but I still felt guilty taking it. Before I left her room, I also helped myself to the snow leopard cape from the shipping trunk.

That night, when I knew I wouldn't be disturbed, I tried on the outfit in my bedroom. The gown was a Balenciaga, timeless in its simplicity and, miraculously, it fitted me perfectly. There was a severe, plain gold underslip with a round neck and sleeves. The overgarment was a black lace shift with a skirt cut on the bias. I twirled, and the heavy lace swirled nicely about my calves. I would wear sheer black stockings, which I could buy with the money I had put away, but I wasn't sure about shoes. My feet were so small that neither my mother's shoes, nor Granny's, fitted me and nothing I had looked right. Oh, but the gown did look nice, and Balenciaga, too! I *had* to wear it. Something in the way of pretty footwear would turn up in time. I had a week and a half. I swirled again and threw back my head and laughed, looking over one shoulder as models did in films. I sniffed: mothballs. I slipped out of the garments and opened the balcony door, carrying out my towel rail. It was cold and very peaceful out there. I could see for miles. There was no moon, but the sky was clear and sparkling with stars. Smoke spiralled up from all the chimneys in the street and I could smell soot and the lighter, more nostalgic scent of wood burning. In the distance I heard a train. It seemed to get closer, then faded away. I laid the two fragile garments over the towel rail and hoped they wouldn't blow away in the night. When I brought them in the next morning, they smelled clean and fresh, of washing hanging on a country line. I buried my face in the fabric and breathed it in, before putting them carefully away at the back of my wardrobe.

A few days later I found my shoes. They were black fabric with a Louis heel and a strap fastening. It had been almost a miracle when I bicycled past the secondhand shop on the way to school and spotted them in the window. I dashed back in the evening to try them on and they fitted perfectly. Like Cinderella's own shoes, they would take me to the ball. 'Ten bob,' the lady had said. I beat her down to four and six, all I had left until I got paid.

As I dressed, on the evening of *Henry V*, the cold, clean smell from the balcony still lingered in Granny's cape and gown. I plastered on makeup, then sprayed on my mother's perfume that I had already stolen. It was nerve-racking creeping out of the house, head to toe in Granny's clothes, I knew that nobody else would notice, but Granny would. She had gimlet eyes and nothing escaped her gaze. I decided that if I left at six o'clock on the dot, she would be listening to the news on the radio. She divided her day by the timing of the news broadcasts and had several radios, each tuned in to a different waveband for her regular programmes. Her favourites was the Home Service, which had the news, and *Woman's Hour* and *Armchair Theatre* late at night, always followed by *A Book at Bedtime*.

Now, as I crept down the stairs carrying my shoes, I could hear the news coming from Granny's room. I closed the front door behind me, slipped on my shoes, and stepped out into the freezing air, glad of the instant warmth and comfort of the thick fur cape. My feet flew along the road as I skirted the black, spooky expanse of the playing fields until I reached the bus stop on the brightly lit main road. I stood waiting in a small queue, feeling slightly incongruous in all my finery. The bus was a while and suddenly I panicked, convinced that Father might drive by and see me. It wasn't my stolen outfit that bothered me, but the certainty that he would offer me a lift to town. He would even try to get a ticket. He would talk, he would ask questions, and how would I manage to escape afterwards to meet Richard? I was on tenterhooks until the big red Number 176 trundled into view down the hill.

Although I went to the theatre alone, I fantasised that Richard had escorted me and that it was the opening night. I pretended that we sat together and he slipped the cloud leopard cape off my shoulders, his fingers kneading into the deep soft pelt. For a brief moment, gazing up at the red velvet curtains with their Greek border design in gold, I flashed back to that enthralling moment during *Under Milk Wood*, when I had first seen him. I hadn't sat so close to the front since then, with my neck tilted up toward the stage. It now seemed too close. I was more used to being high up, and far to the back. That was when it suddenly hit me, why the balcony was called 'the Gods'. It was like being in the clouds on Mount Olympus, where the gods themselves looked down at mere mortals who strutted and fretted their hour on stage. Yet, those watching from the Gods were mostly poor students who couldn't afford better seats. The wealthy people – the actual gods – sat low to the ground at the front, where their viewpoint was looking up, as if in supplication.

The excited, expectant buzz fell silent when the curtain rose. Playing the part of Chorus, John Neville, golden-haired, with fragile, aquiline features, proclaimed the stirring words,

> O for a muse of fire, that would ascend
> The brightest heaven of invention:
> A kingdom for a stage, princes to act,
> And monarchs to behold the swelling scene.
> Then should the warlike Harry, like himself,
> Assume the port of Mars . . .

I sighed as I settled down to absorb the play and tightly held the hand of my invisible lover who was sitting beside me. When he entered, as Henry V, in Scene Two, delighted shrieks came from the bobby-soxers up in the Gods, delaying Henry's first words, 'Where is my gracious Lord of Canterbury?' Insignificant words, and yet they thrilled me, because Richard the actor had become real to me in real life. He quoted lines to me all the time, to me alone, a devoted audience of one. Later, when the Chorus said, 'Now all the youth of England are on fire,' there came another shriek, and then a slight ripple of amusement. Poor Richard, how irritating he must find all this, I thought loftily, wishing they'd all shut up.

In the interval, I remained quietly in my seat so he would know right where I was, just in case he came to get me. I looked hard to see if there was a movement of the curtains: would he be peeping, to see if he could spot me? I longed to go backstage but dared not. I was so tense, so expectant in my fantasy of what might be that I had never known fifteen minutes to pass more slowly. At the end of the interval, I glanced surreptitiously at the returning crowds, especially at those seated closest to me, trying to eavesdrop on their conversations. Were any of them Richard's friends or members of his family? Had they been backstage to see him? I couldn't tell and so gave up, to lose myself in the magnificence of the stirring battle speeches.

When the performance was over, I was in a state of deep emotion, more in love than ever with my golden idol as I rushed to grab a taxi before the crowds spilled out. I pretended that he was sitting beside me as we bowled over Waterloo Bridge and turned into the Strand. When we drew up at the top of Villiers Street, I pretended that it was he who was paying the driver. I walked the few yards down to the Griffin and slipped inside. I was early and he had told me to wait for a half hour, to give him time to take off his stage makeup and get to the flat himself.

'It will be safer if I go straight there,' he'd said. 'If we keep meeting in the pub, someone will be bound to notice and then the cat will be out of the bag.'

I paid for some Rose's lime juice and soda water, the cheapest drink I could think of, and sat in what I thought of as 'our' booth. My small black evening bag, also borrowed from Granny without her knowledge, was too small to have slipped a book in, so I contented myself with looking into the flames of the coke fire and reliving the play. I looked at my watch. The half hour had crawled painfully slowly. I finished my drink, pulled the short cape over my shoulders, and went along to the flat. I had walked along these paving stones a dozen times and yet I still felt that intensely painful stomach-churning sense of anticipation and panic. After seeing him on the stage as the glorious young King Henry V, as powerful and magnificent as the rising sun in all its splendour, I was in love with him all over again. I would have crawled on my hands and knees along those stones to reach him.

He answered the door and blew a soft whistle.

'You look bloody marvellous. Come on in before anyone sees us.'

He bent to kiss me, his mouth grazing my hair and nuzzling into my neck as soon as the door was safely closed – funny, but thinking back, Richard rarely kissed me on the lips – but all I was thinking then was: Please, God, don't let him smell mothballs. Despite the overnight airing, I had sprayed enough of Mother's Givenchy over me to sink a ship.

At first I was shy, still seeing him as the godlike figure on the stage. To cover it up, I acted a part myself, that of a vampish thirties film star to match my clothes. As I walked up the stairs and into the soft lighting and seductive warmth of the flat, I felt the heavy lace skirt of my borrowed finery swirl sensuously against my stockinged calves. I posed in the centre of the room and allowed the cape to slip from my shoulder, while glancing at him demurely. He was extra polite as he poured a glass of champagne and handed it to me with a slight bow.

'To first nights and beautiful women,' he said. He already had a glass of Scotch, half empty on the table. He tossed it back and poured another.

'To first nights and wonderful actors,' I replied, taking a sip.

'Did you enjoy it?'

'Oh yes! You were perfect as Henry. I almost died during the Agincourt speech. I read all the reviews –' I stopped dead. I was gushing and in my nervousness I had almost betrayed myself. I had been about to say, 'I read all the papers in the shop this morning, before doing my paper round.'

'More! More! We crave praise!' he said, clapping. 'Look at me, a short, over-muscled boyo from the Valleys, and yet I play English kings so well, don't you think?' he mocked.

'But you were wonderful!' I protested. 'So . . . so . . . divine.'

'Divine eh? "He wears the rose of youth upon him,"' he said, pouring more champagne for me, more Scotch for himself.

I had no idea where that line came from, but then, Richard did that to me all the time. He could pluck a speech, a sentence out of thin air, leaving me stumbling about in the dark, feeling gauche and ignorant, trying to guess its source, trying to think of a swift, witty response and, usually, failing. I caught a glimpse of myself in a mirror and froze. I looked like an apple-cheeked Renoir girl, my cheeks flushed, my eyes bright, my hair shining with health, but I was like a child who was dressed up, with too slender arms in a frock intended for an older, more sophisticated woman. Even my precocious bosom didn't look as if it belonged to me.

Shut up, Rose, I told myself. Let him do all the talking. He's an actor, he loves to show off. It must have worked, for he basked in my attention and couldn't wait to make love to me.

Later, when we lay entwined before the fire, my head resting on the cape, Richard glanced down at it and allowed his fingers to run through the thick fur.

'This has pretty markings,' he said. 'What is it? Moggie?' I was furious that he would think it a mangy cat's fur, and sat up, covering my nakedness with it.

'No! It's a snow leopard. From the Himalayas.'

'Oh, pardon me,' he mocked. 'Actually, I thought it was lynx, so I'm not too far out. Snow leopard, hmm?'

'They are also called cloud leopards because they live above the cloud line,' I lectured, echoing my grandmother's words. Fascinated and curious, I had looked up the beautiful animals in the library and discovered that in Mongolia a snow leopard pelt was placed in the middle of the temple courtyard and ritual dances called tsam were performed around it. 'They are sacred spirits,' I said, gently stroking the fur as though it were still alive.

'Then it seems a shame to kill them,' Richard said. 'Sacred spirits should be worshipped, not destroyed.'

Mournfully drunk, I nodded, feeling tears well up into my eyes.

'Poor, poor snowy leopard,' I said. Richard took me in his arms.

'Some day,' he said, rocking me gently, 'I'll let you out of the shadows and we'll seek adventures. I'll take you with me. We'll roam the wild places. We'll find snow leopards and yetis and shaman. We'll sleep in icy monasteries above the clouds. We'll find Shangri-la.'

There seemed such a promise in his words, the promise of a shared future. I longed to ask him how this would be, and did he really mean it? My heart wanted to believe him, blindly. Perhaps energised by his success and the wonderful reviews, he made love to me over and over, and between, he described the things we would do together. Some day. But, even after two full bottles of champagne, my mind told me it was all a beautiful fantasy.

Although there never seemed to be anyone around in that little cut-off corner of London, I always left the flat in Buckingham Street alone, often before Richard. He said he didn't want people to notice us always leaving together. Each time he would ask, 'All right for money?' And I always answered, 'Yes, thank you,' too embarrassed to state otherwise. He never pressed, although his hand always went to his wallet when he asked. I knew that he was certain I took a taxi safely home each time I left. This was far from the truth. To save money I would often run up the steep flight of steps in Villiers Street to the station. If the last train had gone, I would linger over a cup of tea. When I was sure that the coast was clear, I would then walk to Trafalgar Square and get on the all-night bus, along with the drunks and the weary people, like waiters, who worked long and difficult hours. Sitting on the bus, I always felt tawdry after a night of such passionate romance. I would gather my crumpled clothes about me and jolt along home in a sea of discarded newspapers, butt ends, and tobacco ash.

On the night of *Henry V*, however, perhaps Richard must have seen that I was stumbling a little as I dressed. He insisted on walking up to the Strand with me, to the cab rank at the station. There, he pressed a note into my hand as he opened the taxi door and then turned away, to grab the taxi waiting behind. I sank back into the seat and closed my eyes. My head was spinning with the cold and the fresh air.

'All right, Miss?' came the voice of the driver.

'Yes, sleepy,' I answered.

'Nap away, love,' he said. 'I'll wake you when we've arrived.'

My hair was tousled and my lipstick worn away with kisses. My sheer black stockings that had been so carefully chosen were now laddered. A night of romance was over. I felt tearfully sentimental, but I refused to cry for I had things to look forward to, sort of. Richard had arranged our next meeting for the following week. 'And then I'll see you one more time before Christmas,' he'd said. 'My family is coming from Wales, see, because I'm working. I can't get away home.' How had I foolishly thought we'd spend Christmas Day together?

'I won't see him at Christmas' was all I could think, as the taxi sped over Westminster Bridge.

When I got home it was almost dawn and the house was dark and still. Not even Jaffa stirred as I crept up to my room. I dragged off all my clothes and bundled them to the back of the wardrobe. Without washing, or bothering to remove the remnants of my makeup, I crawled into an icy single bed, so far removed from the memories of a pink satin eiderdown before a glowing fire. I slept around the clock, missing my paper round, missing school. No one in the family even noticed.

Ten

❦

A couple days after *Henry V*, I was witness to another kind of grand performance. This time it was in the village park. I had seen the boy before. He was always watching me while I delivered the papers to the various big houses, but when he'd seen me look his way, he would bicycle off. He was young, freckled, and with curly ginger hair and not a threat, so I ignored him. One morning – perhaps because it had snowed in the night – another paper boy didn't show up for work. When I came back to return my sack, having finished my rounds, Dick sent me off again, despite my protests that I would be late for school. An unfamiliar route was always a nuisance, with house numbers that couldn't be read and letter boxes that couldn't be found.

Sulkily, I filled the bag, hoisted its heavy weight on to my shoulders, and pedalled off, through the village. The air was very crisp, my breath condensed about the balaclava I wore, and the wheels of my bicycle cut cleanly through the fresh snow in the park. Few people were about and I suddenly realised how beautiful it was. Every tree and shrub was outlined in white. The lake glistened in the rising sun and icicles seemed to chime like bells. In those days there was an aviary by the lake and you could hear the scream of the parrots from some distance away. Often, I would go there just to look at the birds. Ducks, coots, and grey herons lived on the island in the middle of the lake, and I dawdled a little to watch them.

I wasn't sure when I first spotted the boy with the freckles and ginger hair. He was sort of lurking as he spun from shrubbery to shrubbery on his bike. Oh well, I thought, let him play his little games. Boys will be boys. Suddenly, he stepped out on to the path ahead of me, his bicycle lying on the ground where he'd dropped it. He had a startled, almost pleading expression on his face. I went to swerve past him and in that same moment I saw that he had dragged the trousers of his track suit down and was exposing himself. His knees were slightly bent and his belly was thrust forward. It was more comic than frightening, so I started to laugh.

'Silly boy, it'll freeze and drop off!' I shouted as I shot by. From the corner of my eye, I saw him throw himself full length on to the ground and begin rolling in the snow. This was the third time in my short life that a male had exposed himself to me. I wondered if it was common among men, or if I was just unlucky.

Later that morning, at school, sex surfaced in another shape. The rumour flew that our classmate Daphne – we always called her Daffers – was stripping at a local joint, although nobody seemed to know much more than that. Probably she had told a friend and Chinese whispers had done the rest. I didn't know her well, but I had always found her intriguing because of her particular angular beauty, like Vermeer's famous *Girl with a Pearl Earring*, a copy of which my father had bought from the Medici

Society and had hanging in his study. Daffers had an air of loucheness, a worldly-wise look about her. Her gym slips were shorter than ours, she wore stockings instead of socks, and her tie was looped into a kind of bow instead of being neatly knotted. Daffers was the girl who was first to have the latest record. She was the girl who brought in suggestive books and giggled with her friends over them during break. And she was definitely the kind of girl who smoked cigarettes in the toilets and met older boys in the street. We had all noticed that her hair, which she had taken to dying a chestnut colour, had been slowly falling out for weeks. More gossip flew, but she appeared unconcerned by it.

One morning shortly before we broke up for Christmas, Daffers arrived with green hair. Our form mistress immediately singled her out at register.

'Daphne, whatever is wrong with your hair?'

'It must have been the shampoo that turned it this colour, Miss Adams,' Daffers said.

Miss Adams left her desk and walked over to where Daffers was lounging in her seat. She riffled her fingers through Daffers's hair and said, 'Well, it's green right down to the roots. Did you do this on purpose?'

'No, Miss Adams, of course not!' Daffers said, while we all started to giggle.

'If you must dye it, you should have it professionally done. Give it another week or two and you will be completely bald.' Daffers forgot to lounge and sat bolt upright.

'I'll get a wig,' she said, insolently. Miss Adams didn't reply. She returned to her desk, finished register, and we all filed out to our different classes. Daffers had won that preliminary skirmish, we thought, and she went up in our estimation, but something must have been discussed in the staff room because our form prefect was sent for and interrogated.

Nothing much came of that, but later the music mistress opened the local paper and saw an instantly recognisable photograph of Daffers, wearing nothing much more than three fig leaves, in an advertisement for the strip show at the Camberwell Palais, under the heading 'Camberwell Beauties!' This was a pun on the rare butterfly that had first been discovered in Camberwell. A rich velvety blue with a chocolate-brown bloom and a yellow border, it was used as an emblem on many local businesses, including the Palais. Since the strip show was on Friday and Saturday nights, a posse of female teachers arrived at the Palais that very weekend, paid their money for tickets, and waited in a mostly male audience for the show to start. Daffers told us afterwards she was completely unaware that she'd been rumbled as she high-kicked her way on to the stage. The posse said nothing, didn't so much as cough until the dancers started to peel off their clothing. When Daffers was down to her sequined panties, they pounced on her from their darkened seats.

After she was expelled, Daffers came to school to collect her belongings. She tried hard not to appear downhearted over the incident.

'I knew it was all over as soon as I heard Miss Adams shout, "Curtain down! One of those girls is fourteen years old!"' said Daffers.

'But why did you do it?' we all asked her.

'For the money, why else?' she said. 'School's boring, anyway.'

Daffers said it bravely, but I detected regret. She was too young to leave school so was being transferred to a new one. Not only would she be starting in with a black mark against her, but she would have to make new friends. For a time she worried that she would have to go to court, but the school decided not to report it to the police because it would give them a bad name.

In all this, I kept wondering what would be said if 'the posse' knew about my secret life. My time with Richard seemed so remote from school and lessons, as if it were happening to someone else, but I was no different from Daphne, except that I hadn't been exposed. I tried not to think about 'the posse' turning up at the apartment one night, catching me in the act. Would they simply blush to see Richard Burton opening the door, his green eyes mocking them, that lock of hair falling over his brow? Would they have me arrested or would they simply ask for his autograph? At times, I was almost tempted to confide in Betty or the Schultz girls, longing to share my secret, but I had already seen how fast Chinese whispers could spread. Betty might tell her mother, her mother would tell my father. It was a potential nightmare that didn't bear thinking about, so I kept it all to myself. It was never easy; I would agonise over the risks I was running, not to mention my duplicity, I would blush at the slightest remark, I would think well before I spoke. All this was changing me. I was an honest girl, who was living a lie.

—

Our school had a long-held tradition of performing Handel's *Messiah* every Christmas. It needed male voices as well as the sopranos of schoolgirls, so the London male-voice Police Choir was seconded to add weight. The entire school rehearsed our parts for weeks, and then the police came and we all rehearsed together for the real performance, which was sung in Southwark Cathedral. On the day of the performance, something like twenty-seven coaches picked us up and drove us there.

Ever since my walk over Waterloo Bridge with Richard, I had read something of the history of Bankside and had been fascinated to learn that most of the church and priory of St Mary Overie – originally built in the seventh century – had been destroyed in a fire that raged over medieval London Bridge in 1212, killing some three thousand people and destroying many of the wonderful old wattle-and-daub buildings that lined the bridge itself. The church was rebuilt and eventually had been incorporated into what became Southwark Cathedral, the oldest Gothic church in London.

The coaches swept along Redcross Street, where, in Cross Bones Yard – I had read in the *Annals of St Mary Overie* at the library – there had been a patch of unconsecrated earth known as the Single Woman's Burial Ground, which is where all the whores were buried. For me, this was like bringing history alive, and I knew that in this respect, Richard had changed me for ever. I would no longer pass through a place with my eyes blinkered. Everything was now peopled with the spirits of dead souls – if we just paused long enough to let them make contact, then surely we would see them. I reflected on the year, which had started with Richard telling me about the young heiress and her miser of a father, and now here I was, in the very street where she had lived and died – but the biggest change of all had been in me.

Going back to that day in Southwark Cathedral in my memory, I can still hear the surge of the great organ and the sound of our massed schoolgirl and police choirs singing the 'Hallelujah Chorus'. Lessons at school had ensured that we well knew Handel's awestruck words after he had finished composing it in a storm of passion: 'I did think I did see all heaven before me, and the great God himself!' I couldn't wait to share all this with Richard the next time we met. I could almost hear his booming voice saying with a laugh, 'So, you've seen where they buried the whores, have you?' And then we would talk of Handel and other, more lofty things. I wouldn't, of course, tell him that I had sung *The Messiah* with my school.

The following day, at very short notice, Father asked if I would like to go to *La Bohème* with him at Covent Garden, as a special treat for Christmas. This was to become another tradition between us, going once each year for many years. I didn't know when he asked me that he had intended to go with a girlfriend but she had cancelled at the last moment. I really did think it was an outing he had arranged specially for me and I was very touched.

'The story is set in Paris, at Christmas,' Father explained, as he started to sing, '"Your tiny hand is frozen . . . let me warm it into life."' He looked at me. 'You know that, don't you, Rose?' he asked.

I had to admit that I didn't.

'Rodolfo sings it to Mimi when she drops her door key. The candles go out, he finds the key and pockets it, and she searches for it on the floor in the dark. Their hands touch and he lifts her hand up and kisses it. He doesn't know that she is dying of consumption.'

'And this is a Christmas story?' I protested. 'It sounds more like a tragedy.'

'It's wonderful,' Father said. 'You'll enjoy it.'

Full of enthusiasm, Father told me the entire story, punctuating the plot with the odd line of lyrics, singing both the male and female roles. His voice had always been good and, for once, I listened attentively. It suddenly dawned on me that he really did know what he was talking about. This was another side to his normally irritating character and I started to regain a glimmer of the respect for him that I had lost years earlier. There seems a time when a young girl of six or seven is half in love with her father, when he seems to be the epitome of all that is brave and strong and romantic in her unformed mind. Then, one day, perhaps she sees that he has feet of clay and feels let down. This was how it had been with me when I first came to see all of my father's faults. Now, in a strange way, I was gaining a little in maturity and wisdom. For all his bad points, he was my father and the habit of affection was deeply ingrained in me. The irony was, I had come to realise that he loved me as much as he was capable of loving anyone. He loved me almost as much as he loved himself.

The Royal Opera House in Covent Garden was big and grand; the men wore dinner jackets, the perfumed women wore evening gowns and sparkled with jewellery. I had on my usual green taffeta and white bolero beneath my heavy tweed coat. Little white fairy lights festooned the outside of the building and gave it a dreamlike feel. The orchestra was already in place as we found our seats, where Father presented me with a large flat box of chocolates, the height of luxury. We were late because he had fallen into an argument with someone over a parking place while I stood shivering in a biting wind on the pavement. Father won the argument, only because he threatened to ram the other driver if he didn't back out. Nothing, however, could spoil the excitement as the curtains rose on a little garret in Paris. For once, Father didn't ask questions – this was one story he knew backwards, and to prove it, he conducted along with the music, using his finger as a wand while he tapped out the rhythm on his knee with the other hand.

Afterwards, Father took me to supper in a small restaurant just by the flower market. Through the bow windows we could see lorries beginning to arrive and porters unloading as we ate filet of sole mignon and garlicky mushrooms. When he ordered a bottle of white wine, I sighed with pleasure. How I wished that this were Richard with me, sharing the wine, laughing at jokes. I put that thought aside as I listened to my father. He was in fine fettle, telling me stories, discussing music. Suddenly it was almost as if I were looking at him not as his daughter, a fellow dweller in a cold and hostile home, but as a person. I saw what perhaps his friends and girlfriends saw in him, a handsome man who could entertain and amuse. It seemed that, individually, my parents were intelligent, entertaining people, but as a unit they were dysfunctional and destructive. For once, I listened, really listened, to him, putting aside my knowledge of his petty foibles, his womanising, his infringement of our privacy, even his mean little tricks. At face value, my father was quite charming. So this is what all those women saw in him, not knowing him as his family did. That's when he spoiled it for me.

'Well, it wasn't so bad that I was stood up, Rose,' he said. 'It's a pleasure to take my daughter out.'

'Who stood you up?' I asked.

'Oh, nobody,' he chuckled. 'Well, she's a nobody now, for I won't ask her out again. This has been far more fun. You are enjoying yourself, aren't you?'

'Yes, I am,' I said. '*La Bohème* was wonderful. Though it was so sad at the end when Mimi died.'

'Well, that's the story,' Father said. 'That she died. Many people died of TB in those days.' He told me how, when he'd been a boy, many people in his street had died of consumption, as tuberculosis was known. If you had money, you would be sent away to Switzerland to a sanatorium, or to the country. Before the First World War half the population died young of something or another. For once, Father told me about his past, about the backbreaking work he had to do as a child, and the Shetland pony, Dolly, which the greengrocer kept for the deliveries. It was Father's job to curry and feed her, to go to the fields and cut cabbages or dig potatoes.

'In the winter, I would see these icy green balls, rows and rows of cabbages,' he said. 'I'd crunch through the snow and cut a few with my bill hook. I had to stuff them in sacks and then drag them back to the cart. Sometimes, my hands were so frozen I couldn't feel them and I would put them in Dolly's mouth until they thawed.'

'Your tiny hand was frozen,' I said.

'What? Oh, yes!' He roared with laughter. 'Very good, Rose.'

The next day, however, when I came in from my paper round, it was to yet another argument.

'If you tell me one more time what a wonderful evening you had, George, I swear I'll clock you with this frying pan,' Mother said. 'For God's sake, shut up about it.'

'You should come out with me a bit more,' Father whined.

'How can I go out when I am bloody well working?' Mother screamed.

'Anne, you know I detest a woman who swears,' Father said. He turned and walked away, up the hall and through the front door. I could hear him whistling cheerfully before the slam of the door cut it off. Certain he was gone, I came in through the back.

'Didn't you want me to go to the opera last night?' I asked Mother.

'Oh, Rose, of course, I didn't mind that. I just hate it when your stupid father makes stupid statements.' She mimicked him: ' "Anne, you never go out with me!" But how can I go? I work all night at a job I loathe.'

I didn't remind her that she had rarely gone out with him before she worked at nights. They were like oil and water and never enjoyed their outings together. I think Father only asked her to annoy her.

—

Right now though, I had a bigger problem. In every waking minute I was agonising over what to give to Richard for Christmas. This would be my first gift to him, and I wanted it to be perfect. I looked in the shop windows in the village, scoured magazine ads and the pages in newspapers that recommended meerschaum pipes for Father, slippers for Granny, and bath salts for Mother. I'd left it too late to make anything personal, or knit him a sweater. Generously, even though I hadn't knocked on doors for my Christmas tips, most of my paper route customers had brought my Christmas boxes in to the shop, but I would need to use most of that money to buy myself a new rucksack and some walking boots, very practical items. This meant that my small savings would have to stretch a long way to buy gifts for family and friends, not to mention bus fares, stockings, and taxis. My family would be astonished if they knew how often I hopped in and out of taxis – and my mother, who grew giggly on a small glass of sherry, would exile me to Siberia if she knew how much I was drinking.

Richard read books, often one a day, buying half a dozen at a time, so a book would be risky, besides being not different enough. He bought alcohol by the case, and anyway, booze was too expensive for me. Ties, handkerchiefs and gloves were the kind of thing you gave to your father or an uncle. Engraved silver cigarette cases, crocodile cigar cases, briefcases were beyond consideration for the money they would cost. In the end, running out of time, I asked Mr Green, in the art stationer's, to suggest something. Mr Green and his wife owned the toy shop too, at the other end of the village. They were quite old. He had very thick pebble glasses that rested squarely on his nose and Mrs Green was all grey, with her tightly permed grey hair, her grey twinset, and grey pleated skirt. She drifted like smoke about the store, helping customers and chatting.

'Is it for your boyfriend, Rose?' Mr Green asked.

'I don't have a boyfriend, Mr Green,' I said, realising that I was now treading in deep water. If I said it was for a rich cousin, he might mention it to my parents, or to Granny, who was a regular in the shop. If I said it was for Jimmy, who was due home, he might later ask Jimmy how he liked it. 'Actually, it's for a friend of mine who does have a boyfriend, only her parents don't know.'

'Ah, now I see,' said Mr Green. I glanced around the shop, which was crammed with useful things in that artistic community, from oil paints to sketch blocks, wrapping paper to expensive cards, the kind that you couldn't get in Woolworth's. 'And your friend's boyfriend, is he at the College?'

'No, Mr Green, he's . . . he's a student at Oxford. His people are well off, so he has good taste and is used to nice things.'

'And how much can your friend afford?'

'A pound,' I said wildly, now feeling very uncomfortable.

'A pound,' he repeated thoughtfully. His face brightened. 'I have it!'

'You do?'

'Oh yes, Rose. Yes, yes,' he said, rummaging in a sliding cupboard beneath the cards. He emerged with a book and laid it on the counter. 'This is exactly what your friend wants, and it's only ten shillings.'

I took it in my hands. It was an empty journal, bound in a soft brown suede. The paper was handmade, and thick and soft with a torn frilly edge. It was heavy cream, but within that tone was a multitude of subtle tints absorbed from the raw materials used to make it. I could see the shadows of leaves and grasses and the palest blush of petals. I thought it was exquisite. Richard had told me that he kept a journal, as I did. Mine was a cheap exercise book, but he deserved so much more. I could imagine him writing in this, with the fountain pen that he kept filled with black ink.

'It's perfect, Mr Green!' I said. I watched as he wrapped it in white tissue paper and tied some gold ribbon in a bow.

When I left, triumphant, with the gift securely under my arm, it was just beginning to snow again. Small Christmas trees were placed in a row along the line of the shops, each one sparkling with coloured lights. Every lamppost had a big silver star hanging from it and every window was specially decorated. For the first time, holiday excitement started to well up inside me. A small group of Women's Institute members were clustered around a lantern, singing carols on the corner outside the old-fashioned Boot & Shoe shop. As I passed by, one of them held out a tin.

'Happy Christmas,' I said, as I dropped in a shilling and heard it clink as it hit the bottom of the can. I wished the atmosphere at home would be as pleasant as it was in the village, where all the shopkeepers seemed to be smiling. Maybe it was more about the extra money the season meant to them, but that didn't matter.

We had no Christmas tree at home, but Freddy and I had cut some spiky dead branches, which I had painted with a flour and water mixture to resemble snow. The paste had even dripped down and dried to make authentic-looking icicles. A little sprinkle of silver dust and some silver baubles added a crowning touch. When we were younger, presents would appear mysteriously in the night at the foot of our beds, but lately we had started the ritual of putting the gifts out at midnight on Christmas Eve. This would be after the carol service in church, which we sometimes attended. At the stroke of twelve, the whole family would troop into the sitting room and lay our gifts beneath the silver boughs, as if they were offerings.

Richard's present, however, would be hidden away beneath the floorboard in my bedroom as soon as I got home. It would not be joining the others beneath the 'tree'. My greatest fear was that Father would find it on one of his scavenger hunts, rip off the white tissue paper and gold bow, and then exclaim, 'Rose! It's just what I've always wanted!'

Eleven

Two days before Christmas, and with the greatest care, I carried the gift with its gold bow to Richard's apartment. With a nod to the festive season, I think *The Merry Wives of Windsor* was playing that night, with other members of the company acting in it, so he had the night off. Some of his relatives had come from Wales, but he had managed to escape from them to be with me for a few hours.

'The women are all doing late-night shopping,' Richard said with a grin. 'And you know what that means. They'll shop till they're on their knees, and then no doubt they'll be ready for more punishment in the morning.' He seemed remarkably buoyant and I asked if he was happy to have his family in London.

'Well, yes, I love them all,' he said. 'There are dozens of us.'

'Really?' I exclaimed.

'Well, work it out. I was the twelfth of thirteen. The brothers have wives, the sisters have husbands, and then there are the in-laws, the children, the aunties and uncles, the grannies, the cousins. Hell, we're a clan of our own.

The Celts down from the hills, a Welsh invasion.' I was amazed. I still hadn't really come to appreciate that at times he exaggerated, telling many wild and woolly stories with many embellishments for the sake of the story itself, rather than for the truth. In fact, I think that only two or three members of his family had arrived to spend Christmas in London.

'Me, personally, I'd rather be in Wales,' Richard said, 'at home in the Valleys, the land of my fathers. I'm in the grip of hiraeth,' he added mournfully, 'but I'll just have to put up with it.'

'Hiraeth?'

'It's a longing for home. Wherever I go in the world, I can't escape that bloody Valley, nor my family. I'm addicted. Wales is in my blood, my soul.' He nodded to the carrier bag I'd brought into the flat with me. 'And what's in there, girl? I know by your expression you've got my Christmas present and you're bursting to give it. Well, let's have it.'

I blushed and said, 'It's not very much.'

'Well, a little, a lot, it's the thought that counts, eh, love?'

'You mustn't open it before Christmas,' I said, too late, as he untied the ribbon and peeled the tissue paper away.

'What have we here?' he said, lifting the book from its wrappings and rubbing the suede delicately with a finger. The colours changed as he rubbed first one way and then the other. He looked up and smiled. 'That's quality. It's pure velvet like the bloom on a rose petal.'

'The paper's handmade,' I said, almost apologetically, wondering if it was good enough. He quickly opened the journal and held a page up to the light.

'By George, so it is. Handmade, hand beaten, you can

242

see the bloody grass it was made from. Papyrus, do you think? From the Nile? If these were all the riches of Alexandria, I could not like it more.'

'Really?'

'Really. Upon thy cheek I lay this zealous kiss, as seal to the indenture of my love,' he said, as he bent his head and kissed me.

I was enraptured. He had said he loved me. I hoped that I would always remember his words, but were they his, or were they a quote? With him, I never knew. He invented lines, he combined speeches. He could even quote some of Shakespeare's sonnets backwards, and once had confused me by doing so. As seal to the indenture of my love . . . It sounded like a promise. I didn't care if it was a quote or not. I was dazzled.

I watched as Richard then took his fountain pen out of the inside of his jacket and, with a flourish, wrote on the inside page: Richard Jenkins, Christmas 1955.

'Who is Richard Jenkins?' I asked, my heart still bursting with joy. He had said he loved me. Hadn't he? He looked up and smiled.

'Hush, girl.' His pen wrote on, a black scrawl across the soft white paper. Then he showed me what he had inscribed on the virgin sheet. 'Biting my truant pen, beating myself for spite: "Fool," said my Muse to me, "look in thy heart, and write." '

I looked it up later, and found that it was by Sir Philip Sidney, poet nephew of Queen Elizabeth's favourite, the man everyone expected her to marry, Robert Dudley, Earl of Leicester. I learned so much by listening to Richard and following it through by reading on, but, when I once commented on how much he was teaching me, he'd said, 'You teach me more.'

'Who is Richard Jenkins?' I asked again.

'I am Richard Jenkins,' he said. 'Little Richie, the boyo from the Valleys who made good. It is Richie Jenkins who will write in this book, not Richard Burton, the bloody pouf and fraudulent actor. I have diaries filled in by Burton. Believe not a word in them.'

'Burton is your stage name?'

'No, Burton is the name of my adopted father. I took his name. He said it sounded better on stage than vulgar Jenkins. He is the man who took the crude Welsh out of me and brought me out of Wales. He made me what I am, Burton of Blundels. That's what my joker friends called me at Oxford to give me a class I didn't possess nor crave.' He went across to the table and picked up a record album. 'And this is what he made me. "A wandering minstrel, I, a thing of shreds and patches," a teller of tales. Sorry it's not wrapped, love,' he said, changing his voice. 'Somebody else does all that for me, but this time, well, I forgot. Still, I've signed it for you.'

He handed me a copy of Dylan Thomas's *Under Milk Wood* that he had recorded with the BBC. He had written: To Rosemary, my dream girl, all my love, always. The words jumped up at me and I blushed an even deeper, fiery red. I could feel the flush travelling up my neck and over my face.

'Come here,' he said, when I started to cry. He took me in his arms and held me close, murmuring sweet endearments, soothing words. When I had got control of my emotions, I said, muffled into his chest, 'I have loved *Under Milk Wood* since I first heard it, but I didn't know you had made a record.'

'Oh yes, I'm a man of many talents. Are you all right now?' I nodded, sniffling into his shirt.

'I'm so happy,' I said.

'Bloody hell, girl, they all say that. Now don't you start.' I pulled away.

'No, I won't. I'm not happy. I'm miserable, and you're horrible.'

'Good. That's better. Come on,' he suddenly said, 'let's go out.' This was unexpected.

'Out?'

'Yes, it's Christmas! Let's look at the lights, have a drink, eat something.' It was so surprising that I stepped back and stared. He laughed to see my astonished face. 'London is full of Jenkins women running about. I'll say you're one of them if we're asked, not that I expect to be asked. "Good evening, Mr Burton, who's the bloody bird with you?" "None of your bloody business, arsehole." '

He grabbed his camel-hair coat and my tweed, swallowed his drink, and practically pushed me out of the flat. Perhaps things were getting too intense, too emotional. I had noticed that he didn't like to give much of himself unless he'd drunk too much, and then he could get very depressed and morose.

Snow still lingered in the gutters from the fall a few days earlier. It was bitterly cold, and the wind had a sharp edge. We wandered into Trafalgar Square, where even in the depth of winter, on the coldest night, a few people always seemed to congregate like pigeons. Long icicles shimmered on the frozen fountain, against the backdrop of the National Gallery. The traditional Christmas tree was festooned in tiny white lights, its graceful green boughs rimed in snow. There was a cluster of carol singers on the steps of St Martin's and we walked over to listen. As we stood next to one of the big bronze lions on its plinth, Richard put his arm around my shoulders and pulled me close.

'Warm enough?' he whispered. Too choked with emotion to speak, I could only nod wordlessly. The smell of chestnuts roasting on a brazier blew on the cold wind, which whipped a newspaper around our ankles. 'Let's find something to eat. I know a little place in Covent Garden that stays open all night.'

As we walked, Richard talked about his childhood in Wales. I loved it when he told me these stories about his homeland. Sometimes, when it was dark, to get some fresh air, we would walk along the Embankment in the privacy of the night, watching the ebb and flow of the river. Perhaps it was the smell of the water, or perhaps the constant movement, suggesting that there was a rhythm to life, but he would talk then about his dreams and his memories. Now, on this night so close to Christmas, as we walked along Maiden Lane and the warren of little streets in the elbow of the Strand and St Martin-in-the-Fields, where violin-makers and artists like Turner and John Nash had once lived when they were young and poor, Richard described drab little Welsh villages tumbling down the valley toward Port Talbot, where the big steel mills were. You could always smell the coke furnaces, and at night, Richard said, there would be sparks and flames shooting high into the sky. Above them on the barren slopes were coal tips.

'They would deliver coal free to a miner's family, a ton at a time, dumping it on the pavement,' he told me, as we walked along, chilled to the bone. 'The houses, in terraces, opened straight on to the street. All the kids had to run back and forth with buckets and shovels, carrying it through the house, over the slate flagstones that their mam had scrubbed each day on her hands and knees, over the cement step that she got gleaming white like a bone. Coal dust would fall in a fine mist, casting a malignant bloom over everything. We could taste it, bite it on our teeth, it was that gritty. We breathed it in, it soaked into our skin. The miners, men like my da, had blue skin, pitted it was, with coal chips from the mines, like tattooing, see. And we had no baths, no running water, to get it off easy. We would have to drag the tin tub in from its nail in the yard and fill it with water from buckets on the stove. The youngest and cleanest first in, the oldest and dirtiest last. The water was like ink by then.'

I noticed that when Richard talked of Wales, his accent thickened, the rhythms and cadences of the Valleys returned. He had spoken Welsh as a child and had learned English as a second language when he went to school. He told me that Philip Burton had struggled for months to rid him of his crude Welsh accent, to modulate his voice with a posh English overtone, but he still spoke fluent Welsh and it was Welsh that he dreamed in. Even so, when he spoke like that, I never knew if he was mocking himself or not. Sometimes, I detected a sense of irony and bitterness in him that was strongest when he mentioned two men: his father and his foster father. I knew that his mother had died of blood poisoning when he was two or three, within days of the birth of his younger brother, Graham.

'Do you miss your mother?' I asked, knowing how the holidays can make one mourn for loved ones lost.

'I never thought of her again once she died,' he answered. 'Cissie, my beloved Cissie, who came at once and took me home with her, tells me that I went from following my mother around like a puppy, never letting her out of my sight, to never mentioning her name again. I don't remember her.'

'What about your father? Didn't he want to keep you?'

'No, he had no regard for us. He was a seventeen-pints-a-day man, lost in his booze, his whippets, and the betting shop.' He said this quite bitterly. 'He let me go then without a bloody murmur when I was two, and he let me go again when I was seventeen. He allowed me to be signed away without even a protest. I lost my name and my birthright. I went from being Dic Jenkins's son to being Phil Burton's creature, a thing to be shaped and moulded, not in his image but in the image of the man he wanted to be, had he been a real man. Phil Burton saw a beauty in this pockmarked face that sang to him. He worshipped Hamlet and glorious Henry and Prince Hal, and if he couldn't be any of them, then I would be. I would even be his Romeo and his Juliet. I would be the light shining in every one of his bloody windows.'

'You call everybody a poof,' I said, hesitantly, not sure how he would react to my question. 'Was Mr Burton really one?' At this, Richard sped up. He had a sailor's roll, an aggressive walk. I almost ran to keep up with him.

'A bloody arse-bandit?' he snarled. 'You betcha he was. If I wasn't sitting on it, studying all those bloody books he set me, he would have stuffed himself up it. He was my schoolteacher, my English teacher. A Welshman from up the Valley who taught English. That made him different, see, not as other men. He took me in to live with him. Ask yourself, is that usual unless you've got buggery on your mind?'

I was shocked. I truly hadn't expected this sort of honesty and bluntness, not even from Richard, and I had never heard him talk like this before, not even when he was drunk. He went on to describe how he had been a good student, but as a teenager started to throw his weight about a bit at home. His sister tried to keep the peace between Richard and her husband, but money was always in short supply. At the age of fourteen, more to teach his brother-in-law a lesson so he'd be sorry, Richard abandoned grammar school and started work, serving behind the counter in a clothing store. However, the person who was sorriest was Richard himself. He was humiliated being an apprentice at everybody's beck and call while his jeering school friends walked by to their lessons.

'Not even extra drink and fags, nor being able to afford to play snooker down in Port Talbot, made up for the sense of inferiority that being a shop boy instilled in me,' he said. 'I should have gone down the mines, not been standing there like a pimply faced twit, selling men's socks and underpants to miners' wives. They would pat me on my curly head like a puppy, and I would wag my miserable tail at them.'

'And then? What happened then?'

'Philip Burton came riding to the rescue, my knight on a bloody white horse. "Come varlet, I'll give you the ride of your life!" he cried. Bloody right, he did. He took me in, crammed me with learning and a little more besides, put me back in school, and shoved me all the way to Oxford University. He pushed and beat the doors down until he got me on stage. "The voice, lad, the voice, it must be heard, and by George it shall be heard!" '

Even now, from a distance of forty-five years, I can hear the fury, remember his words – oh, perhaps not exactly every one, but he revealed more to me then, in that Christmas walk, than he ever had before. I saw a little boy whose mother had died, whose father didn't seem to care, a child who, when he met his brother at the age of seven or eight, the brother whose birth had led to their mother's death, had only then realised that they were brothers. It had been the moment when all the grief of separation had hit him, but he had kept it bottled up. By the time Philip Burton, his peculiar mentor, had taken him in hand, Richard had resolved that he would continue to bottle up his feelings, he would do anything to show his da, little Dic Bach as they called him, that he could make something of himself.

'But, it was all a waste of time,' Richard said. 'I could be a flea jumping on the back of one of his whippets for all I mean to him – and he's the one man in all the world with the power to destroy me, an ugly little waster of a man, no higher than my knee. So why do I care so much?'

I knew that he didn't really want me to answer. This walk perhaps was cathartic in some way, striding out anonymously in the cold air, among people glowing with food and wine and cheer, spilling out of bars or restaurants after their Christmas parties. He had already told me that being on stage, playing Henry, had been a great strain, particularly after the poor reviews of some of his films. Even films for which he had been nominated for an Oscar had not done all that well, and though he professed not to care a jot, he was always shaken and cut to the quick. The stage was where he could shine, but it bored him to tears, and the constant struggle of proving himself when in his heart he didn't think he deserved it, exhausted him. 'I'm a fake,' Richard often said to me. 'A bloody big fake.'

By the time we reached the bustling cobbled streets around Covent Garden, where traders were shouting above the noise of lorries delivering fruit and flowers, his mood had changed. He was open, expansive, embroidering stories that I knew weren't true, but that made me laugh. We sat in the café that the porters used, eating bacon sandwiches and Richard's favourite greasy chips sprinkled with vinegar and salt and drinking mugs of hot, sweet tea, while he talked of food and travel and books. He described the tea and sop they'd have at home as dessert. The black tea would be sweetened with big dollops of condensed milk, bread broken up in it, and the whole mess would be eaten with a spoon, he said. He smiled when he described it. Perhaps he thought it would disgust me. Instead I told him about the roti muchi chini I ate as a child in India, bread and milk and sugar.

'On the ship coming home, we were given diluted sweet condensed milk to drink,' I said. 'It was delicious, served icy cold. I loved it so much that I used to steal condensed milk from the pantry and eat it straight from the tin with a spoon.'

I felt very grown up and important when I was able to make Richard laugh, to amuse him, as he did me, and so I told him about the dog. It was when we lived in Wimbledon and my father suddenly appeared with a big boxer dog that he had agreed to look after for a friend. The dog would lie at the top of the stairs, looking out of the fanlight, as if looking for its owner to return. One night, when I was creeping down to the kitchen, an open tin of condensed milk on my mind, I tripped over the dog and fell all the way down, breaking the bottom step and badly bruising the base of my spine.

'No doubt you woke up the house,' Richard said.

'No, they all carried on sleeping,' I admitted. 'I could have been a burglar and they wouldn't have moved. Even the dog didn't move till I stepped on him. I staggered into the kitchen, demolished the tin of condensed milk, and next day, I threw up. I thought it was my greed that had made me so ill, but in fact, I was sickening for the mumps.'

'At Oxford some idiot spiked my beer with wood alcohol,' Richard recalled. 'I could hardly stand, let alone see. I fell down a steep flight of stairs and nearly broke my back. I still suffer from back pain and find fight scenes hard to do.'

We were talking to each other like old friends on a Christmas outing. I couldn't believe how wonderful it was, no more hiding in the flat. Surely, this was the beginning of a new relationship between us, a more adult, honest one than before. Outside, a Salvation Army band started to play, with brass instruments tiddly-pom-pomming, the drums and tambourines pounding a rhythm. 'God rest ye merry gentlemen, let nothing you dismay . . .' Richard sang along. He had a good tenor. Two Salvation women in their navy uniforms and poke bonnets tied under their chins with starched ribbon came inside, shaking their collection bags and Richard dug into his pocket and poured in a handful of change.

'Happy Christmas,' he said.

'God bless you,' they chorused. I wondered if they recognised him, but if they did, they made no comment.

'What are you doing for Christmas?' Richard asked me. 'Going down to your pile in the country?'

'Something like that,' I said airily. 'My brother, Jimmy, will be home. I miss him.'

'Is he at boarding school?'

'He's in the RAF.'

'Is he, by Jove! A pilot, no doubt. I was in the RAF during the war, you know . . .' And then he was off, with yarns of the air cadets at Oxford and joining up as a navigator, before being sent to Canada. 'I joined too late to be any use, but I could navigate to Berlin and back, provided I didn't get the map upside down.' I didn't tell him that

Jimmy was at the bottom of the heap, an RAF student-cadet.

Wistfully, I wished every time we had together could be spent like this, taking a stroll, eating food, enjoying the spark of London, but, as always happened, reality leaked its way into a perfect evening.

'We need to get back, love,' Richard said, and I knew in my heart that he wouldn't be prepared to risk an outing such as this too often. So we returned to the flat, where, after our usual lovemaking, I took my precious album and allowed him to pay for a taxi home. As the cab drove through the chilly night, I ran my finger over the album cover. It was in *Under Milk Wood* that I had first seen him, heard him, before I ever knew his name: 'To begin at the beginning . . .'

—

Jimmy arrived next morning. I felt shy with him. In the six months since he had last been at home on leave he had sprung up like a sapling and now towered even more above Father. His grey-blue uniform suited him. His short dark hair and peaked cap seemed to accent the more angular lines of his face.

'You look like my brother, Bill,' Mother said at once. 'Exactly like him!'

'No he doesn't,' Father said sourly. Bill had been the brother sent by her parents to fetch my mother home to England when she announced her engagement to my father.

'Yes, he does,' Mother insisted. 'Mum, what do you think?'

'Yes, he resembles Bill,' Granny agreed. 'Thank God.' I could see at once that things were not going to be all that comfortable, especially when Mother tried to get Jimmy

253

and my father lined up, back to back, to measure the difference in their heights. Father flatly refused.

'Well, it's plain to see that Jimmy is already much taller,' Mother said. 'He takes after my brothers.'

'Yes, yes he does,' Granny said again. At this, my father's face blackened with anger and he stalked off upstairs to his study, slamming every door in the house on his way.

Later, Jimmy went up to make his peace, but within twenty minutes we could hear raised voices floating down the stairs.

'Your father should not have had sons,' Mother said. 'He sees them as a threat and a competition, and his expectations are too high.' She told me how, when Jimmy was a baby, Father had bought him a set of wooden alphabet blocks and expected him to make words out of them right away. 'All Jimmy could say was "goo-goo" but that stupid man upstairs expected him to spell out the dictionary. Of course, he lost his temper, as he always does. He slapped Jimmy, and him just a little baby! I told him that if he ever laid a hand on any child of mine again, he would have a knife in his back.'

I knew that this threat hadn't stopped Father. He continued to lash out – once, he had beaten me with a hairbrush – but for some reason it was Freddy he really laid into, with a belt. That had been during the years when Mother had been breaking down. The worse she was, the more of a bully Father became. Since she had become stronger, it hadn't happened again. It was as if she had finally come awake enough to be the protective barrier between us and Father's worst nature.

Freddy, however, had already retreated into himself by this time. Once, Mother had remarked that she hadn't seen Freddy for a few days and sent me up to see if he was all right. His bed was just behind the door of his freezing attic room. As I peered round, I could see from the immobile hump under the blankets that he was in bed. There was no movement whatsoever and I immediately sensed that something was wrong. I quickly went in and pulled the blanket back. Freddy was lying there unconscious, and his left eye, the one closest to me, had popped out of its socket. It looked unbelievably ghoulish. I screamed and ran to the top of the stairs, where I carried on shrieking. Everyone came running up and an ambulance was called. Freddy had developed an abscess in the space behind the eye socket, and it had pushed his eye outward. He was only a few hours from septicaemia and death – but nobody in that strange and insular house of ours even remarked on how Freddy could lie alone and unconscious in bed for so long and not be missed.

Jimmy had grown so fast that none of his civilian clothes fitted him. In the afternoon, Mother took him shopping. They returned burdened with packages containing a tweed jacket and flannels and some shirts. When Father saw the quantity of clothing, he exploded, even though Mother protested that this was Jimmy's Christmas present.

'He can't be expected to walk around in his blues when he's home on leave,' she said.

'Why not?' Father demanded. 'I did when I was his age. I didn't have a mother to squander money on my back. Whatever I got, I had to pay for myself. Jimmy has chosen to leave home, now it's up to him to keep himself.' Mother saw red. In her mind, it was all Father's fault that her beloved elder son had had to go. She screamed at Father that he had spent all her money on God knew what nefarious schemes, on women, and on clothes for his own back.

While the battle raged, Jimmy and I caught the bus to Herne Hill, where I introduced him to Betty and the Padsmeres. Their house, with comfortable chintz-covered sofas and armchairs, thick carpets, and a family who sat in the sitting room before the fire together, watching TV, seemed an actual home. In the same way that we didn't possess a refrigerator, nor a washing machine, neither did we have a television set. The sum total of our entertainment was listening to the radio, reading, and playing games. In fact, the television was the real reason why I went to visit them. The BBC was the only channel available. The evening started off with *Children's Hour*, followed by the news. Then there was a 'toddlers' truce' when the airwaves went dead so mothers could get the children to bed. After dinner, adult viewing consisted of a discussion or a panel game, a play, and the news again. 'God Save the Queen' concluded the evening, and in homes up and down the land people really did stand up in respectful silence while it was played.

Father thought none of this was worth watching. 'What is the point of spending so much on buying a television set for just three hours' viewing a night?' was his opinion. 'It's no different from the radio, only you can see their faces, and ugly ones at that.' He could have added that he was never in during the evenings to watch it in any case, so why did we need to be indulged?

The Padsmeres had mince pies, shortbread, and sherry to hand around to their guests. Mr and Mrs Padsmere drank neat gin. We played cards for an hour, but, fuelled by booze, it wasn't long before Betty's parents started to quarrel. At first, they directed little barbs at each other, but soon these grew more spiteful in tone. I was sad that her parents seemed as bad as mine. I looked at Jimmy and he nodded, as if answering me – it was time for us to go, before things got too heated.

'Next time you come, you lovely boy, bring Georgie-Porgie with you,' Mrs Padsmere giggled, plastering Jimmy with wet kisses. 'Georgie-boy's a real man, unlike my dear husband, who's just a fat slob, ain't that so, fat slob?' I froze. It seemed that even if my father wasn't present, he could still start a quarrel.

'Shut up, you bitch,' Mr Padsmere retorted, gin dripping off his handlebar moustache.

Jimmy and I quickly left, walking home through light snow. When we got to the corner of Half Moon Lane and Village Way, we saw, backlit by a street light, a glorious sight: with branches laced with snow, an almond tree had forgotten the season and was in bloom, floating above the pavement like a Degas dancer. I stopped to absorb the scene.

'Everything is so beautiful,' I finally sighed.

'No it's not,' said Jimmy. 'I wish I could have finished school and stayed at home – but how could I with him here?'

'Oh, Jimmy, do you hate it?'

'It's all right,' he shrugged. 'I'm doing fine, but I do get lonely.' I suddenly had the overwhelming urge to tell Jimmy about Richard, about the happiness I had reached out for on those nights at the flat. I wanted my brother to know that happiness did exist somewhere, along with peace, but I was just too ashamed. I knew Jimmy would be utterly shocked. So, instead, as we walked, sliding on icy pavements, I talked of other things, none of them really important. I tried to capture the way we had been together, before he'd left home, but Jimmy had changed too much during the time he'd been away. We turned up our street. From the church opposite, carols floated on the night air. It was midnight as the two of us stood there, side by side, staring at the house, the night, the stars overhead. It felt good to have my brother next to me again. Had he noticed how much his younger sister had changed? If so, he didn't say. But I had. More than he, or even I, realised.

'Remember how much fun we had in Cornwall?' Jimmy suddenly asked. 'When we were kids? Remember how I'd take you hunting?' I nodded. I did remember.

'Let's go in,' I said. The cold was eating its way beneath my coat. While we stood lingering outside by the gate, reluctant to go in, I could see the shimmer of my frosted 'tree' in the window of the sitting room. 'They'll be waiting up for us to put out the Christmas presents.'

In the morning, after breakfast, Mother told me to take some of my mince pies and a Christmas card round to the Schultzes, our Jewish neighbours. I wrapped the warm plate in a clean cloth and put it in the basket. As I walked the few doors up the street in my new red jersey that Mother had managed to find the time to knit, I could smell the heady perfume Jimmy had given me. It was a new variety, Coty's 'Lily of the Valley', which came in a little white bottle with a kind of plastic wand attached to the top that you dipped in, then dabbed behind the ears and on the wrists.

'Come in, Rose, come on in,' Mrs Schultz greeted me warmly. 'Happy Christmas to you!'

'I wasn't sure if you celebrated Christmas,' I said.

'Oh, Christmas, ja, we celebrate everything.' She laughed at her joke and took the basket, peeping under the cloth. 'Mince pies! Are they kosher?'

I hesitated. 'Well, I'm not sure. How would I tell?'

'You made the pastry with butter, ja?' I nodded. 'And what about the filling? Does it have suet in it?'

'I suppose so,' I said.

'Never mind, it's Christmas. We can ignore kosher for Christmas,' she laughed.

I went into their kitchen, which was warm and, as usual, smelled deliciously of coffee. Ruth and Clara were there, still eating breakfast. They chorused 'Happy Christmas!'

'See what Rose has brought,' Mrs Schultz said. 'Come and sit down, Rose. Have a cup of coffee with us and one of your delicious mince pies.' I sat at the table as the coffee was poured. In the warmth, the strong smell of Lily of the Valley rose up and threatened to swamp me. Suddenly, my mouth filled with acid and I got up and ran to the kitchen sink. It was filled with pans, so I flew through the back door and was sick on the path.

'Oh, too much chocolate in your Christmas stocking, I think,' Mrs Schultz said, following me. 'I tell Ruthie and Clara, watch the chocolates.' After a while, I was able to return indoors and sit at the table again.

'A glass of cold water, hey?' Mrs Schultz said, offering me some. 'Drink it, you'll feel better in a moment.'

But I knew I wouldn't be feeling better for a long time, for I suddenly realised what I had been avoiding.

Christmas Day passed in a blur. I was too numb with the enormity of my situation to enjoy it. Even cooking the traditional fat goose made me so nauseous I couldn't eat it. Crazily, I saw bizarre irony in that. My goose was cooked, all right, thoroughly cooked, and I was the one who would be growing fat. Alone in the icy cavern of my room, my breath rising like a cloud above my head, I started to laugh hysterically. What would be the solution? Gin in the bathtub? Jumping out of the window?

Granny came upstairs to see me, worried because I had refused to eat lunch. Perhaps she was wiser than I realised, this woman who had seen so much. She sat on my bed, huddled into a thick woolly.

'Not even a dog could be expected to sleep in a room as cold as this,' Granny remarked. 'Why don't you light the fire?'

'Daddy doesn't let us have coal for our bedrooms,' I said.

'No wonder you're ill,' she said.

'I'm not ill.'

Granny looked at me keenly. 'You look ill, Rose. You look feverish. Have you taken your temperature?'

'No,' I muttered, seeing that perhaps I had better let everyone think I was poorly. How else could I explain the state I was in? 'I might have caught the flu at Betty's yesterday.'

'Aspirin, hot water and lemon, and a hot water bottle in bed,' she prescribed, getting up. 'I only hope I don't catch it. The elderly are susceptible to influenza. Do you want the doctor?'

I shook my head. 'I'll go to bed, Granny. I'll be all right in a day or two.'

⏤

That year Boxing Day was on a Monday, meaning all theatres were closed. On Tuesday afternoon I got up and dressed and caught the bus up to the Old Vic. I didn't even know if there was a matinée that day, and if there was, of which play. Richard wasn't expecting me, so the only way I would be able to see him, short of hanging about outside, or waiting in the Cave for hours, was to try to bluff my way in at the stage door. I told the doorman that I was Richard

Burton's cousin, just down from Wales. Unfortunately, many fans often had the same idea and used the same ruse. And then he electrified me: 'Mr Burton was here earlier, with his wife, but they've gone now in any case.'

His wife! I thanked him and numbly turned away. I reached St George's Circus and looked around in confusion. Disoriented by the many roads, and not having noticed in which direction I had walked, I was quite lost. I walked some more until I recognised the Imperial War Museum with its big guns outside. Its dome had once been the organ room of the Bedlam madhouse. I knew it only because I had been here once before with the school. I looked around for a bus, but it was that time of the day when nothing seemed to be running. In the end, I stopped someone in the street and asked the way to Camberwell. After that, I would know the way home. I trudged all the way, arriving with feet and legs sore, my heart broken, my world destroyed, my foolish fantasies shredded. It is almost impossible to describe or to recapture that particular degree of adolescent agony. It was so devastating, so utter, that I truly believed I would never survive it.

The sense of shock and grief lasted for days. It was his deceit that slew me. 'Some day . . . we'll seek adventures. I'll take you with me,' he had said. He had made that promise. He had said that he loved me. Hadn't he?

Early in the New Year, I telephoned the stage door from the red phone box at the bottom of our road, pushing the penny into the slot with frozen fingers. I called an hour before the performance when I knew that Richard would be there, getting ready. The doorman was very reluctant, but I convinced him that it was an emergency. I can't remember what I said, but I must have sounded so desperate that he called Richard to the phone. When Richard came on the line, I blurted, 'It's Rose.'

It was so unusual for me to phone, that for a moment he was confused. 'Who?'

'Rose, it's Rose.'

'What the hell!' he exclaimed, angry. 'You can't do this. I've a good mind to hang up.'

'No!' I said. 'Please don't!'

'Well, then, what is it?'

'I have to see you.'

I think he knew from the tone of my voice. After a silence, he sighed. 'I'll be in the flat tomorrow afternoon, at noon. Will that do?'

'Yes, thank you,' I said humbly, and hung up.

It seemed hours until the next day. When we met, he didn't greet me normally, as he usually did, and I felt very unsure of myself and afraid. My voice wavered horribly as I blurted out the news. I made it sound muddled: I started to tell him about the Lily of the Valley, then I changed tack and said how much I loved the scent of the flowers, I even digressed to say we had some growing in the front garden, while he grew impatient and strode about the room, drumming his fingers on the furniture.

'Get to the point, get to the point,' he said. 'What's this all about?'

So I had to tell him.

'I'm pregnant,' I said, the first time I, myself, heard the words spoken. Even though he must have expected this, he was still shocked. He stared at me for a long time.

'Are you sure? Yes, you would be. Well, it was inevitable. Damn, damn, damn!'

While he raged, I sat in a chair, watching him anxiously.

'Well, you'll have to get rid of it,' he finally said.

'Yes, I know. I know you're married.'

'Well, it's no secret.' He had never once mentioned a wife to me, but now he no longer seemed to care about the deceit. He came over to where I was huddled in an armchair and crouched before me. He took my hands between his and looked into my eyes. 'Look, love, it will be all right, I promise. I'll take care of everything. Okay? Can you meet me here tomorrow? I'll have it sorted out.'

That night, I slept badly, not worried about the right or wrong, but scared about what was going to happen. There was no question in my mind. I couldn't go through with having a child; it was a shame I couldn't face. I would rather have thrown myself off Waterloo Bridge. Just thinking of the strife and tension that already existed in my home life was enough to make me realise this was my only real choice. My fear was that, whatever it was they did, it would hurt. That's what old wives' tales taught us: pain, disgrace, blood poisoning, and even death.

When we met the following day, Richard said it was all arranged for two days' time. He couldn't go with me, but he gave me some cash 'for expenses'.

'Everything else has been paid for,' he assured me. 'You don't have to worry about a thing.' I wanted to say, 'Oh, but I am worried, I am sick to my heart with fear,' but I was too numb to do more than stumble through what had to be done. I had already told Mother that I would be going youth hostelling, so she didn't ask any searching questions. I knew she wouldn't check up on me. I was to go to the doctor's surgery in Fulham with a bag packed with the things I would need for a two-day stay in hospital.

Dr D. – I will not divulge his real name – was expecting me. He was a short, quick man, with a high-domed forehead and round, owlish glasses with gold frames. After a brief examination, we went out to his car and he drove me across London to the cluster of streets behind Harley Street, to an expensive clinic where film stars and sheikhs went for treatment.

'Don't forget, the nurses will be told that you have bad period pains and we're treating you for that,' Dr D. instructed me. 'Don't tell them anything.'

'Won't they guess?' I asked.

'No, not the staff nurses who will look after you afterwards,' he said. Afterwards. To be an afterwards, there had to be a before and during. I started to panic. Dr D. looked at me intently, as if guessing. He squeezed my arm.

'You'll be all right,' he promised. 'This is just routine.'

I was shaking as we went up the steps and in through the doors. The receptionist looked up and smiled.

'Hello, dear. Your parents are abroad, are they?' I nodded.

'Well, Dr D. and we will take good care of you,' she said. 'You're in room six.'

———

This was nothing like I had expected. After the bloody waste and rats I'd seen outside our flat in Dalston, my idea of an abortion was sordid and terrifying. This was clean, soothing, and normal. It was quite apparent that the rich and famous had a different set of rules. When I woke from the anaesthetic, I felt nothing. I was floating on a cloud of painkillers. Nurses came and went and tended to me with gentle hands while I drifted between wake and sleep. While I slept, my body and the heartache of betrayal healed. I remember little of that quiet room, where even the sounds of traffic were subdued. There was no clock, so I had no concept of time. Hours were marked only by the changing angle of light through the tall window. I could see the sky, sometimes pale, sometimes dark and heavy with snow. A storm blew in, piling snow along the windowsill, and then ice formed on the outside of the double glazing, but all was warm and calm within. After a while, I noticed that a pigeon was crouched, out of the wind, in a corner of the windowsill. Sometimes a little gust would ruffle its feathers, but the bird didn't move. I worried that perhaps its red feet had frozen to the sill. Or perhaps, unable to fly away, it had starved to death.

I lay in my bed and worried about the pigeon, which at least took my mind off myself. I recited a little poem I remembered from my early childhood: Birdie, rest a little longer, till the little wings are stronger. So she rests a little longer, then she flies away. In the morning, the bird was still there. The angle of the sun moved round the side of the building and warmed the sill a little. As I watched, the pigeon stood up. Dipping its head up and down as if eating corn, it walked back and forth in the snow. I was relieved, and asked a nurse to feed it. She said she wasn't allowed to open the windows, and that they were in any case sealed.

I continued to watch that bird walk and nod and sometimes crouch in the corner until I drifted off. When I awoke, it had flown. In my naïve and girlish mind, it was a sign, a romantic omen straight from a Jane Austen novel that I would one day fly myself. When I came to leave, I felt nothing: no grief, no shame, no shock. It was as if the abortion had never happened, or, at least, as if it had happened to another girl. In fact, I had so much money left over, I even went shopping in Oxford Street and bought myself a new coat with a band of fur at the bottom, and some Russian-style suede boots with crossover lacing.

It was only the next day, when the painkillers wore off, that I felt extreme flashes of pain, but even that soon passed. A few days later, I read that Richard Burton had won the Evening Standard Drama Award. I stood on the dusty bare floorboards of the back room of Dick's shop, surrounded by bundles of newspapers, staring at my lover's photograph. He was wearing a dinner jacket, with a big bow tie. It was made so apparent to me that he and I lived in two different worlds. I tore out the page and stuffed it in my pocket, to read again later. After my recent experience, I had decided that the relationship with Richard was just too risky. I was determined to end it.

In fact, however, it was Richard who ended it, by simply not getting in touch. He had promised me, the last time I had seen him, that he would drop me a postcard with a date and a time when he would be at the flat. Because my family had no telephone, and although I had been reluctant to give him my home address, it seemed the only way that he could get in touch. But, no card came. I was both frantic and relieved. It was time to put Richard Burton behind me.

Twelve

❦

The Christmas holidays dragged drearily along. I returned to school, feeling low and depressed, unable to concentrate. Everything seemed so pointless. I started to spend more time with Betty Padsmere, going to her house once school was done for the day and I had prepared dinner at home and lit the fire. I would have tea with the Padsmere children, bread and butter and jam and cake.

After tea, Betty and I did our homework companionably in the comfort of her warm bedroom, listening to Radio Luxembourg on a little green and cream portable wireless with a pop-up lid, the replica of my own. Mr Padsmere worked in advertising and would arrive home drunk from a boozy day spent glad-handing his clients. It wasn't long before the arguments started. To drown it out, Betty would increase the volume on the radio in ratio to their nightly battles and we would work on, finishing essays, struggling with maths. The knowledge that we were in the same boat drew Betty and me closer for a while, but I still didn't feel sure enough of her to tell her my secrets. I think the real reason for holding back was that

Betty went to church twice on a Sunday, and I worried she would be more shocked than sympathetic.

Sometimes, as Betty and I worked, I would hear my father's voice floating up from downstairs, or his laughter joining Mrs Padsmere's piccolo giggle and Mr Padsmere's deep bass boom. When it was time for me to go home, usually around nine o'clock, I would creep down the stairs and out of the door, hoping I wouldn't be noticed and invited into the sitting room where the drinks were flowing and the air was thick with smoke. Once outside, invariably I would see Mr Padsmere's red Jaguar parked at a crazy angle, proof that he'd come home in jocular mood.

If Mother heard me come in, she would call from her room, 'Rose, is that you?' I would go in to see what she wanted, and she'd point at her bedside table, which was right next to her bed, and ask for her cigarettes, or her glasses. She could have reached them perfectly well, but I knew she was lonely and wanted someone to talk to, so I would get her a cup of tea and then perch on her bed while she sat up and drank it.

'Did you see your father there?' she always asked, not bothering to say where 'there' was.

I usually answered truthfully, 'No', since I hadn't really seen him, but Mother always knew.

'Why do you cover up for him, Rose?' she would sigh.

'I'm not,' I'd protest. 'I didn't see him.' Then I would let myself down by muttering something like, 'He wasn't doing anything.'

I think I said it more to keep the peace and to make Mother feel better, than to defend Father. We never talked about what he could have been up to, what 'doing anything' could have been. I knew he was a philanderer. What I didn't realise, because she seemed so old and my father's women were all young, was that in Mrs Padsmere, my father saw a soul mate, a woman who enjoyed a good time.

The seventh day of February was memorable that year for two things: it was the Lenten Eve, which in those more religious times we took note of, at least to the extent of giving up some small pleasure for a few weeks, and, more memorably, the Padsmeres decided to throw a party. They said it was 'to get the fasting off to a bang'. They weren't serious about the fasting, of course. When we were asked at school in religion class what our sacrifice was to be, I said that I would give up my passion, Fry's peppermint cream bars. Privately, it was Richard whom I told myself I would give up totally and for ever. If he sent that card during Lent, I would ignore it. I was certain.

Mother had also been invited to the 'Lenten Frolic' at the Padsmeres', and, as usual, she had declined, but her intuition must have been working overtime because she suddenly changed her mind.

'It's about time I saw what the old goat is up to over there,' she said.

'All they do is drink,' I assured her. 'It's very boring.'

'Well, boring or not, I'm going,' she stubbornly declared.

I had been asked to go to keep Betty company. Her little brothers were spending the night with their grandmother, but Betty was remaining at home. That night, it started to snow again. Father had a problem with the windscreen wipers, which didn't seem to like the weight of it. He cursed and swore as we juddered along in fits and starts while he crouched over the wheel peering through the smeared windscreen. 'George, we should get out and walk,' Mother said, several times, but Father just kept on going.

By the time we got to there, the party was in full swing. Mrs Padsmere's idea of a good party was plenty to drink, and playing what she called parlour games. The first, in keeping with the theme of the evening, was for everyone to stand up and confess what they would be giving up for Lent. Betty and I had planned to stay in her room out of harm's way, but Mrs Padsmere, splashing gin all the way up the stairs to the top of their tall house, came to fetch us.

'Now, girls, don't be so standoffish,' she said. 'Everyone's asking for you.' She wouldn't take no for an answer so, reluctantly, Betty and I went down.

'Look what I found lurking in the ivory tower!' Mrs Padsmere shouted, as she pointed at Betty and me. 'The two virgins!'

Everyone cheered and clapped while Betty and I stood in a blush of embarrassment.

'Leave them alone,' my mother said, quite distinctly.

'Oh, it's only fun, don't be such a bore,' said Mr Padsmere. He was over at the well-stocked bar. 'Come on, let's play the game.'

'The game, the game,' Mrs Padsmere warbled, pushing us on to the sofa. 'Me first! For Lent, I shall give up . . . yes, I shall give up Gordon's!' She emptied her glass and sashayed across to the bar, holding it out for a refill. 'From now on I shall drink Tanqueray!' she said, and everyone laughed.

'Did you know that Tanqueray comes from Malacca? The Dutch invented it,' my mother noted, speaking to no one in particular.

'Come on, Anne,' my father said. 'No one wants to know that.'

'No, we just want to drink it!' someone shouted. More laughter ricocheted about the room while my mother flushed red. The game progressed, becoming noisier and crueller and cruder in tone. Mrs Padsmere pushed her way forward again and shrieked that she was giving up wearing any undies and, with a quick flash, lifted her skirt. Everyone screamed again with laughter, like parrots at the zoo, while I watched my mother grow more stiff and awkward, her conversation more stilted. She interrupted at all the wrong times. It was evident that nobody wanted to listen to anything she had to say. For a woman who could be very funny, she seemed to freeze and become rigid when with strangers. I couldn't bear it any longer, so Betty and I escaped back to the sanctuary of her room. Betty threw herself on to her bed.

'I loathe them! They're so moronic,' she said.

The party continued downstairs. We could hear the racket even above the records we played. Nobody came to get me to say that it was time to go home, and eventually I fell asleep on Betty's divan that was heaped with cushions and doubled as a sofa.

When I woke in the morning, Betty was asleep in her bed. Everything seemed very quiet. I crept downstairs and into a sub-layer of stale perfume, drink, and tobacco. Empty bottles littered the hall and half-filled glasses were on every surface, as if guests had abandoned their drinks on the way out of the door. I peeped into the sitting room. The curtains were still drawn and a few lights were on in the dining room beyond the double doors. There, wreathed in clouds of smoke, I saw my father, Mr Padsmere, and two other men in the midst of a card game. There was no sign of Mrs Padsmere. My mother was asleep on one of the big chintz sofas, covered with her coat. Even in repose, her face looked tired and sad.

As I was about to back out of the room, Mother opened an eye.

'Rose, is that you?' she whispered. 'I want to go home.'

Nobody noticed. The game of cards didn't even falter as I helped her up. In the hall, Mother and I put on our coats and boots and escaped into the dazzling icy white world beyond the front door. The street was hushed and quiet. The bare branches of the ornamental cherry trees, denuded of their leaves, were like the naked spokes of big black umbrellas against all that whiteness. Our footsteps broke the untouched layer of snow along the pavement. Despite the fact that it was a normal working day, it seemed as if Londoners had taken one look out of their windows and returned to bed.

We reached the main road running alongside Brockwell Park, which rose to the skyline in a gentle sweep. Once this road had been the bed of the Effra stream, along whose shallow, gravelled bed wagoners and carters had travelled with their heavy loads. Now, empty of traffic, it looked like that long-lost stream again as it might have done when covered with ice in the depth of winter.

'There won't be any buses,' I said.

'No, we'll walk,' said Mother. She was brooding and silent, hunched in her coat. At the park gates, she said fretfully, 'I don't want to go home. Let's walk in the park.'

'But, Mother, it's freezing. And what about Gracie?'

'I keep telling your father, we really should have a telephone, but he refuses to listen. Your grandmother is there, she'll see to Gracie. I don't want to go home yet.'

'The path is steep and looks icy,' I protested. 'You might fall.'

She didn't answer, so we turned in to the big cast-iron gates. Swaddled in warm clothing, our heads festooned in woollen scarves, we must have looked like medieval shepherds setting off across the fields in search of lost sheep.

Holding on to each other, we crunched up between wintry trees. The distinctive trident marks where birds had hopped earlier, looking for food, made long lines in the snow, but apart from that there was no other sign of life. At the top, the path widened into a sweeping forecourt lined with park benches. Each bench was piled with snow that had taken the shape of a sleeping person. Dead men could be lying there, as if in a morgue, and we would never have known.

After the effort of the walk my face glowed and I unwound the scarf. We could see for miles in every direction over a vast expanse of billowing snowfield. To our left was Brixton, ahead was the long ridge of Herne Hill, and to our right was the wonderfully named Knight's Hill, where knights really had jousted once. Beyond that, on the horizon, lay Dulwich Woods. I tried to imagine what all this had been like when it had been the private gardens of the beautiful old mansion behind us. What views those long-ago Georgians must have enjoyed as they strolled along this terrace in their curled and powdered wigs, the women in their crinolines.

Mother sighed wearily.

'How did I ever get to be here?' she asked. I didn't know if she meant this literally or philosophically. 'Well, let's walk,' she said, 'it's cold just standing.'

We followed the walls of the house toward the back. To the side, three cedar trees stood, dark sentinels against the glittering field of snow. Mother drew her breath and stopped.

'A deodar!' she exclaimed, for the first time showing signs of animation.

'They look like cedars,' I said.

'The one on the left is a blue Atlas, from the Atlas

Mountains,' she told me. 'The one on the right is a cedar of Lebanon, and the middle one is a deodar. It's sacred to Hindus and comes from the Himalayas. Go and have a look at the deodar. Its needles are almost two inches long. The cones are as big as a man's fist and grow only on the female and bisexual trees.'

This was how Mother had spoken the previous night, full of information that no one wanted to listen to at a wild party. She had a natural interest in everything, and knew so much. At one time, she had studied botany and horticulture at Calcutta University and had gone for many long orchid-collecting trips in the mountains.

'Do you mean that there are three types, male, female, and bisexual?' I asked, and she nodded, as if pleased that someone finally wanted to have a conversation with her.

'Absolutely,' she said. 'I used to walk beneath forests of huge deodars in Amritsar. There's a luminous lake which the locals say is mist that traps moonlight and starlight. The Milky Way makes a great arc across the sky, and when the sun rises and hits the glaciers, it's as if they're on fire. From across the valleys you can hear the crackle and snap of the ice warming.'

'I remember the smell of the pines and the snow,' I replied, suddenly caught up in her memory. 'The snow was higher than me, and they used to shovel deep paths through it. It towered above my head.'

'You were born in a thunderstorm,' Mother said, almost dreamily. She didn't seem to feel the cold at all now, although my feet were frozen in their fur boots. 'We had rented a cottage at Jutogh, on one of the seven ranges of Simla. There was no running water, no electricity, just oil lamps. I was alone, except for the servants. Your father was in New Delhi. The storms can be terrifying and last for hours, and we were right in the middle of one so violent that the house shook. They have even been known to start avalanches. My contractions began, so I sent the gardener to fetch the doctor. He took hours and I was on the point of giving birth to you when he finally arrived. He got me up and out of my bedroom and on to the kitchen table. There was a lantern swinging overhead and he had the ayah standing by. All the servants were huddled on the porch. The doctor wouldn't have them in the house because they were men. They were terrorised by the spirits that were causing the storm and wept and wailed like banshees. It set the dogs howling, and then the wolves. You could hear them howling from peak to peak. In my delirium, I heard the roar of tigers and the shriek of owls. A bad omen. In the convent I used to hear the screams of victims being murdered by thugees in the forest outside. I heard it again, then, and I knew I was going to die.'

'It sounds very dramatic,' I said. It was the first time that I had heard this.

'It was dreadful, quite awful,' Mother continued. 'The storm raged and raged, and you could hear my screams above it. Dr Macmillan told me to stop it, that it would upset Jimmy. But how could I stop? I was going out of my mind with pain. You were the wrong way round and just wouldn't come out. I was in labour for twenty hours, and in the end, he had to cut you out.'

'A caesarean?' I said, shocked.

'No, he cut me below, as if he were gutting a fish, and dragged you out.'

'Oh, Mother,' I said.

'Then he sewed me together, but complained he couldn't see properly in the light of the lamp. He had no anaesthetic whatsoever. He'd come with nothing, just some forceps and a few needles.'

'I'm surprised you had any more babies after me,' I said.

'That was your father. He was thoroughly selfish. It was always what he wanted, never any consideration for others.' She spoke bitterly, but now I saw, or thought I saw, what was the cause of all the conflict between them.

At the back of the house the path wound by the lovely old stable block, with a weather vane hanging with icicles, and led to a walled garden. We passed through the iron gate, pushing it against the snow that lay thick on the ground. A flock of white gulls rose from the lawn that surrounded the frozen pond in the centre. They screamed angrily before taking off over the roof of the mansion. Espaliered trees, symmetrically carved shrubs, and neat yew hedges were all hidden beneath a thick blanket of snow. The path, visible only because of a slight indentation, followed the walls, past a well, toward a small summer house in the far corner that was overhung by a black mulberry, its dark trunk and branches looking sooty against the snow.

'Shall we go in the shelter?' I asked.

'No, it will be too cold,' Mother replied. She turned and walked on, so I had no choice but to follow. In the far corner, almost hidden behind some kind of climbing plant, probably a wisteria judging by the thickness of the trunk, was a small sundial. It was on a tiny brick pier that jutted out from the wall. I wondered how it could tell the time since the sun would not be overhead here all day. Much of the time, the dial would be in shadow. On it was carved the date, 1775, and an inscription: 'So Doct. Ho In D.'

'That means sol docet horas in die,' something like, "the sun tells the time, the hours, during the day".'

'But not today,' I said. 'There's no sun.'

'No. And we had better go home.' But she stood without moving. She sighed again. 'I wish I could live in a walled garden. I should have been a nun in a cloister.'

'But then you wouldn't have had us.'

'Oh, you would have had some other mother. It wouldn't have made that much difference.'

'How could we have had another mother? We wouldn't have existed.'

Again, my mother surprised me. 'In the greater scheme of things your souls would have found their way to other vehicles.'

'You mean, like reincarnation?'

'Of course,' she said. 'Your destiny is in being reborn, not who you're reborn as. It's what billions of Hindus and Buddhists believe. Who are we to say they are wrong?'

'You don't really believe that, do you?' I asked.

'I don't believe in God, at least, not in the god painted on the walls of the convent chapel, along with all the demons that scared me to death as a child,' she replied. 'Sitting in chapel, gazing upward at it all, with no one to tell me I wasn't about to be stuck on a pitchfork and grilled, I was so scared I could hardly breathe.' She smiled briefly. 'Come on, Rose, let's go home.'

That afternoon, several more feet of snow were dumped across much of the country. By evening, the vale of Dulwich and its surrounding hills were cut off. London came to a standstill. Driving was impossible and Father used it as an excuse to stay on at the Padsmeres' doing, as Granny put it, God knows what, for another night.

A few days later, it was Saint Valentine's Day. It was also Mother's birthday. We hadn't had any post for days, but, nevertheless, I was downstairs hovering in the freezing mausoleum of the hall in the morning, half convinced that now Richard had my address, there would be a Valentine's card or a letter for me. There was nothing. The postman didn't come. I went back upstairs and found Mother's card and present and took them into her room, where she was still in bed, snatching another half hour before she had to go to work.

'Happy birthday!' I said, hiding my misery with a false cheerfulness.

Mother kept the blankets over her head and an arm emerged.

'Let me see,' she said. I sat down next to her and opened the envelope. The card had violets on it, the early spring flower I have always associated with my mother. 'Open the present too,' she said.

'Don't you want to do it?'

'No, Rose, you do it for me.'

I untied the pink ribbon and spread the wrapping paper out. I had bought her two pairs of thick ribbed stockings and a pretty silk scarf.

'Very nice, Rose, you're a good girl,' Mother said. 'Put them in my top drawer.'

'Shall I bring you breakfast in bed?' I offered.

'No, make me some coffee and I'll come down in a moment. I dread going out in this weather.'

'Mother, don't you like your birthday? You never seem to enjoy it.' My question seemed to pain her.

'I hate it,' she said. 'I always have. I don't know if your grandmother has ever mentioned Donald.'

'Yes, she showed me his photograph. The baby who died.'

'Well, he died on my birthday. February fourteenth,

1917. I committed an unforgivable sin. I survived and Baby Donald died. He could do no wrong. All of my brothers were sacred, but Donald was the apple of my mother's eye. His death turned her hair grey overnight.'

'But Granny said her hair turned grey after it was cut off when she got malaria.'

'She got malaria because she spent night after night lying on his grave without a mosquito net,' said Mother. 'She's lucky she wasn't carried off by a tiger, though perhaps she wanted to die. At Donald's funeral she attacked me and screamed that I should have died. That's why I was sent away to school when I was just three and a half years old. She wanted me out of her sight.'

'Oh, Mother, that's so sad,' I said. Gracie was four and a half. I couldn't imagine her being sent away to school. Mother shrugged.

'I remember praying to Jesus in the convent, asking him to take me instead and send Baby back. I didn't go home again until I was nine. Oh, my father would come to visit me if I was in trouble and the nuns sent for him, but my mother never came.'

Moved by those images of a lost and lonely little girl, I wanted to say something nice, perhaps even kiss her, but I knew she would rear away. We didn't have that kind of relationship, none of us did. Her childhood had been so cold and unloving, she found it hard to show need or warmth. Everything was so locked inside her own heart, like a tight knot, that it had become the pattern of our family, each one of us insular and isolated under the same roof.

Downstairs, as I made Mother's coffee, I noticed that Granny was pale and withdrawn, with dark shadows beneath her eyes, as if she hadn't slept well.

'Good morning, Granny,' I said.

'Good for some,' she replied dourly. She took her breakfast into her room and closed her door, something she had never done before. I sighed and put an extra spoonful of sugar in the coffee, hoping, somehow, that it might sweeten the day a little.

Thirteen

❦

Early in March, at the end of our English class, Miss Wilton produced a small flyer.

'We're going to see *Othello*,' she announced with a smile. 'I have managed to get tickets for the entire class. It has come out of the school fund.' Everyone gasped and there was a buzz of conversation. I sat frozen in my seat. I decided instantly that I would pretend to be ill, and therefore exempt from going, but as the hours and days ticked away, just the thought of seeing Richard again, if only at a distance, was too overpowering.

The next Saturday, we all piled on to several differently numbered buses that ran through Camberwell straight up to Waterloo, where the Old Vic was. We were required to wear our school uniforms so that we would be able to find each other on arrival at the theatre, like coloured ants reassembling. As we lined up, I felt very conspicuous, and much too mature for the rest of my class, who were all laughing and twittering like birds on the pavement. That's when I glanced up and saw Richard walking by with that quick, almost aggressive stride, looking preoccupied, as all the actors did when hurrying past fans to get to the stage door. Something, electricity, intuition, call it what you will, made him glance my way. Our gazes locked. As he took in my navy-blue school uniform and the neat little velour hat, he looked visibly shocked. His eyes widened, his stride faltered, before he went on, disappearing behind the heavy door.

It felt strange to sit in a sea of schoolgirls who giggled and gossiped, like a flock of magpies. I was a part of them, yet I also felt estranged and remote. After all, I was the girl who'd made love to one of the actors who was about to come on stage. The tension was almost unbearable until the house lights dimmed and the curtain slowly rose on a street in Venice. Tall, graceful John Neville, as Iago, appeared with Roderigo. I sat in a state of high tension as the first scene continued, barely taking it in, aflame for when Othello would finally appear in Scene Two. When Richard stepped on stage, I barely contained a gasp. He looked terrifying, dark and dangerous. He seemed to glare out over the auditorium like a black panther through the bars of a cage. I didn't recognise him at all. Suddenly I felt a burning desire rise up inside me. It took me quite by surprise, caught me unawares. I wanted this powerful person, this actor, this man named Richard Burton to make love to me so badly that I trembled. I think perhaps this was the first time I felt a purely physical longing for Richard. This feeling wasn't about his wit, or his ability to quote poets at the drop of a hat. It had to do with the dark and dangerous ache that ran through my young body.

Miss Wilton had informed us that we were free to go home on our own after the play if we wished to do so. I waited in line with my friends since they were intent on getting autographs. My feelings standing there with them were very mixed. He had already seen me, so what difference did it make? But then I didn't want to seem like the other screaming teenage girls. I suppose I had secretly hoped all along that he would notice me when he came in to the theatre, perhaps send me a signal. If he didn't, I might never see him again and the thought of that was too overwhelming.

Twenty minutes later, when the stage door at the side of the theatre finally opened and Richard stepped out, he was instantly mobbed. Dashing forward, my classmates thrust their programmes at him to sign, while I stood to one side, just absorbing him. He looked tired, his dark hair curled in damp tendrils on his neck and brow, as if he had just showered. Thinking I was staring too hard, as if for attention, I dropped my eyes. When I looked up again, I saw that he was staring right at me. He quickly scribbled on a piece of paper what would seem to be his autograph, and handed it to me. I waited until he was gone and I'd broken away from the other girls, before I read it. It was a note. 'Come to the flat in half an hour. Don't change.'

When Richard opened the door at the flat, he stood looking down at me, at my school uniform.

'Well, well, well,' he said at last. 'Come on in.'

Sheepishly, I went ahead of him up the stairs. I could feel his eyes burning a hole in me as he took in my bare legs and neat white socks. Upstairs, he closed the door and then turned.

'Are you all right, love?' he asked.

I knew what he meant. I blushed and nodded. The awkward moment was over. He indicated my uniform.

'Who would have guessed,' he said. 'You do realise, don't you, this is every man's fantasy?'

I didn't know what he meant, so I asked him. His sweep of the hand took me in, from head to foot.

'The shy schoolgirl. Bugger me, Miss Austen, it's incredible.'

'You must have known I was quite young,' I said, forgetting that I had done all in my power to dress and look older than I was.

'Of course I knew,' he said. 'But I thought you were seventeen or so. How old are you? Sixteen? At least you're not below the age of consent. Are you?'

'I'm fourteen,' I admitted sheepishly. 'I'll be fifteen in July.' I didn't add, 'I was still thirteen when we first met,' because he looked shocked enough as it was.

'Bloody hell. Is that the truth? Yes, you wouldn't lie about that.' He walked to the window and closed the curtains. 'You realise what this means, don't you?' I shook my head. 'Underage sex. Don't you know how many years I could get? A lot more than poor old Oscar Wilde got for buggering the Marquess of Queensberry's pretty young boy.'

Still, I didn't get it. I stood there like a schoolgirl on the mat, up before the head.

'Years? What do you mean, years?'

'Having sex with a minor is a crime. Perhaps not as bad as being sent down for being a queer, but nevertheless, it's against the law. I could get seven years in the clink if this ever comes out.'

'Seven years!' Now it was my turn to be shocked. 'But you must have guessed I was under age, even with the lipstick and the heels I didn't look that grown up.' It was true. He was too old, too sophisticated, too well-travelled not to have recognised my inexperience.

'Sixteen, maybe, but not this young.'

'Well, it's a bit like locking the stable door after the

horse has bolted, isn't it?' He reached out and touched my face with the back of his fingers. 'What's done is done. You're here now, and I'd better live up to my reputation of a cad by taking full advantage of you.'

'You do want me to stay?' I asked.

He grasped me firmly by both shoulders, and looked down at me.

'Rose, this is the most dangerous thing I have ever done,' he said. 'Possibly the most foolish thing I have ever done. But yes, I want you to stay.'

Then he asked that I not take off my uniform.

'Why?'

'Because I want to make love to you just as you are,' he said.

What I recall most clearly about that day is the smell of the greasepaint. Even though he had washed most of the stuff away, there were remnants here and there on his face and neck, and the deeply evocative smell still lingered. But there was another smell lingering in the air as well, that of lemons. When I used the bathroom, jealous curiosity made me open the medicine cabinet. On the shelf was a bottle of Jean Naté body splash. I stared at the yellow and black label as if it were a serpent coiled there, something dangerous to the touch, but I reached out my hand anyway and grasped it. I unscrewed the silver cap and sniffed. Lemons. Richard had never used cologne, nor did he ever smell of lemons. 'Lemon' was a female kind of smell, wasn't it? This bottle of Jean Naté was not his. So whose was it?

When our allotted hour was up, abruptly, Richard asked if I would wear my school uniform sometimes when we met. From that request, I knew that he intended our affair to continue, and this became a frequent theme between us from then on. I went to the flat after that day perhaps a dozen times wearing my school uniform, the blue serge tunic and white blouse, all neat and starched and perfect.

He also said that he wanted to give me the money for a taxi home each time: 'I know I'm a disreputable bastard, but at least let me do that much.'

So I rode home in a taxi, not as Miss Austen, the provocative ingénue, but as Rose, the schoolgirl in her neat uniform, bare knees primly together, wearing her white socks and lace-up brown brogues. This was a different feeling. It was as if I were finally given permission to have this grown-up relationship, and yet still be the young girl I truly was.

———

When I returned home that evening, with the taxi dropping me off just up the street from my house, I found my mother in tears. She was at the piano in the sitting room, her hands idle in her lap, her face white and strained. She didn't ask if I had enjoyed the theatre.

'Mr Padsmere came,' she said immediately. 'He had something to tell me.'

'Betty's father?'

'Yes, your friend's father. Horrible man, with his quivering belly and moustache. He leered at me. He seemed to think that he and I could get together.'

My head was still full of the events of the evening. I wanted to retreat to my room and relive it all, but instead, I sat and listened.

'Did you know about this, Rose?' she asked. There was that eerie, quiet frenzy about her that used to put me instantly on my guard. It seemed another nervous breakdown lurked at each and every corner these days.

'Know about what?' I asked, cautiously.

'Your father and Mrs Padsmere have been having an

affair,' Mother said. 'It's been going on for weeks. They meet at her house in the afternoons.'

I stared at her, not knowing what to say, but not in the least bit surprised. The truth was, I think I had known it from the start. I had recognised the signs, but didn't want to admit them to anyone, not even myself, and especially not to Mother. The miracle was that my father hadn't blurted it out as he always did. A thought should have occurred to me at that moment: Richard was married too. Was his wife somewhere, wringing her hands all evening, wondering where her handsome husband was this time?

—

Richard and I began to see each other more frequently and would meet at the Cave now and then, but I always kept away from him. I remember one night, vividly. Richard, Keith Michell, Jeremy Brett, and Derek New – I think it was Derek New – were sitting in the booth nearest the door and having a grand time. It was remarkable how noisy and boisterous they got on innumerable cups of tea; although, having seen Richard's ever-present little flask, the innocent-looking tea could have been topped up with rivers or even lakes of Scotch.

I remember that Keith Michell was pretending his bra strap had broken and so he was fishing inside his sweater and plumping up his pretend 'boobs'. This was when Richard, talking in a falsetto lisp, pretended to be his 'friend', a female hairdresser. 'My falsies are always slipping, love,' Richard lisped. It was an hilarious sketch, and I began giggling from my own booth. When they realised they had a small audience, they started to play to the gallery. I think that was the one and only time that I felt a part of that exciting inner circle of actors, even if it was only at a distance. Richard and I never addressed each other directly at the Cave. My being dressed in gym slip and blazer, at his request, was like being camouflaged. A schoolgirl is a schoolgirl, after all, not someone whom a thirty-year-old well-known actor would be sleeping with.

In the midst of all the jokes, I heard Keith Michell ask, 'Rich, how's the lovely Claire?'

'She's well, just splendid,' Richard replied.

From the laughter, I suddenly knew that the 'lovely Claire' was another one of Richard's conquests. I felt a surge of jealousy. I wondered who she was, and when and where he met her. Did she also come to the flat? Was she the girl who used Jean Naté? How could I be so naïve as to think I was the only one? He was a lustful man, a man with strong sexual energy. During those two months while we had been apart, there would have been someone else. Wounded as I was, however, I knew I wouldn't stop our affair because I loved him with all the desperate intensity of youth.

As usual, we left separately. I went first, and he caught up with me. I couldn't help myself, my first words were, 'Who's Claire?'

'Ah,' he said. 'I wondered if you'd heard.'

'Yes, I heard. I bet she uses Jean Naté,' I said bitchily. 'It smells of lemons.'

'No, I don't believe Claire smells of lemons,' he mused. 'Claire was a girl I knew in Spain. I loved her once, but now I love you. Claire was a dry martini. You, my love, are a cup of tea, and I can't do without my egg and chips and a cup of tea.' I started to laugh.

That night, in the flat, Richard got very drunk. Sometimes, I think it was the only way he could get to the sadder, more hurtful places inside himself. He was not talkative otherwise, but more the performer, quoting and reciting and singing. As much as he was virile, often making love several times in an evening, he didn't talk while it was happening. Only booze could fuel him to say more private things. This night, I kept on about the Jean Naté in the cabinet until he stormed into the bathroom, grabbed the bottle, brought it back to where I lay on the pink counterpane before the fire, and tipped its contents all over me.

'Here!' he shouted. 'You want bloody lemons, well, I'll give you lemons!' Then he bent and rubbed the cologne into my skin. '"Oranges and lemons, say the bells of Saint Clement's" . . . you want five farthings too? Here, have bloody five farthings.' At that, he grabbed his trousers and stood, emptying a pocket of change over me, shouting, 'Here comes the chopper to chop off your head, chip-chop-chip-chop!' The rain of coins hurt and I started to cry. At once, he stooped down and cradled me in his arms. 'Oh love, oh love, I can't help myself, I'm a bastard, I know it.' He reached out and grasped the bottle of whisky, swallowing directly from it, and I knew that the night would grow darker in mood. I had drunk a lot of champagne, too, and together we grew maudlin and tearful over the abortion. Then Richard started to ramble.

'We wanted a child so much, we've been trying for years, and when I get a girl with child, I have to destroy it, and this destroyed me,' he said. That's when I realised that it wasn't me this remorse was directed at, but his childless marriage. 'Ah, my dear Rose, do you really know, or care, what that did to me? The very essence of man is to give life, not to take it.'

Although we were drunk, this was serious, it felt too intense and searing for the moment. I was almost frightened by the enormity of the subject – I, too, had been feeling so much guilt over what had happened – but Richard wasn't finished with the self-flagellation. He talked of torn promises, of the things he had destroyed, of a childhood of emotional deprivation, of not being wanted, of his father who didn't give a toss about him, a man who cared for nothing, not for God nor even himself.

'How can I help being a mess?' he said, his words slurring as he gazed into the fire. 'How can I help it, pock-faced, driven by shame and guilt?' He was gone, sunk into depression, repeating himself, brooding and mumbling. He was angry at himself, and yet, when we made love again, there was a hint of desperate violence about it. We were like two lost souls who needed each other. We climaxed in a frenzy and again he came inside me, the painful lessons we'd just learned already forgotten in the heat of the moment. I crawled away from his embrace and shakily got to my feet. For the first time, I pulled back the covers and got into the neatly made bed in the unused bedroom. The sheets were cold and smooth, the pillows soft. My head sank deeply into them and I slept.

When I woke, Richard was dressed and moving around, clearing up the mess from the night before. He brought me my clothes, and a cup of tea. There was milk in the tea and I wondered where it had come from. Perhaps a milkman had left a pint on a nearby office doorstep, one that the tramps hadn't managed to steal before Richard did. Or, perhaps he had gone up to the Charing Cross Hotel, a couple of hundred yards away. Wherever he had found the milk, it was now in my cup of tea and I was quite pleased over his kind gesture.

'Come on love, drink up,' Richard said. 'People will be arriving for work soon.'

At Easter, I had arranged to go youth hostelling with some of my girlfriends, to Tanner's Hatch in Surrey. I had been hostelling before, but generally, since travelling was so expensive, I stuck to areas around London. The hostels were primitive, usually a bunk bed in a shared room, but were very inexpensive, considering the price also included breakfast. In exchange, we did a few chores which kept down the cost of running them. When I told Richard where I'd be going, he instantly said that he had most of Easter off and he would love to meet me there.

'You want to stay in the youth hostel with us?' I asked, astonished. 'With me and my friends?'

'No, of course not. We'll go to a hotel, you and I, make a night of it.' If he kept his word, which in my heart I doubted, it would be the first time I had ever seen him outside London, the first time we would be sharing a bed together.

As the weekend approached, I grew more excited. The plan was that I would spend the first night at the hostel, then somehow lose the others to meet him in the grounds of a nearby big house that was open to the public.

Tanner's Hatch was buried deep in the chalk escarpment area near Box Hill and was reached from a small railway halt. We left the train, shouldered our knapsacks, and looked on the map to find the Trackway, the old footpath that dated from Iron Age times across southern England, from Stonehenge to the Thames. Tanner's Hatch was a fourteenth-century cottage with wattle-and-daub walls and a thatched roof. There was no electricity and the water came from a well. Hidden in a hollow on the edge of a bluebell wood and surrounded by a flowering blackthorn hedge, it was enchanting, like something from a fairy story.

You could almost expect Snow White, or a gnarled witch, to greet you on the doorstep.

That night, tired from our long walk and replete with cheesy potatoes baked in the old bread oven, we sat by the inglenook fire and told each other ghost stories. The moon was just past its fullness that night, but it was hidden behind a thick layer of clouds in the overcast sky. When there was a scream in the wood, we almost leaped out of our skins.

'It's all right,' said the hostel warden. 'It's only a fox.'

In the morning I woke in my cramped little bunk beneath the thatched eaves. I was warm in my down sleeping bag, and for a few moments I snuggled cosily, relishing the warmth and the sweet smell of the wood fire drifting up from below. The room appeared strangely bright and white and I craned my head, trying to see out of the low dormer window. I unzipped my bag from the inside, and leaned on one elbow, all I had room for in the tight triangle of the thatch. I saw that my sleeping bag was covered with a white fluff. At first, I thought that it had burst, then I saw that it was snow, snow that had blown in through a hole in the roof in the night.

'It's snowing!' I shouted to the other girls. I scrambled out of the sleeping bag and, still in my pyjamas, ran across the bare floor to the little low window. I knelt there and peered out into a bright landscape. Snow billowed over grass and shrub and hedge, over the old well in the garden, softening the landscape, making it astonishingly beautiful.

I had already thought of my cover story on the way down the previous day. Box Hill, named after the great number of full-size box trees growing on its chalky flanks, had been the scene of a few picnics when I was a child and lived in Downside. I told my friends that while they rambled along the Trackway, I was going off to stay with an old friend in one of the nearby farms. I said I might stay the night, so not to expect me back that evening. They accepted that without question, and, immediately after breakfast I shouldered my knapsack and walked through the woods to the beautiful old estate of Polesden Lacey, where Richard had promised to be waiting. The path I followed was a sunken one between high banks on top of which were overgrown hedgerows on each side. Flocks of little birds, mostly finches, constantly flew across the lane ahead of me in groups as thick as clouds of butterflies.

I crossed the park and entered the gardens, following a wide flagstone path to a series of long ponds that were surrounded by tall cedars and the dark green of rhododendron bushes. It was a secluded spot, ferny and green and almost deserted, except for a solitary figure that walked along the far side of a pond. It was Richard. He was there! I was quite astonished to see him, on time and so out of place. To me, he represented the city, the lights and streets of London, the Old Vic and the Cave. Now, here he was, in a thick white fisherman's sweater. As he walked toward me, with his abundant dark curls and sculptured bones, all I could think of was *Wuthering Heights*. 'It's Heathcliff,' I told myself, smiling.

The snow had melted in the hot sun, but the hedges were filled with great drifts of blackthorn and cherry blossom, like snow overhead. We walked along the sunken path I had found that morning and again finches flew in excited flocks back and forth just ahead of us. It was amazing to see so many different varieties flying together: the gold, black and red flashes of goldfinches; the brilliant pink of the bullfinches' breasts, with their sooty black heads; the greenfinches' lime-green feathers; and chaffinches with their softer pinks and greys.

'It's a charm of finches,' I said.

'Yes, a watch of nightingales, a descent of woodpeckers, a congress of ravens, an ostentation of peacocks, and a tiding of magpies,' Richard replied. 'Not to mention a shiver of sharks and an ambush of tigers. It's like being in the middle of *The Magic Flute*.' Softly, he started to la-la the tune, then sang some of the words in perfect Italian. 'Do you know the story?' he asked.

'Yes, I went with my father to Covent Garden. It's about trials that people must go through to find their true love.'

'Some day, I'll take you to the opera and the ballet,' Richard promised. He paused. 'No, not the bloody ballet. I can't stand the bloody ballet. It's full of big muscly pansies, leaping and twirling about like fairies.'

At the end of the lane we crossed the field, toward a hilly wood. On the edge, where snow still lingered in drifts, there was a kind of little dell surrounded by a grove of silver birch just brushed with green, and a cherry tree that hung low. The entire bank was covered with purple violets and golden primroses. Richard stopped and pulled me down.

'What better place to make love than on Titania's floral bank,' he said.

'Here, in the open?'

'"Yet mark'd I where the bolt of Cupid fell . . ."' he quoted. 'And it's fallen right here. I want you now. "The lunatic, the lover and the poet, are of imagination all compact." Well, imagine it's a bank in Tuscany in the hot sun, and we are surrounded by the scent of wild thyme and rosemary.'

'You are a lunatic,' I laughed. 'We'll get soaking wet. There's still snow about.'

'Well, you've got a sleeping bag in that rucksack, haven't you? Get it out, Miss Austen. Get it out!'

I spread my sleeping bag and we made love out in the open. It was a wonderful experience to feel so abandoned and entirely natural, at one with the scents and smells of the countryside and warmed by the sun. The whole experience had a sweetness about it that I had never felt in the flat. That was enclosed, shaded in secrets. This was joyful and open.

Afterwards, I asked his plans. Would we walk perhaps to Box Hill and then find a hotel later? 'There's one near Box Hill,' I said, having discreetly asked the hostel warden. I had said it was for my parents, who wanted to walk in the area. Richard's words were a blow.

'I can't, love, it's too risky. You do see that, don't you? I mean, it would be risky enough if you were eighteen, but can you imagine me trying to sneak *you* in?'

Feeling rejected and let down, I walked back with him to where he had left his car.

'Do you want a lift back?' he asked nodding toward a grey Jaguar. I shook my head and he kissed me lightly on the cheek as he said good-bye. I watched as the big car spun around, leaving tyre tracks on the damp earth, and then disappeared back toward London. Saddened, I stayed for some time, watching the finches and listening to the quiet of the woods before I returned to the youth hostel to join my well-scrubbed, rosy-cheeked friends for supper. They looked so normal, but then, they hadn't been making love on a bank of wildflowers with a married older actor – they had been getting healthy exercise as befitted their age. I was the odd one out. With Richard's cautionary words still sounding in my head, I felt more than ever that my life was getting out of control. Being a living secret was getting too great a burden for a girl who was not yet fifteen.

―

When I returned home, it was to learn there had been a ruction at the Padsmeres'. Mr and Mrs Padsmere had drunk too much over Easter and had had a fight for the record books. They had ended up in the street, my father with them, all screaming at each other. When my father tried to drive away, Mrs Padsmere had flung herself across the bonnet of his car and Mr Padsmere had dragged her off by her ankles. Neighbours called the police.

'The police!' my mother cried, as she told me the story. 'Our family, involved with the police. I shall never live this down.'

Granny was grimly delighted.

'I knew things in that direction were getting out of control,' she noted. 'If the police bring charges against you, George, perhaps being locked up will do you some good. You'll have time to reflect.'

For once, Father sat there with a hangdog expression, not arguing. I think he really did feel remorseful.

'Do you think they'll press charges?' he asked.

'They certainly should,' said Granny.

'It was getting that car,' Mother moaned. I think she was more terrified that he could lose his job and we would end up destitute. 'I knew nothing good would come of it. It's made you too mobile. If I could meet the woman who gave you the money – and don't argue for I know you got it from a woman – I would wring her neck.'

Making his usual pained face, Father astounded us by letting slip that Granny had given him the money for the car.

'I got it aboveboard,' he declared. 'No woman was involved. Just her.'

'What?' Mother asked, astonished. She turned to look at my grandmother. Granny was instantly defensive.

'He told me I could find somewhere else to live if I didn't give it to him,' she said, and then she looked instantly sorry. Mother turned her anger back at my father.

'You blackmailed my mother?' she asked, incredulous. 'George, I will never forgive you for this. Never.'

I said nothing, just took my rucksack and went on up to my bedroom. I knew she would forgive him. She always did.

Fourteen

I could tell by the odd explosion when he swore nonstop, viciously and eloquently, about things I didn't understand, that Richard was no longer happy at the Old Vic. I gathered it was because he got bored with acting. He told me that real actors treated it as an art, their life, but to him it was just something at which he was good, something he could switch on and off. Once, I asked if there was anything that really interested him, that was his passion above all else.

'Rugby,' he said. 'Then, when I got too old to play, I'd turn to books, to reading, writing, learning.' When he spoke of these things, his face was always animated. His dream, he said, was to live in a house that was essentially a huge library with a few living rooms off it. 'Like a scriptorium in a priory.'

'And rugby? You don't play, do you?'

'Not any more, not since the competition decided that they'd rather kick me than the ball. After all, any moron can kick a ball, but how many can say they've kicked the crap out of a famous film star's head?'

I smiled at his description of himself. Usually, he was

extraordinarily modest. He went on to say that when he was a child all he had ever wanted to do was to play for Wales at Cardiff Arms Park. 'And if we were to beat England at Twickenham, then I'd die happy.'

One night he told me that he was breaking his contract with the Old Vic on doctor's orders, due to 'exhaustion'. In fact, it started off as a row over the design of the costumes to be used in *Troilus and Cressida*. He loathed what he described as 'a Ruritanian version' of the play in which all the actors were to wear uniforms like toy soldiers. He also loathed Michael Benthall, whom he called 'an upstart of a director'. It had escalated until the face-saver was the medical note he produced that said he was too tired to continue, but he confessed to me that he was breaking his contract in order to make a film in Jamaica.

'I'm paid forty-five pounds at the Vic, and a bloody sight more in films,' he said.

Money as such didn't interest Richard, however, and he was always giving it away. It was his dream to see every one of his brothers and sisters in their own houses and dragged up out of poverty, or at least poverty as he saw it.

'I'm working for them, really,' he said, 'not for myself.' He assured me that he would see me again on his return. Besides, he hadn't gone yet, so I knew that there would be plenty of time to make our good-byes.

—

It was at this time that Mother's certification proving her qualifications finally arrived from India. Now she could give up the hated job in the hospital and become a science teacher. To celebrate her rise in status and income, she had a phone put in. It was the first time we had had one, and to this day I can remember the thrill of seeing it sitting there on the table in the hall. I even got up in the night to gaze down the stairs at it. When Richard announced he was shortly leaving for the Caribbean to start filming, the pain of separation was diluted a fraction because now I was able to give him my telephone number, even though I warned him that he mustn't use it. A man's voice asking for me would cause so much consternation and curiosity at home, I said, I would never be able to get away with it.

'A gentleman friend calling Miss Austen!' he said, with a laugh. 'Break out the smelling salts!'

I may have felt lonely after Richard had gone, but at least I wasn't pregnant. By then I was sitting exams at school and was cramming in every spare moment. After they were over, the next important event at school was Prize Day, and the guest speaker earnestly entreated us to read good books.

'When you reach my age,' he said, 'you come to appreciate that life is only so long. For every bad-quality book you read, you have deprived yourself of the joy and educational value of a good one.' Then he went on to say that being future mothers was an important thing in itself, and that the best mothers were educated women, that giving birth to our babies would be a glorious occasion, a moment in which to be thoughtful, to realise that we were holding the future of society in our arms. We all giggled and blushed at this. That a man should mention the words mother and birth in an all-girls school was embarrassing.

That summer seemed much too long. A tall, fair-haired German boy came to stay with the two elderly spinsters who lived next door. One day, one of the women called to me over the garden fence.

'Wolfgang is your age, Rose,' she said, a glimmer in her eye. 'Would you play with him?' Did I want to play with

Wolfgang? I looked at her, so earnest with her straggly bun and owl's glasses, and didn't know whether to laugh. I had turned fifteen in July, although, like most of my birthdays it hardly registered at home.

'Miss Plowman,' I said gently, 'I think we're too old to play together, but I will show him around.' She seemed relieved.

'We're letting him ride one of our bicycles,' she said. 'Perhaps you can go on picnics.'

So Wolfgang and I took long bicycle rides to Keston Ponds, where we would lie on a grassy bank and watch great blue dragonflies dart over yellow flags, and a kingfisher dive for minnows. Sometimes a heron came to fish and there were always sooty coots with white faces, and little russet moorhens with their flirty white flashes under their tails. The longest ride of all was into the heart of the Kentish countryside, to Chartwell, Churchill's country home, which Wolfgang's father had insisted he visit, if he could. I didn't realise the significance of this trip, until many years later I was told that Wolfgang's father had been one of the Luftwaffe pilots involved in the dogfights over Kent and Sussex during the Battle of Britain.

The lane leading to Chartwell was marked on an old black and white fingerpost. We rode to start with, then, as the lane rose, we got off and pushed. I was hot and sweaty by the time we reached the high brick walls.

'Oh,' I said, disappointed. 'We can't see the house.'

Wolfgang pointed out a stile leading into a field on the rising land opposite.

'Look, we can go into that field and have our picnic,' he said. 'We can look down on the house.'

We leaned our bikes in the hedge and emptied our packed lunch from the saddlebags. The stile had not been crossed for some time and was overgrown. Brambles and nettles clutched at our legs and tore my bare skin. We walked through meadowsweet and tall ox-eye daisies. The whole world was white and green and smelled of flowers and hot earth. Finally, we found the perfect spot where we could look down the hill at the rambling red-brick house. The gardens were a riot of roses, so much colour it seemed to merge into pastel drifts, like a picture on a jigsaw puzzle or a box of chocolates. Someone was at work on the wall at the back.

'Do you think it's Churchill himself?' Wolfgang asked excitedly. 'I would like to meet him.'

'It's hard to tell from here,' I said, taking a long gulp from the bottle of Tizer.

'I like you, Rose,' Wolfgang turned to look at me. 'Can I be your boyfriend?'

'Oh no, Wolfgang,' I replied. 'I'm far too young for such things.'

What I didn't tell Wolfgang that day, or my classmates at Prize Day, was the truth about how I suddenly felt about boys, and love, and marriage, and being a mother, and all those things. I had already come very close to being a mother at the age of fourteen. I was already in love as deeply as any young girl could be, and it was with a man who was closer to the age of Wolfgang's father, than to Wolfgang – older, wittier, wiser, more sophisticated than any teenage boy. How could they compete now? The truth was that they couldn't, and they didn't. I wouldn't fall in love again until I was twenty.

In October, the Hungarian Uprising occurred. I joined in the anti-Communist protests and started to hang out with an artsy crowd. I was already beginning a new period of my life without realising it, becoming quite beatnik, dressed all in black, with maroon velvet flatties that were so cheap I got two pairs for five shillings. I was changing, getting more outward-looking, developing new interests. Instead of spending my nights after school with Richard, I spent them in coffee bars, and jazz and folk clubs, listening to music. The hit songs that autumn of 1956 were Guy Mitchell's 'Singing the Blues', Jim Lowe's 'Green Door', Fats Domino's 'Blueberry Hill', and Elvis Presley's 'Love Me Tender'. I bought them all and played them loudly. My mother didn't mind since she liked them too. Father, as usual, was never there.

All I was doing was killing time until Richard returned from Jamaica. I kept up with my newspaper delivery, since I needed money for my outings to the local clubs and cafés. It was early one Saturday morning in December, and I had just come in from my round, when the phone rang loudly in the hall as I was passing by. I was still not used to the sound of it and stared, mesmerised, before snatching it up. Politely, I gave the number as I had been taught to do.

'Gypsy Hill, one-six one-eight,' I said.

'May I speak to Rose?' How could one ever mistake that voice? I will remember for ever the thrill of hearing it on the phone that day. I will remember it until I am nailed snugly into my coffin. It was Richard. Richard Burton, telephoning me. I sagged against the carved elephant's head on the leg of one of Granny's ebony tables.

'Hello?' he said.

'Richard,' I whispered.

'Is that you, Miss Austen?'

I nodded, then realised that he couldn't see me.

'Yes,' I managed. 'It's me.'

'Well then, are we going to meet? Can you come up?'

In half an hour I was at the door of his flat. It was like old times, except that now I was wearing my beatnik regalia, the black drainpipe trousers and polo-necked sweater with a black cloak lined in purple satin with a lion's-head clasp.

'Bloody hell, you've gone all Left Bank on me!' Richard exclaimed, when he opened the door and saw me standing there. He could have laughed, but he didn't. Instead, he walked circles around me, taking it all in. 'Well, it suits you, but I must say I miss my little schoolgirl. Champagne?' I smiled at this. He had remembered.

'I haven't had champagne since the last time I was here,' I said.

We made frenzied love, and I was eager for it. It felt good to be held in such strong arms. It felt safe. I always felt safe when I was in the shadow of Richard's strength and personality. Afterwards, while we lay on the magical pink eiderdown, he told me that he was going home to Wales for Christmas. I knew how much he loved his entire family there, for he'd said so often. Now, I thought, now he's going to say that he loves me, too, there'll be a future for us. I really did believe this.

Instead, as he poured the last of the second bottle of champagne into my glass, he told me that it was over.

'I'm going to miss you, Rose,' he said. Just like that. I stared at him, not fully understanding.

'Are you going to Wales immediately?' I asked.

'Soon,' Richard replied. 'But, Rose, this is good-bye. We won't be meeting again.'

'Is it something I've done?' I asked, my voice tiny. I felt suddenly unsafe. I couldn't think of any other reason for his words. After all, we'd only just got back together again after those months apart, and the last few hours had been magical, at least to me.

'I can't make any money in this country, Rose,' he explained. 'For every one hundred thousand pounds I earn, the bastards take ninety thousand in tax. It's outrageous. I'm going to live in Switzerland.'

I had been dreaming of his return for so long that this news was a terrible blow. I sobered up fast. He talked of other things then – films, books, I can't remember what – as I dressed. Back on went the black drainpipe trousers and polo-necked sweater. I tried not to meet his eyes as I flung the black cloak around my shoulders.

'Good-bye,' I said. 'I need to rush. I have to meet my friends. I'll be late.' I knew if I didn't leave right away I would cry, and that would spoil our last time together. Richard merely nodded. I suspect he knew that I was trying to save face.

'I'll walk you to a taxi,' he said. He smiled, briefly. 'All right for money?'

'Yes,' I said, airily. 'I'm fine.'

Perhaps he wanted to spin the moment out, because, instead of putting me in a taxi at the end of the road, he walked with me. When we left the flat, instead of turning right, as he always did, he turned to the left, to the end of the short street. We passed through the big iron gates in front of the Watergate that once led into the courtyard of the Duke of Buckingham's grand house on the banks of the river. Nothing remained of all those acres of lawns and pastures but the narrow strip of the Victoria Embankment Gardens. We crossed the road to the Embankment itself, with its massive plane trees and the iron dolphins gambolling and twining over every lamppost and bench. This was where we had walked and talked, almost two years earlier, and Richard had thrilled me with his knowledge of things: *All history has been here, Rose. Traitors, kings, emperors. When the river froze, they held ice fairs on the ice . . .*

So much had happened since those first days of our affair. I had been changed for ever. Now, Richard was about to change my life again, but this time, he would take away the excitement he had brought to me, leaving me in his wake, leaving my days bleak and mundane. I wondered, as we walked, if I would feel like a schoolgirl again, once he was gone. I couldn't imagine ever going out with another man. What would I possibly do without him? I had set my calendar by him for so long now. Everything pointed to when I might see him again. I turned to him, trying to fight the tears.

'We really won't meet again, will we?' I asked. There was a nostalgia in him now, a sorrow.

'No, I don't think so, Rose,' he answered, 'but it's better like this. You'll see.'

I knew then that it was really over. This was the end.

'Can I write to you?' I asked hopelessly.

'There's no point,' he said. 'I'll be living abroad. Oh, I'll come to London again, but I can only stay here for a short time or the taxman will be after me. My life's getting to be very crowded. And you, Miss Austen, you will grow up. You'll find someone else.'

'No!' I clutched his hand. 'There'll never be anyone else. You're unique.' He laughed to hear me say this, his deep resonant laugh.

'I'm a rogue and a rascal,' he said, 'but I'm glad I knew you, Rose. You're very special, and don't you forget it.' Platitudes that I hugged to my heart to be remembered later.

Breaking his rule, Richard bent his head then and kissed

me in broad daylight. Once, I would have been thrilled, but now I was too numb to feel a thing. It was an awkward, fumbling kiss before he stepped back. I couldn't say a single word at that moment. Instead, I ran to the edge of the pavement and flagged down a taxi. When it pulled up, I quickly jumped in.

As we eased away from the kerb and speeded up into traffic, I turned my head and looked back. Richard was standing, staring after my cab. Behind his shoulders, the cold, pale sun was casting long shadows from the bare trees. I kept my eyes on him, that familiar outline, there in his dark overcoat. Then, before the taxi turned the corner, I saw him turn and walk away, with that same brisk stride I had come to know so well. It would be the last time I would ever see Richard Burton again, alive and human, and not some Hollywood actor on a television set.

In the taxi, I sank back in my seat and gave in to the tears that had been trying to fall.

'Are you all right, Miss?' the driver asked. I couldn't answer, and my tears turned to sobs. My stomach hurt so much that I almost couldn't bear it. The tension, along with the motion of the car, made me feel desperately ill. 'Are you all right, Miss?' he asked again.

'No, I'm going to be sick.'

The taxi slowed and the driver picked up the nearest thing he had. It was his lunch box. He tipped out the sandwiches and handed it to me through the sliding window.

'Here,' he said. 'Don't make a mess in my cab. It's the devil to clean up.'

I clutched it and fell back into the seat. The taxi speeded up a little, the driver keeping a cautious eye on me in his mirror.

'Oh love, oh love,' he said, as I finally vomited into his box.

When we arrived at my house, I stumbled out. The last of the autumn leaves were thick and slick on the pavement, and falling from the tree outside the gate, like gold confetti in the sun.

'Do you want your lunch box back?' I asked the poor driver.

'No, Miss, you can keep it,' he said. 'And buy yourself some flowers, love. You look like you could do with cheering up.' Off he went, without taking my money.

⟶

At Christmas, I wrote Richard a long and tearful letter. Then, with it tucked into my shoulder bag, I tried to find his house off Hampstead Heath. Even if he had already gone to Wales, at least I could leave the letter in his box. I knew his street address from dropped bits of conversation during our times together, but not the actual number of his house. Then, in a flash of logic, I wondered what I would say if Richard or his wife – that woman with the silver-grey hair and the sweet face – came to the door. I panicked at the thought of this disruption to their lives, and fled, instead, to the Heath. I sat on a bench where I took the letter out and read it slowly, my eyes filling with tears. It contained the foolish words of a foolish girl, and I was about to tear it up when I stopped. No, I'll keep it as a memento, I thought, so I slipped it back into my bag.

I got up from the bench, and began to walk. It was cold and frosty. There was a pink light over London with a wonderful view of St Paul's rising out of the river mist. *Did you know that lightning struck St Paul's once, Rose, even before the Great Fire destroyed her? Can you imagine how amazed everyone was when Wren started to build her back, that great dome rising high, the largest in Europe at the time?* I would remember Richard's lovely lectures for all my life. His interest in such things would give me an interest, too, not just in history, but in art and in writing. *They all said it would fall down. Even the king asked Wren if he knew what the hell he was doing. But, the bloody thing stayed up. When Wren called the king in to look, he invited him up to the whispering gallery where you can hear a mouse scampering across the tiles of the floor far below. The king was astonished but some of the courtiers screamed and fled. They were lucky not to break their bloody necks. They thought the place was haunted, Rose . . .*

I suddenly felt very connected, a tiny part of the whole, in that immortal way in which the poets write. I took deep breaths of the cold, clean air. My lungs hurt, but the air was cleansing. The oxygen seemed to fill my body with energy and hope. My spirits lifted. *And you, Miss Austen, you will grow up. You'll find someone else . . . I'm glad I knew you, Rose. You're very special, and don't you forget it.* I could sense, sense in the way the young can, that Richard was just an episode in my life that I was lucky to have experienced – but there were many other wonderful experiences waiting up ahead for me. I was certain of it. My life was still waiting to be lived.

Epilogue

❦

L ife did indeed go on
In 1960, my father finally met the love of his life, or
so he said, and began an affair with her. Tina was an
exciting but ruthless and mercenary red-haired French-
woman with the slender ankles of a racehorse. Her story,
however, was dark. Her head had once been shaved and
she had been tarred and feathered by the French
Resistance, after the war, for being a traitor. Her hot and
torrid affair with Father continued for years. Often, he
even took Gracie along with him, telling her not to breathe
a word to Mother. Stunned and ashamed, Gracie once
stood in the garden with Tina's two very young children
as all three stared in through the windows, watching Father
and Tina making passionate love. Eventually, after constant
fights with both women, and perhaps overwhelmed with
guilt, my father decided he couldn't choose between my
mother and Tina, so he gave both an overdose. His
reasoning was that the woman who survived would win
him. He took my mother a cup of coffee in bed – she
should have been immediately suspicious – laced with
powdered sedatives. Tina always claimed, proudly, that she

took her pills voluntarily. At any rate, after spending a day dashing from house to house, watching two unconscious women slip away, my father's nerve gave and he sent for two ambulances and Tina and Mother ended up in different hospitals. A psychiatrist came to discuss this suicide attempt with my mother, to judge her state of mind and whether or not she could be sent home. 'I didn't try to kill myself, you fool!' she screamed at him. 'My husband did!' Nobody believed her but us children.

Finally, after reconciliations and bitter arguments with both women, Father chose Tina. Angered and hurt, Mother sought a judicial separation because divorce was against her 'religion', which was a newly discovered and nonexistent Catholicism. Then, she tried to get my father fired from his job by writing to everyone she could think of, his superiors, the Archbishop of Canterbury, and even the prime minister. In the end, Father put all that he possessed in Tina's name – we learned later that he'd hidden away many assets from Mother – and he and the love of his life left London.

I was already twenty by this time but, since Mother couldn't make ends meet on her own, she begged me not to move out. Mother forbade me to visit Father, but I did anyway; he was my father, despite all that he'd done.

The fight between my parents was very bitter and protracted and in the years he stayed gone, my mother went mad and was mad for a long time. She started taking prescription tranquillisers and then became an alcoholic.

I think my mother worshipped my father. I know she both loved and hated him. She certainly couldn't let him go. She would have taken him back, no matter what he did. But I don't think my father ever really loved my mother. He thought she would have money when he married her, but my grandparents made certain she never did. Father was angry about that. Mostly, as he always pointed out, they were too different, opposites. 'I want a woman who enjoys life and parties as I do,' he often told me. 'I don't want an insular bookworm. I want a woman with slender ankles.' He got the woman he wanted for a time when he ran away with Tina.

—

To escape the tension and the madness of home, I promptly took up with Gerald Kingsland, a journalist, when I was twenty years old, and became a journalist myself. He was a kind man, but one whose moods were as changeable as Richard's. Like Richard, he could be warm and affectionate one moment, and then sink into deep black depressions the next.

When I took our firstborn son to meet my father, Mother found out about it. It so angered her that she refused to speak to me, so Gerald and I moved to Windsor, where a second son was born. Then Wales, and a third son. Three sons in three years, but Mother didn't speak to me for two of those years, she was still so angry over my visit to Father.

My life with Gerald was erratic but exciting. I know I was happy some of the time. I went on to travel the world, live in many cultures, write books, edit magazines, work in film and television: a life in pursuit of the arts. It was while I was living in Italy, in 1976, that Granny died back in London. Going against her stated wishes, my mother had her cremated.

Granny's ashes were scattered in a local crematorium: her half of the grave at the little cemetery in Patcham, where she buried Granddad, is still waiting for her.

Long years passed before I split from the father of my

three sons. Then, I met someone else, Neil, a composer. He and I spent several years in the United States before returning to Britain because my father had cancer. When I walked through the door of the Gypsy Hill house after so much time away, the memories and the anguish all came rushing back. I wrote to a friend, 'The house is dark and black with hate.' It was. I couldn't live in it. Neil and I bought a Gothic old ruin in West Wales, close to the sea. It had rare bats in the attic and birds I hadn't seen for a very long time flying across the wild and lovely landscape. My sons drifted back from the Pacific islands where they had been living with their nomad of a father (the film *Castaway*, starring Oliver Reed, is about Gerald Kingsland's adventures), and they helped to nurture our acres.

Mother and Father finally divorced in 1970. In the meantime he had split with Tina and married an alcoholic woman who was younger than I, but the details of this adventure of his are far too awful for me to relate. In 1978, Father returned to live with my mother again, in the house at Gypsy Hill. I won't say they lived in harmony, for now the anger of years was unleashed. They didn't care how much they hurt each other, and the rows were bitter in the extreme.

As usual, I was still caught in the maelstrom, driving down from Wales every week to do some shopping and housework, but then, my father's cancer started to slowly spread. He lost his sight. That's when my mother told me that her heart had 'gone'. The time had come to move in with them in order to take care of them as they required.

Over the next six months Mother's heartbeat slowly declined. It just grew softer and weaker, like the last haunting notes on the piano she no longer played. She wouldn't have a nurse or even the doctor in. Caring for her became an exhausting and full-time job.

Finally, despite her protests, I realised that I had no choice but to send her to hospital. I went with her as she left the house for the last time, carried on a stretcher, wrapped in a red wool blanket. Her terrified eyes met mine.

'I won't be back, will I, Rose?' she asked. She looked around and then said, 'Well, good-bye,' as if she were addressing all her memories as her eyes travelled up the stairs, where my father hovered just out of sight on the landing. She would not have him anywhere near her until right at the end, at the hospital, when I asked if she was sure she didn't want to see him.

'He's asking,' I said. 'He wants to talk to you.'

'Let him come if he wants,' she said, completely uninterested.

'Don't cause a row,' I warned him, as we walked into the long ward. I looked at the expression in her eyes when he approached the bed, then walked away in tears, feeling the pain, the tragedy of two ruined lives: so much love and hate and anger and regret all fighting to find a place in the last few hours. He sat close to her and took her hand.

'Anne, it's George,' I heard him say, 'your suer qe butcha.' Son of a pig. It seemed a shocking oath, yet in the early days, that had been what she had called him in hatred, and at times in love.

'Well, George,' she said. 'You won – but I'll be there waiting.'

I gave them privacy for a while. Then he bent and kissed her as he left. She gazed after him as he shuffled away. I didn't want to press on the drive home by asking him what was said, that was between the two of them, but he was very tearful all the way, stumbling up the steps of the house, and wiping his eyes with his handkerchief.

'I've known her longer than anyone else,' was all he said. He spoke as if he knew for certain that she would be gone very soon.

Mother died early the next morning, 20 June 1996.

—

Mother's coffin was white cardboard, organic, as she had requested. She hated trees to be cut down and used to abuse the neighbours for doing so. We didn't get a wreath. Instead, early in the morning, I cut a great sheaf of her pink roses, orange blossom, white daisies, and white foxgloves from her garden, with bay leaves and rosemary. She had asked for no ceremony, no religious music. As bizarre as it sounds, she wanted a tape of Elvis Presley songs, so Neil made one for her, choosing the songs she had requested.

Mother had planted a rambling red rose that now grows about twenty feet up into the pear tree, and it was around this that her ashes were scattered. That night, as I sat under the apple tree, the air rich with the heady perfume of my mother's roses, lilies, lavender, and orange blossom, she came and sat with me.

'I'm fine, Rose,' she said. 'It's all right,' and I knew that while happiness had eluded her so often here on earth she had found it, finally. She was at peace.

—

In November of 1999, Gerald Kingsland, the father of my three sons, came home from Western Samoa to die. This was following a bawdy life of adventure all around the world, one that had kept the newspapers, and those of us who loved him, well entertained. We took him into the house at Gypsy Hill and cared for him until his death from colon cancer on 20 March 2000.

My father hung on for four more years after Mother died. Fighting ferociously against death, I think he thought he could live for ever. He refused to acknowledge that he was ninety-one and blind and, almost to the end, dressed immaculately as he had always done. With his white cane twirling, as if to imply that he didn't need it, he would saunter off to meet his friends at the pub. He still had ladies in to read poetry to him, provided they were young. There were times I would have sworn that he could see when he sensed a female presence in the room. The decline, when it came, was very rapid. Just before he died, in March of 2001, he did nothing but talk of his mother. 'Why did she give me away?' he asked me, tears in his eyes. 'Do you think she ever missed me, Rose? Do you think she was sad?'

On the day of his funeral, I was up at dawn. There was a steady, cold, and sleety rain falling, but I went out into the garden to pick forsythia, daffodils, and bay branches for his wreath. The ceremony itself was almost Gothic, a wet and windy day in a truly ancient graveyard. Men in top hats and tails carried in the coffin, which was white cardboard, and organic, just like Mother's. We wanted to make them equals, at last, even if in death, but we did leave Father in the graveyard. As crazy as this sounds, I wanted to avoid any spooky conflict somewhere in the afterlife. I couldn't bear the thought of the two of them going at it again, out in the back garden, under the climbing rose.

I went home to the house at Gypsy Hill and fell into a deep depression for days. How could it all be over? How could those two remarkable human beings be gone? My job for so many years had been to act as a kind of moderator between them, and now that job was over. The silence without them was deafening.

———

When you write such a detailed and intimate memoir, there is always the question: Will I hurt anyone? I have tried where possible to obviate this. I have changed names sometimes, and, sometimes, only lightly sketched in details. I have finally told my family of this early adventure of mine. They are supportive, even curious, certainly surprised. But, ultimately, this was part of *my* life. This happened to me, not to someone else. This is something that has shaped my life, for better or worse. If you were to ask me, I'd say it was all for the better.

First love is sometimes the deepest, often the sweetest. It is the one you never forget. Nowadays, I am aware of the passage of time, and it's true what they say about it passing faster as one grows older. Richard wasn't old when we were lovers. He was only twenty-nine when we first met, younger than my sons are now. Yet, he both loved and feared my youth. I was a dangerous temptation he couldn't resist. At times, with a bottle of Scotch consumed and lying empty on the floor between us, he would get a bit maudlin as he stroked my honeyed skin. ' "Golden lads and girls all must, as chimney-sweepers, come to dust," ' he once recited to me. Then, perhaps overwhelmed by that Welsh working-class morality he could never outrun, he said, almost spitefully, 'You realise that, don't you, Rose? That we'll all grow old and die, nothing but food for the bloody worms, so "gather ye rosebuds while ye may".'

The words, in that unmistakable voice, even with an edge of cynicism, did not upset me. I was a golden girl, his golden girl, and life seemed eternal then. It's hard to grasp that more now lies behind me than ahead.

Richard's story is well documented. Based in Switzerland, he and his wife, Sybil, had two daughters before he left them for the great love of his life, Elizabeth Taylor, with whom he became involved while filming with her in Rome in 1961–62. They were starring as Antony and Cleopatra. Played out in the full glare of the media for decades, their love story eclipsed even that legendary historic romance.

It was not until recently, when I read actress Claire Bloom's autobiography, that I realised that she was the Claire whom Richard had been teased about that night at the Cave. Their affair started in 1953, when they were performing *Hamlet* together. She writes that she hated him, thought him uncouth, and so she became a challenge to him. Richard then bet his friends that he would have her. The affair continued in Spain, during the 1955 filming of *Alexander the Great*. They split up for a time, and then continued again, in London. Claire wrote that sometimes she let Richard into her Chelsea house very late, hours after the theatre was closed. It occurred to me that he may have just come from his rendezvous with me – and it's very possible that the Jean Naté was Claire's. What had he told me? *No, I don't believe Claire smells of lemons. Claire was a girl I knew in Spain. I loved her once, but now I love you.* I have to smile when I think of this now.

I never saw nor heard from Richard Burton again. Sometimes, now and then in the course of time, as the years spun away with us both, I'd see him on television doing an interview about some upcoming movie. He was witty and dashing as ever, until the later years when one could see the ravages that alcohol had made upon him. I was always saddened that his beauty and the golden promise of his youth had been so dissipated. I couldn't help but wonder if he ever thought of me, or if he ever mentioned me, in one of those pensive, maudlin moments

I'd known him to have. I was living a simple life out of touch with the larger world when Richard Burton died in 1984, so I missed the moment of his passing. I can only hope that he lived his life as he wanted it to be.

Until recently, I never told anyone of my love affair with Richard. It has been my secret for all these years. So why am I telling it now? Well, a mixture of nostalgia and regret, I suppose. When I decided to begin writing this book, I was facing one of those 'significant' birthdays and was looking back, as one does when one grows older. Trying to remember it all, has certainly been painful – not just the part that included Richard, but recalling all those bittersweet years of growing up in a home filled with strife – but once the door to the past was opened, the memories seemed unstoppable.

It was only after writing this book that I knew why I'd waited so long to put my story down. I couldn't have done it while my parents were alive. And only now that the story is finished do I realise that it's as much about them as my brief affair with Richard. I hear them both all the time. I seem to catch their ghosts unawares, here in these same rooms that held some of our joy and so much of our pain. I have made Mother's downstairs bedroom my office. I painted the walls tobacco brown, the woodwork white, a cosy, womb-like den. At night, the shadows draw about me and I often see my mother there. Sometimes, I can almost hear Father singing, *Remember the vows that you made to your Mary. Remember the bower where you vowed to be true. Oh don't deceive me; Oh nevere leave me! How could you use a poor maiden so?*

At other times, the light shines through the windows at certain hours of the day, and then it all comes back: it's Shrove Tuesday and we're standing at the front door, with its stained-glass sailing ship on a blue sea. There is fresh, white snow all around us. Father has the key. We wait ceremoniously – Mother, Gracie, Jimmy, Freddy, and I – as he puts the key in the lock and turns it. 'Welcome home!' Father says, and quickly steps in ahead of Mother. 'George, you're uncouth,' she tells him, as she glances down the hall. 'But it all looks very nice.'